See the Wider picture

The eccentric Cadillac Ranch, Amarillo, Texas, USA

Three artists built Cadillac Ranch in 1974 beside the famous Route 66. They created the installation by half-burying 10 old Cadillacs nose down in the ground. The cars are placed at the same angle as the face of the Great Pyramid of Giza in Egypt. You can add your own graffiti, but make sure you take a photo because it will soon be painted over by someone else.

What would you paint?

CONTENTS

		STARTER UNIT Welcome to Woodley Bridge	0.1 INTRODUCING TOMMO Activities and interests; Likes and dislikes; Home and furniture; *There is/are* with *some/any*; Possessive adjectives and possessive *'s* pp. 4–5		0.2 INTRODUCING SKYE Jobs; Present Simple with adverbs of frequency p. 6
		VOCABULARY	**GRAMMAR**	**READING and VOCABULARY**	**GRAMMAR**
UNIT 1 That's my world		Talk about everyday technology VOX POPS ▶ pp. 10–11	Use different tenses to talk about the present • Present Simple • Present Continuous • State verbs p. 12 VOX POPS ▶	Find specific detail in an article and talk about gadgets p. 13	Use verb constructions with *to*-infinitives and *-ing* forms • verb + *-ing* • verb + *to*-infinitive VIDEO ⓖ *Woodley Bridge* p. 14
UNIT 2 Wild nature		Talk about the weather and natural disasters pp. 22–23	Use regular and irregular verbs to talk about the past • Past Simple p. 24	Find specific detail in an article and talk about culture p. 25	Talk about an event in the past and what was happening around it • Past Simple and Past Continuous VIDEO ⓖ *Woodley Bridge* p. 26 VOX POPS ▶
UNIT 3 The taste test		Talk about food and drink pp. 34–35	Use the Present Perfect with *ever, never, just, already* and *yet* VIDEO ⓖ *Woodley Bridge* p. 36 VOX POPS ▶	Find specific detail in an article and use *make* and *do* accurately p. 37	Talk about duration of time, and be general and specific about experiences • Present Perfect with *for* and *since* • Present Perfect and Past Simple p. 38
UNIT 4 Curtain up!		Talk about films and television VOX POPS ▶ pp. 46–47	Compare different things • Comparatives and superlatives p. 48 VOX POPS ▶	Understand the main points of an article and talk about entertainment p. 49	Talk about quantities of countable and uncountable nouns • Quantifiers VIDEO ⓖ *Woodley Bridge* p. 50
UNIT 5 The big match!		Talk about sports and sports events pp. 58–59	Talk about plans, predictions, arrangements and timetables • The future: *will / going to* / Present Continuous VIDEO ⓖ *Woodley Bridge* p. 60	Identify specific detail in an article and talk about volunteering at a sports event p. 61 VOX POPS ▶	Talk about possible future situations • First Conditional + *if/unless* p. 62 VOX POPS ▶
UNIT 6 See the world!		Talk about holidays and travelling VOX POPS ▶ pp. 70–71	Talk about obligation, prohibition and advice • Modal verbs: *must, have to, ought to, should* VIDEO ⓖ *Woodley Bridge* p. 72 VOX POPS ▶	Find specific detail in an article and talk about travelling p. 73	Speculate about the present • Modal verbs: *must, could, might, may, can't* p. 74
UNIT 7 Getting to know you		Talk about relationships with family and friends pp. 82–83	Talk about imaginary situations • Second Conditional VIDEO ⓖ *Woodley Bridge* p. 84 VOX POPS ▶	Find specific detail in an article and talk about friends p. 85	Be specific about people, things and places • Defining and non-defining relative clauses p. 86
UNIT 8 No time for crime		Talk about crime and criminals pp. 94–95	Use verbs in the Passive • Present Simple Passive and Past Simple Passive p. 96	Find specific detail in an article and talk about solving crimes p. 97	Use the construction *have/get something done* VIDEO ⓖ *Woodley Bridge* p. 98
UNIT 9 Think outside the box		Talk about school life pp. 106–107	Make questions with the correct word order VIDEO ⓖ *Woodley Bridge* p. 108	Find specific detail in an article and talk about intelligence p. 109	Use a variety of tenses p. 110 VOX POPS ▶

IRREGULAR VERBS p. 127   STUDENT ACTIVITIES p. 144   CLIL   ART: 3D printer sculpture p. 139   SCIENCE: Cooking p. 140

0.3 INTRODUCING DAN Clothes and accessories; Present Continuous; Talking about feelings p.7		**0.4 INTRODUCING ALISHA** Countries and languages; *was/were*, *there was/were*; Past Simple: regular verbs p. 8		**CHARACTER QUIZ** p. 9
LISTENING and VOCABULARY	SPEAKING	WRITING / ENGLISH IN USE		BBC CULTURE
Understand the main point and find specific details in a radio programme, and talk about using technology p. 15	Make and respond to suggestions VIDEO *Woodley Bridge* p. 16	Write a description of places and lifestyles p. 17	WORDLIST p. 18 REVISION p. 19 GRAMMAR TIME 1 p. 118	Do smartphones make you smarter? VIDEO *Addicted to screens* pp. 20–21
Identify specific detail in a conversation and talk about being in the wild p. 27	Criticise and explain when things go wrong VIDEO *Woodley Bridge* p. 28 VOX POPS	Use adverbs and indefinite pronouns p. 29	WORDLIST p. 30 REVISION p. 31 GRAMMAR TIME 2 p. 119	Nice day, innit? VIDEO *Severe weather* pp. 32–33
Identify specific detail in speech and describe food VOX POPS p. 39	Order food in a café or restaurant VIDEO *Woodley Bridge* p. 40	Write an email to a friend p. 41	WORDLIST p. 42 REVISION p. 43 GRAMMAR TIME 3 p. 120 EXAM TIME 1 pp. 130–132	What do the British really eat? VIDEO *Indian food Liverpool style* pp. 44–45
Identify specific detail in an interview and talk about festivals p. 51	Ask about, express and explain preferences VIDEO *Woodley Bridge* p. 52	Describe how people do things • Adverbs of manner p. 53	WORDLIST p. 54 REVISION p. 55 GRAMMAR TIME 4 p. 121	How do you like to celebrate? VIDEO *London celebrates* pp. 56–57
Identify specific detail in a conversation and talk about sports training p. 63	Can ask and talk about plans VIDEO *Woodley Bridge* p. 64	Write notes and make requests p. 65	WORDLIST p. 66 REVISION p. 67 GRAMMAR TIME 5 p. 122	Where do they toss the caber? VIDEO *The Highland Games* pp. 68–69
Identify specific detail in a conversation and talk about trips and excursions p. 75	Clarify what I have said and ask for clarification VIDEO *Woodley Bridge* p. 76	Use time clauses p. 77	WORDLIST p. 78 REVISION p. 79 GRAMMAR TIME 6 p. 123 EXAM TIME 2 pp. 133–135	Can ironing make holidays exciting? VIDEO *Adventures of a lifetime* pp. 80–81
Identify specific information in a monologue and talk about pets p. 87 VOX POPS	Explain who I am talking about VIDEO *Woodley Bridge* p. 88	Write a short story p. 89	WORDLIST p. 90 REVISION p. 91 GRAMMAR TIME 7 p. 124	Is moving house good for you? VIDEO *On the move* pp. 92–93
Identify the main points of a monologue and talk about discovering a crime p. 99 VOX POPS	Persuade and reassure someone VIDEO *Woodley Bridge* p. 100	Form and use negative adjectives VOX POPS p. 101	WORDLIST p. 102 REVISION p. 103 GRAMMAR TIME 8 p. 125	Is chewing gum a crime? VIDEO *A famous robbery* pp. 104–105
Identify specific information in a dialogue and talk about awkward moments p. 111 VOX POPS	Have a casual conversation VIDEO *Woodley Bridge* p. 112	Write a letter giving information p. 113	WORDLIST p. 114 REVISION p. 115 GRAMMAR TIME 9 p. 126 EXAM TIME 3 pp. 136–138	Can school be fun? VIDEO *Two very different schools* pp. 116–117

DRAMA: Zigger Zagger p. 141   **GEOGRAPHY:** International Date Line p. 142   **SCIENCE:** Forensics p. 143
CULTURE 1: Explore India p. 143   2: Explore New Zealand p. 144

0

Welcome to Woodley Bridge

VOCABULARY
Activities and interests | Home and furniture | Jobs | Clothes and accessories | Countries and languages

GRAMMAR
There is/are with *some/any* | Possessive adjectives and possessive *'s* | Present Simple with adverbs of frequency | Present Continuous | *was/were, there was/were* | Past Simple: regular verbs

SPEAKING
Likes and dislikes | Talking about feelings

0.1 INTRODUCING TOMMO

Activities and interests; Likes and dislikes; Home and furniture; *There is/are* with *some/any*; Possessive adjectives and possessive *'s*

1 🔊 **1.02** Read the text. Name the person and objects in the photo.

> My name's Alexi Thomas, but my nickname is Tommo. I'm fifteen and I'm from Woodley Bridge, a small town in the UK. My mum is a nurse at the local hospital and my dad is a carpenter. We've got a very unusual home, a canal boat called *Ocean Princess*. It's small, but I haven't got any brothers or sisters, so there's enough space for the three of us. I've got a cat called Hissy. She's a wild cat and she isn't very friendly!
>
> Life on a boat is fun and it's a great place for my favourite hobby, kayaking. I've got my own kayak and I like going out on the canal before school. I'm interested in nature, and I love drawing and painting wildlife, too, so this is the perfect home for me.

2 Work in pairs. Mark the sentences T (true) or F (false). Correct the false sentences.

1. ☐ Tommo's real name is Alexi.
2. ☐ Tommo's parents are doctors.
3. ☐ His home isn't very big.
4. ☐ Tommo's got a younger brother.
5. ☐ He hasn't got any pets.
6. ☐ Tommo often goes kayaking before school.

3 Read the text again. What are Tommo's hobbies and interests?

4 🔊 **1.03** **I KNOW!** Work in pairs. How many activities and interests can you add to the Vocabulary A box in three minutes?

Vocabulary A	Activities and interests

doing nothing　going to the cinema　listening to music
playing computer games　reading books or magazines　taking photos

5 Use the Speaking box to tell your partner about your favourite activities and interests.

Speaking	Likes and dislikes
I love … / I like … / He loves … I don't mind … / She doesn't mind … I can't stand … / He can't stand …	

I love taking photos.

6 🔊 **1.04** Check that you understand the words in the Vocabulary B box. Listen and tick the words that you hear.

Vocabulary B	Home and furniture
bath bathroom bed bedroom ceiling cupboard dining room floor garage garden kitchen mirror roof shower wall window	

Skye: Can you teach me to kayak some time?
Tommo: Sure, but not today. My kayak's in the garage.
Skye: But you haven't got a garage.
Tommo: No, *we* haven't, but my dad's friend has got a garage. My kayak's in there at the moment. Dad makes his furniture there, too. It's like a workshop for him.
Skye: What's that noise? Is it something on the roof?
Tommo: That? Oh, it's probably Hissy in the garden.
Skye: What garden?
Tommo: Well, it's not *really* a garden. Mum's got some flowers in plant pots up on the roof. She calls it a garden. You know, that's her idea of a joke. Come and see. Oh no! Hissy!
Skye: What a mess! Hissy's really dirty! Can we put her in the bath?
Tommo: Well, we haven't got a bath because the bathroom's too small.
Skye: Oh yes! But we can wash her in the shower. Come on, Hissy. There's a good girl.
Tommo: Have you got her? Right. There are some towels in the cupboard there. Oh dear! She can't stand showers.

7 **I KNOW!** Work in pairs. How many items can you add to the Vocabulary B box in three minutes?

8 Study the Grammar A box. Look at the photo and complete the sentences with *there is/are* or *there isn't/aren't*.

Grammar A	There is/are with some/any	
	Singular	**Plural**
+	There's (there is) a bed.	There are **some** clothes.
−	There isn't a desk.	There aren't **any** shops.
?	Is there a chair?	Are there **any** books?

1 *There's* a red rug on the floor.
2 _____ any pictures on the wall.
3 _____ a bed next to the window.
4 _____ curtains.
5 _____ a TV.

9 In pairs, make more sentences about the photo, using *There is/are* and the prepositions below.

between   in   near   next to
on   opposite   under

10 Study the Grammar B box. Complete the sentences with possessive adjectives or possessive *'s*.

Grammar B	Possessive adjectives and possessive *'s*
's = singular	the cat**'s** toys
s' = plural	my parents**'** boat
adjectives	my/your/his/her/its/our/their bedroom

1 Whose book is it?
  It's Tommo*'s* mum*'s* book.
2 Is it Hissy____ ball?
  Yes, it's ____ ball.
3 Is that Tommo____ room?
  No, it's ____ mum and dad____ room.
4 Is this ____ cat?
  No, it's my friend____ cat.

11 Write three sentences about your home.

There's a big mirror in my parents' room.

Starter Unit **5**

0.2 INTRODUCING SKYE

Jobs; Present Simple with adverbs of frequency

1 🔊 **1.05** Read the text. Find:
1 a surname _Winter-Fox_
2 three jobs _____ _____ _____
3 two things to eat _____ _____
4 an animal _____
5 two sports _____ _____
6 two places _____ _____

Hi! I'm Skye Winter-Fox and I'm 15. I live with my Gran because my parents are scientists and they often work abroad. They are in New Zealand at the moment. Gran's really sporty. She's a yoga teacher and she swims every morning. I sometimes go with her but I don't like getting up early!

We usually have breakfast together, then I feed my pet snake. Yes! I've got a beautiful snake called Basil. I have lunch at school, but it's always boring because I have cheese sandwiches every day. After school, I see my friends Tommo, Dan and Alisha. Dan and I like running together. Sometimes we all meet at the café on the canal.

In the evenings, I do my homework and Gran makes dinner. Does she cook every day? Yes, she does. She's the best cook in the world, and she makes a brilliant chilli!

2 🔊 **1.06** Study the Vocabulary box. Can you add more words?

Vocabulary	Jobs
cook/chef farmer hairdresser	
mechanic nurse scientist	

3 In pairs, describe a job from the Vocabulary box. Your partner has to guess which job it is.

This person can make you better when you are ill. A nurse.
This person likes working with animals …

4 Study the Grammar box. Find more examples of the Present Simple in the text.

Grammar	Present Simple with adverbs of frequency
Affirmative	**Negative**
I live with my Gran.	I don't swim every day.
My parents travel a lot.	They don't live in this country.
Questions	**Short answers**
Do you live near the school?	Yes, I do. / No, I don't.
Does she cook everyday?	Yes, she does. / No, she doesn't.

> _Always, usually, often, sometimes, never_ go before most verbs, but after the verb _to be_.   **Watch OUT!**

5 Complete the sentences with the correct form of the verbs in brackets.
1 We _don't go_ (not go) to school on Saturdays.
2 She _____ (often/be) with her friends in the park café.
3 Mum and Dad _____ (never/sleep) after 8 a.m.
4 _____ (you/live) in a big house?
5 Emma _____ (not eat) lunch at school.
6 Jake _____ (always/cook) for my birthday.

6 **WORD FRIENDS** Study the phrases and underline those that are in the text. Can you add more everyday actions?

> do homework   get dressed   get home   get up early/late
> go to school / go out   have a shower
> have breakfast/lunch/dinner   see friends

7 In pairs, describe a school day.

I always wake up at six o'clock.
I never get dressed before breakfast.

8 In pairs, describe the people in your house. What do they do? What's their routine?

I live with my mum and my dog. Mum gets up early every day. She's a dentist.

0.3 INTRODUCING DAN

Clothes and accessories; Present Continuous; Talking about feelings

1 **CLASS VOTE** Look at the photo. Do you think the boys are family or friends?

2 🔊 **1.07** Read the text. Mark the sentences T (true) or F (false).

> Hi, I'm Dan. This is a photo of my older brother, Ed, and me. In the photo, we're both wearing sports clothes. I'm wearing my favourite football T-shirt, and Ed's wearing his baseball cap and his favourite hoodie. We're smiling in the photo because Ed's telling a stupid joke! Ed and I were born in the USA. My dad's family is originally from Mexico and we both speak Spanish. I'm in England now because Mum's working at a school here. Ed's at university in New York and he's having a great time. Mum and I are making plans to visit him this summer, and we're really excited. I'm enjoying my new school in England but I don't like the school uniform! I'm glad I've got friends like Tommo, Skye and Alisha. I'm shy, but they're always around when I'm worried about something.

1. [F] Dan is older than Ed.
2. [ ] Dan and Ed were born in Mexico.
3. [ ] Dan and Ed don't speak Spanish.
4. [ ] Ed's in New York at the moment.
5. [ ] Dan likes the school uniform in England.

3 🔊 **1.08** Study the Vocabulary box. Which clothes and accessories can you see in the photo?

Vocabulary	Clothes and accessories
baseball cap earrings hoodie jacket school uniform T-shirt watch	

4 **I KNOW!** Work in pairs. How many words can you add to the Vocabulary box in two minutes?

5 Study the Grammar box. Find more examples of the Present Continuous in the text.

Grammar	Present Continuous

Affirmative
I'm wearing my favourite shirt.
He's wearing a hat.
They're wearing hats.

Negative
I'm not wearing my favourite shirt.
He isn't wearing a hat.
They aren't wearing hats.

Questions
Are you wearing a tie?
Is she wearing a tie?

Short answers
Yes, I am. / No, I'm not.
Yes, she is. / No, she isn't.

6 Order the words to make questions. Answer the questions to make them true for you.
1. you / are / going out / ?
   Are you going out? No, I'm not.
2. are / wearing / an earring / ? / you
   _____
3. the students / are / talking / ? _____
4. doing / this exercise / your friend / is / ?
   _____
5. you / looking at / are / your phone / ?
   _____

7 Study the Speaking box. Can you add more words to describe feelings?

Speaking	Talking about feelings

I'm ... annoyed / bored / excited / frightened / irritated / nervous / relaxed / sad / shocked / tired / worried.

8 🔊 **1.09** Listen and answer the questions.
1. What is Dan's problem?
2. How does Dan feel about the party?

9 In pairs, describe how you usually feel:
1. before an exam
2. on your birthday
3. after a party
4. on holiday

0.4 INTRODUCING ALISHA

Countries and languages; *was/were*, *there was/were*; Past Simple: regular verbs

1 🔊 **1.10** Add the words below to the correct categories in the Vocabulary box.

> China   Chinese   France   French   German
> Germany   Italian   Italy   Poland   Polish
> Portugal   Portuguese   Turkey   Turkish

Vocabulary	Countries and languages
Countries	**Languages**
India	Hindi
Spain	Spanish
_____	_____
_____	_____
_____	_____
_____	_____
_____	_____

2 **I KNOW!** Work in pairs. How many countries can you name for each letter of the alphabet?

A – Argentina, B – Belgium …

3 🔊 **1.11** Read the text. Find two countries and two languages.

Hi or 'Namaste'! My name's Alisha and I'm half-English and half-Indian. My dad's from India and my mum's from England, so I speak Hindi and English. Dad's family is very big and I've got lots of cousins. We weren't in India last summer but this year we're planning to be there for a whole month. I've got an older brother called Damian. He's funny but also a bit annoying! I'm really into computers and I want to be an IT specialist one day. I like helping my friends when they've got problems. I'm not crazy about sport but I'm fit and very strong. Skye and I were in a kickboxing class at school last year, and I really liked it because it was fun and there were lots of useful exercises. Our kickboxing teacher invited us to do it again this year, and we want to try!

4 Read the text again, and then cover it. Write three things about Alisha.
1 *She's got an older brother.*
2 *She can speak …*

5 Study the Grammar A box. Complete the sentences with *was/were* and *wasn't/weren't*.

Grammar A	*was/were, there was/were*
Affirmative	**Negative**
He **was** on holiday.	He **wasn't** on holiday.
We **were** on holiday.	We **weren't** on holiday.
There **was** a party.	There **wasn't** a party.
There **were** lots of people.	There **weren't** lots of people.
Questions	**Short answers**
Was it fun?	Yes, it **was**. / No, it **wasn't**.
Were they at home?	Yes, there **were**. / No, there **weren't**.
Was there a party?	Yes, there **was**. / No, there **wasn't**.
Were there many people?	Yes, there **were**. / No, there **weren't**.

1 Naomi and her parents _were_ on holiday in Spain but the weather _____ terrible.
2 _____ you at the cinema last night? No, I _____.
3 The film festival _____ fun and there _____ lots of films to watch.
4 _____ your parents angry when you _____ late home?
5 Liam _____ only 10 years old in 1999.
6 _____ the English test difficult? Yes, it _____. There _____ lots of difficult exercises.

6 🔊 **1.12** Study the Grammar B box. Listen and answer the questions.

Grammar B	Past Simple: regular verbs
He **lived** in California.	
They **didn't invite** her.	
Did you **like** the film?	

1 What was Dan like on his first day at school?
2 Who did Dan live with last year?
3 What language does Alisha want to learn?

7 In pairs, tell your partner about five things that were true for you last year, but are NOT true now.

I was in a different class.
I wasn't in the basketball team.

Starter Unit

0.5 CHARACTER QUIZ

1 In pairs, describe the photo. Make as many sentences as possible. What do you think life is like in Woodley Bridge?

2 🔊 1.13 Listen and mark the sentences T (true) or F (false).

1. ☐ The café is closed.
2. ☐ The café sells lemonade.
3. ☐ Dan hasn't got a mobile phone.
4. ☐ Dan is waiting outside the café.
5. ☐ Dan likes the café.
6. ☐ There are lots of places to hang out in Woodley Bridge.

3 Complete the questions with one word in each gap.

The BIG Character Quiz

1. _____ Dan and his brother from the UK?
2. Where _____ Tommo live?
3. Where _____ Alisha's dad's family from?
4. _____ Skye live with her parents?
5. What _____ Dan's brother's name?
6. _____ lived in America last year?
7. _____ Dan and Alisha speak other languages?
8. _____ Skye and Tommo got pets?
9. Why _____ Dan's mum sad?
10. _____ Skye's parents doctors?
11. _____ Tommo got a kayak?
12. _____ Tommo, Dan, Alisha and Skye often meet in a café?

4 In groups, do the quiz about the young people from Woodley Bridge. Use the texts in Lessons 1–4 to help you. How much can you remember?

5 In pairs, write two similar kinds of questions about yourselves. Hand the questions to your teacher and have a class quiz with two teams.

And YOU

Starter Unit 9

1

That's my world!

VOCABULARY
Everyday technology | Adjectives of opinion | Time

GRAMMAR
Present Simple, Present Continuous and state verbs | verb + *ing* / verb + *to*-infinitive

Grammar: It's upside down

Speaking: Let's go in

BBC Culture: Addicted to screens

Workbook p. 16

BBC VOX POPS ▶
CLIL 1 > p. 139

1.1 VOCABULARY Lifestyle
I can talk about everyday technology.

1 **CLASS VOTE** Do you take photos with your mobile phone? What do you take photos of? People? Places? Other things?

2 Match photos 1–6 with sentences a–f. What do the photos tell you about the person's life?

He/She likes reading.   He/She's got a cat.

a ☐ **sunny01**   She's up to mischief again!
b ☐ **jacko999**   Friends + chocolate cake #agreatday!
c ☐ **ninab98**   Come on rain! We've got the right boots.
d ☐ **singingboy98**   Dan's singing again! ;)
e ☐ **robbie2**   It's film time … yay!
f ☐ **paul13**   Ready for our trip!

3 🔊 **1.14** Listen and check you understand the words in the Vocabulary A box. What objects can you see in the pictures?

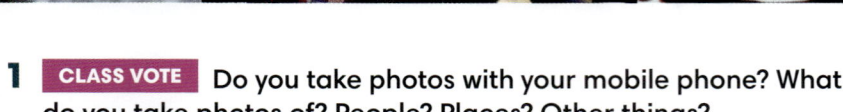

Vocabulary A	Everyday technology
battery cable charger earphones plug selfie stick speaker tablet	

4 **I KNOW!** Can you add more words to the Vocabulary A box?

5 🔊 **1.15** Listen to speakers 1–4 and write the presents. Use the Vocabulary A box to help you.

1 _____   2 _____   3 _____   4 _____

6 Which object would be the best present for you? Why?
I'd like a selfie stick because my friends and I love taking photos.

I want to listen to music but I can't find my ¹*earphones* / *plugs* because my brother is using them! 'They're better than mine', he says. 'It's OK,' I say. I can use my new ²*battery* / *speaker* that plays music *really* loud. However, when I look inside, the ³*plug* / *battery* isn't there because it's in my brother's digital camera and, guess what? His friend's got it at the moment. In the end I decide to watch a funny film on my ⁴*cable* / *tablet* but I can't find it. I look in my brother's bedroom. On his desk there's a pile of ⁵*earphones* / *cables* that are all different lengths. I finally find the short black one with the right ⁶*plug* / *selfie stick* on the end of it for my tablet. 'OK, where is it?' I ask him again. Then I hear Mum's voice. 'Are you looking for this, love?' she asks. 'I'm just buying some shoes but it's nearly dead. Can you get me the ⁷*battery* / *charger*, please?'

7 🔊 1.16 Read the text. Choose the correct options. Listen and check. Is it the same in your house?

8 🔊 1.17 **WORD FRIENDS** Listen to people talking about their phones and mark ✓ the expressions you hear.

Word Friends	
chat with friends	**download** songs
go online	**listen** to music
make/film a video	**play** games
read e-books	**send/get** instant messages
share photos	**text** friends/parents
upload pictures	**watch** music videos

9 In pairs, ask and answer the questions.
1 How many instant messages do you send and get in a day?
   I send about ten instant messages in a day and I get about twenty.
2 Do you know somebody who reads e-books?
3 When do you listen to music?
4 How often do you download songs?
5 Would you like to make a video with friends in your school?
6 What games do you play on the computer?
7 When do you usually text your parents?
8 What type of photos do you usually upload?

10 🔊 1.18 Write the words in the correct column below. Listen and check.

Vocabulary B	Adjectives of opinion
all right amazing awesome awful boring brilliant cool disgusting exciting funny lovely nice noisy OK old-fashioned perfect strange terrible useful	

😊	🙂	😐	🙁	☹️
amazing awesome brilliant	*cool funny*	*all right nice*	*boring noisy*	*awful disgusting*

11 Write two things that are:
1 useful   4 strange
2 awesome   5 terrible
3 old-fashioned

12 Compare your ideas with the class.

13 [VOX POPS ▶ 1.1] Who in your family uses technology the most? What do they use it for?

My brother loves his gadgets. He's older than me and he's got a really good tablet. He shops online, watches films, and he uses it for studying.

Unit 1   11

1.2 GRAMMAR Present Simple, Present Continuous and state verbs

I can use different tenses to talk about the present.

1 **CLASS VOTE** Do you watch music videos? Yes or No? What are some of your favourites?

2 🔊 1.19 Look at the photo. What can you see? Read the text.

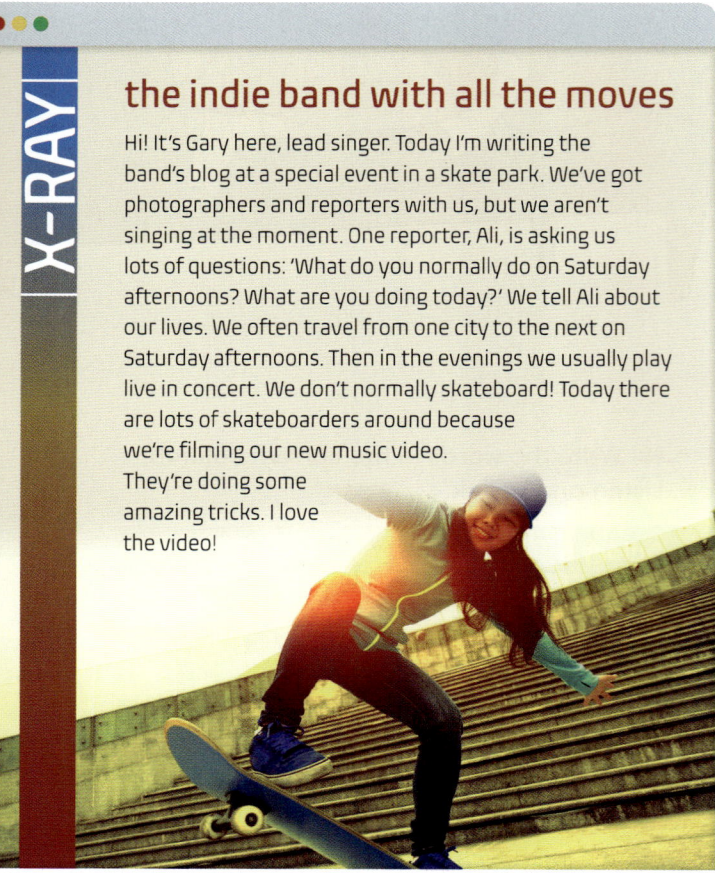

X-RAY

the indie band with all the moves

Hi! It's Gary here, lead singer. Today I'm writing the band's blog at a special event in a skate park. We've got photographers and reporters with us, but we aren't singing at the moment. One reporter, Ali, is asking us lots of questions: 'What do you normally do on Saturday afternoons? What are you doing today?' We tell Ali about our lives. We often travel from one city to the next on Saturday afternoons. Then in the evenings we usually play live in concert. We don't normally skateboard! Today there are lots of skateboarders around because we're filming our new music video. They're doing some amazing tricks. I love the video!

3 Study the Grammar box. Find examples of the Present Simple, Present Continuous and state verbs in the text.

Grammar	Present Simple, Present Continuous and state verbs

Present Simple
They usually *travel* on a tour bus.
He *doesn't write* his blog every day.
Do they *speak* English? Yes, they *do*.

Present Continuous
He*'s travelling* a lot these days.
They *aren't recording* a song at the moment.
Is she *skateboarding* now? No, she *isn't*.

State verbs
Verbs with no continuous form: *love, like, hate, know, think, see, feel, understand, want, need*

GRAMMAR TIME > PAGE 118

4 🔊 1.20 Choose the correct option. Listen and check.
1 Ali and Gary *sit* / (*are sitting*) on a bench at the skate park.
2 Gary usually *sings* / *is singing* in concerts on Saturday evenings.
3 The band members *don't often visit* / *aren't often visiting* skate parks.
4 The skateboarders *do* / *are doing* some fantastic skateboard tricks at the moment.
5 Sara *always wears* / *is always wearing* her lucky blue helmet.
6 Several people *film* / *are filming* the skateboarders.

5 Use the Present Simple or Present Continuous to write questions about the text in Exercise 2. In pairs, ask and answer the questions.
1 the people in the park / film / the skateboarders?
Are the people in the park filming the skateboarders?
2 Gary / work / as a reporter?
3 Ali / ask / questions at the moment?
4 Sara / wear / a helmet in the photo?
5 the band members / usually play / live in concert on Saturdays?
6 the skateboarders / perform / in a competition today?

6 🔊 1.21 Complete the text with the correct form of the verbs in brackets. Listen and check.

My name's Sara. I ¹*love* (love) skateboarding. I'm a real fan. I ² _____ (practise) at a local park every weekend. I ³ _____ (not/often/do) competitions because I'm from a small town.

I'm very excited today because I ⁴ _____ (perform) in a video for a famous band. At the moment we ⁵ _____ (get) ready. Lots of people ⁶ _____ (come) into the park now. My mum and dad ⁷ _____ (sit) near the front because they ⁸ _____ (want) to upload photos for their friends!

7 [VOX POPS ▶ 1.2] In pairs, tell your partner about a hobby/sport you like. Complete the sentences to make them true for you.

I really like/love … because …
I usually/never/don't often …
I want …

Unit 1

1.3 READING and VOCABULARY   Are all gadgets useful?

I can find specific detail in an article and talk about unusual objects.

A

B

Gadget testers for a day! By Max Stevens and Tina Wallis

Today we're going to school by bus as usual. We normally leave home at 8 a.m., but we're leaving early because we're testing some new gadgets for this month's report. All these gadgets are useful when you're travelling. So, what have we got?

First up is the **Briefskate**. It's made of wood, so it looks like a normal skateboard, but you can open the top. Inside there's space for books and a mobile or a tablet. In my opinion, it's useful and fun, but Tina and I can't skate, so we can't test it …

Next, we're trying the **Sospendo**. It's a strange plastic gadget which works like an extra pair of hands to hold your phone or tablet. Tina's wearing it at the moment. She won't drop her tablet, but people are staring at her. I'm sure they're thinking, 'What on earth is she doing?'. Tina doesn't like this gadget!

Max

Now it's my turn. The next gadget is a tiny **controller**. You put it on your mobile or tablet so that you can play games. It looks cool, but I don't need this to play games on my phone.

I normally take a rucksack to school every day, but today I'm testing a **Defender** bag. It's like a rucksack. You can wear it on your back or on your front. When it's in front of you, you can use it like a small table. I don't like it because it looks ugly. Right now, Max is using the **Phorce** bag. You can use it to charge your phone or tablet. I often forget to charge my phone before I leave the house, so I think this is a brilliant idea. Max loves it, too. It's our favourite gadget!

Tina

1 **CLASS VOTE** Would you like to test new gadgets for teenage students? Yes or No?

2 🔊 **1.22** Find the names of the gadgets in bold in the text. Read the text and match two of the gadgets with pictures A and B.

3 Read the article. Choose the correct answers.
1 Max and Tina normally get the bus to school.
  a True   b False   c Doesn't say
2 Tina is going to school on the Briefskate today.
  a True   b False   c Doesn't say
3 The Sospendo is heavy.
  a True   b False   c Doesn't say
4 Tina thinks the controller is useful for her.
  a True   b False   c Doesn't say
5 You need to put the Defender bag on a table to use it.
  a True   b False   c Doesn't say
6 Tina forgot to charge her phone today.
  a True   b False   c Doesn't say

4 What is Max and Tina's opinion of each object? Use the adjectives below to help you.

| boring   clever   cool   fun   normal
| strange   ugly   unusual   useful

They think the Briefskate looks quite normal.

5 What do you think of the gadgets in the report? Which do you like?

I like the Defender bag, but I don't want to look stupid at school!

6 In pairs, describe the things below.

| something in your bag
| your favourite gadget

It's made of plastic.
You can use it to charge your phone.
It's boring.

Unit 1   13

1.4 GRAMMAR Verb + *ing* / verb + *to*-infinitive

I can use verb constructions with *to*-infinitives and *-ing* forms.

VIDEO   IT'S UPSIDE DOWN

Tommo: Hi, Alisha. Are you busy?
Alisha: Yes. I'm trying to finish my homework but it's taking ages. I'd love to be outside in this weather.
Tommo: Me too, but I've got a problem with my computer. Dan says you're good at fixing things.
Alisha: Well, I enjoy trying. What's up?
Tommo: I'm making a poster for a competition. I prefer using my own photos but when I upload them from my phone to the computer, they're upside down.
Alisha: That's strange.
Tommo: It's really annoying. I want to put the posters up in town but now I've got ten photos … upside down!
Alisha: Tommo, the problem is your settings.
Tommo: Oh, so what can I do?
Alisha: I can't explain now but I don't mind coming to your boat later.
Tommo: OK … but don't forget to bring a snack. It could take a long time.
Alisha: Tommo!

It's upside down.   It's taking ages.   It's really annoying.   **OUT of class**

1 **CLASS VOTE** Who do you speak to when you've got a problem with your computer, tablet or phone?

parent?   friend?   shop assistant?   teacher?

2 ▶ 1.3 🔊 1.23 Watch or listen. Why does Tommo want Alisha to help him?

3 Study the Grammar box. Find more examples of verbs + *ing* or verbs + *to*-infinitive in the dialogue.

Grammar | verb + *ing* and verb + *to*-infinitive

verb + *ing*
After: *avoid, can't stand, enjoy, finish, look forward to, (not) mind, miss, practise, stop*, and after prepositions
I **don't mind coming** to your house.
She's good **at fixing** things.

verb + *to*-infinitive
After: *agree, allow, ask, choose, decide, forget, hope, learn, offer, plan, try, want, would like/love*
I **'d love to be** in the park in this weather.

verb + *ing* or *to*-infinitive
After: *like, love, hate, prefer, start*
I **prefer making** my own posters. / I **prefer to make** my own posters.

GRAMMAR TIME > PAGE 118

4 Choose the correct option.
1 There's a concert on TV tonight. I hope *watching* / *to watch* it when I get home.
2 Our friends are coming to the park. We enjoy *meeting* / *to meet* here after school.
3 My cousin's learning Chinese and would like *to visit* / *visiting* China one day.
4 Homemade pizza is amazing but I'm not very good at *making* / *to make* it.
5 Naomi misses *to see* / *seeing* her friends from her old school.

5 Complete the advert with the correct form of the verbs below.

put   ~~take~~   come   meet   do   bring

School photography club!

Are you interested in ¹*taking* better photos?

Then don't forget ² _____ to the new photography club. It's the place where you can enjoy ³ _____ something different. This week our theme is buildings and we want you ⁴ _____ some of your best photos to the club. We hope ⁵ _____ our favourite ones on display in the school library. We're looking forward to ⁶ _____ you!

6 In pairs, write an advert for a new club at your school. Compare your ideas with the class.

1.5 LISTENING and VOCABULARY   Are you technology crazy?

I can identify specific detail in a radio programme and talk about using technology.

1 **CLASS VOTE** Do you think you spend too much time on your phone or on the computer?

2 Is it time for time out? Do the quiz and compare your results with the class. Then go to page 144 to read what your answers say about you.

1 When do you first look at your phone or use the internet?
  a In the evening.
  b Probably at lunchtime.
  c The minute I wake up.

2 When is it too late to text somebody?
  a On a weekday, after 10 p.m.
  b At midnight.
  c It's never too late.

3 What do you do when you have a free moment?
  a I listen to music.
  b I read a book.
  c I go online.

4 How often do you check your text messages?
  a Once a day. I don't get many.
  b At school I check them at break time.
  c I check them all the time.

3 🔊 **1.24** Complete the gaps with words from the quiz. Listen and check.

Vocabulary	Time
second, *minute*, hour	
6 a.m., _____	
in the morning / the afternoon / _____	
on a schoolday/_____/Sunday(s)	
at the weekend/_____/mealtimes/lunchtime	
_____/twice/three times a day / a week / a month / a year	

4 In pairs, ask and answer the questions. Compare your ideas with the class.

1 What's your favourite mealtime? Why?
  I love lunchtime because I eat with my friends.
2 What time do you go to bed at the weekend?
3 How many seconds are there in five minutes?
4 What time do you get up on a schoolday?
5 What do you normally do at break time?
6 What do you do the minute you wake up?

5 🔊 **1.25** Listen to the first part of a radio programme. What is the programme about? Choose the correct answer.
  a The number of families that use phones or tablets in their free time.
  b How much time families spend on their phones or tablets.

6 🔊 **1.26** Listen to the second part of the programme. Mark the sentences T (true) or F (false).

1 ☐ Everybody in Gemma's family has a smartphone.
2 ☐ First Gemma gets up and then she checks her messages.
3 ☐ Gemma's mum uses her smartphone to read the news.
4 ☐ A phone app helps Gemma's mum when she's running.
5 ☐ Sometimes Gemma's brother doesn't hear his mum's questions.
6 ☐ Gemma thinks they should talk more in her family.

7 How important is technology in your life? What technology do you use and what do you like doing? Write five sentences.

Technology is very important to me. It's useful because I can go online and do my homework and I can chat with friends. In my free time I listen to lots of music ...

And YOU?

1.6 SPEAKING Making suggestions

I can make and respond to suggestions.

VIDEO LET'S GO IN

Tommo: Hi, Alisha. Welcome to my canal boat. Let's go in.
Alisha: This is so cool! So, are you doing your poster?
Tommo: No, not now. I'm filming my cat for an online video. Like these.
Alisha: Aah! I love Ninja Cat! Your cat can be famous too.
Tommo: You could help me.
Alisha: OK, cool. Where's your cat? What's his name?
Tommo: *Her* name is Hissy. She's a girl.
Alisha: Oops, sorry! So, where is she?
Tommo: Er, I don't know. She usually hides from visitors.
Alisha: Why don't we look for her? Maybe she's behind the sofa.
Tommo: I can't see her. Oh yes, she's there, but she isn't coming out.
Alisha: What about putting some food down?
Tommo: Good idea. Dinner time, Hissy!
Alisha: Look! I can see her eyes. Shall we film her there?
Tommo: Yeah, why not? She looks funny.
Hissy: Hissssss!
Alisha: What's up? Oh, she doesn't like the camera.
Tommo: Hissy! Where are you going? Come back!
Alisha: Don't worry! You can call the video 'Cross Cat'!

> *Good idea.   Come back.*
> *This is so cool!*

OUT of class

1 CLASS VOTE Describe each cat. Which video would you like to watch?

Scary Cat   Ninja Cat   Wet Cat

2 ▶ 1.4 🔊 1.27 Watch or listen and answer the questions.
1 What's Alisha's opinion of the canal boat?
2 What's Tommo doing?
3 How does Hissy react to visitors?
4 Where's Hissy hiding?

3 Study the Speaking box. Find more examples of suggestions in the dialogue.

> **Speaking Suggestions**
>
> **Making suggestions**
> You could look online.
> Let's look for it.
> What about texting her?
> Why don't you charge it?
> Shall we watch *Friends*?
>
> **Accepting or rejecting suggestions**
> Yes, great idea. / Yes, why not? / OK, cool.
> I'm not sure. / I'd rather not.

4 🔊 1.28 Listen to six speakers and respond. Use the Speaking box to help you.

5 In pairs, follow the instructions.

Student A: choose a situation from the list.
Student B: respond with a suitable suggestion.

> I need some information for my project.
> The teacher's late.   I can't see the board.
> It's really cold in here.   I can't swim.

6 In pairs, plan a funny video. Discuss what you want to film and where. Make suggestions and respond.

a dog with a stick – in a park
my sister at dinnertime – at the table

1.7 WRITING A description of your dream lifestyle

I can describe places and lifestyles.

1 **CLASS VOTE** Which of these would be your dream home?

- a modern caravan
- a castle in Scotland
- a beach hut on an exotic island
- a terraced house in a small town
- a massive skyscraper   a villa in Spain
- a cottage in the mountains
- a flat in a block of flats

2 Read the text. Which of the things below does Skye write about in paragraph 1? Which are in paragraph 2?

sports _2_   home ___   hobbies ___
friends ___   place ___   daily routine ___

My Dream Lifestyle
by Skye Winter-Fox

In my everyday life, I live in a terraced house near Oxford with my grandma, because my parents are in New Zealand. But my dream home is a beach hut in Bali. The beach hut has got one bedroom and a living room. As well as a huge touch screen TV, there's a fast internet connection in case I want to share videos with friends! Although it's small, outside there's a veranda so I have a perfect view of the sea.

In real life I go to Cherwell School on weekdays. I usually swim before school and I try to write at the weekend. However, in my dream lifestyle, I sit outside and write my novel on my laptop every morning. Then in the afternoon I swim and go surfing, too. Friends often visit me at the weekend and we have amazing barbecues on the beach.

3 In pairs, find four differences between Skye's real life and her dream lifestyle.

In her real life Skye lives near Oxford, but in her dream lifestyle she lives in Bali.

4 How is your dream lifestyle similar or different to Skye's?

Skye's dream lifestyle is a beach hut in Bali, but I'd like to live in a villa in Spain.

5 Complete the sentences to make them true for you.

Writing	A description of your dream lifestyle

Real home and dream home
I live in _____ . / My home is in _____ .
My dream home is a _____ in _____ .
It's near a beach / a cliff / _____ .
It has got _____ .
Outside/Inside there is/are _____ .
I have a view of _____ .

Daily life and dream life
In real life I go to _____ school.
I usually/often/sometimes/never _____ .
I _____ on weekdays / at the weekend.
In my dream lifestyle, I often _____ in the morning.

6 Complete the gaps with connectors from the text, matching the connectors with their function.

Adding similar detail: also, _____ , _____ , _____
Showing contrast: although, _____ , _____
Giving reasons: in case, _____ , _____

7 Complete the sentences with connectors from Exercise 6.

1 _____ playing the violin, I have singing lessons _____ .
2 My dream home is small. _____ , it's perfect for me!
3 _____ I love dancing, I'm not very good at it.
4 I want to live near the sea _____ I can swim every day.

Writing Time

8 Write a description of your dream lifestyle for a school magazine. Follow the instructions below.

Paragraph 1: Real home and dream home
Paragraph 2: Daily life and dream life

TIP
Use the Present Simple and adverbs of frequency.

Unit 1 17

WORDLIST Everyday technology | Adjectives of opinion | Time

alarm /əˈlɑːm/
all right /ˌɔːl ˈraɪt/
amazing /əˈmeɪzɪŋ/
at mealtimes, /ət ˈmiːltaɪmz/
at break time /ət ˈbreɪk taɪm/
at midday/midnight /ət ˌmɪdˈdeɪ ˈmɪdnaɪt/
at the weekend /ət ðə ˌwiːkˈend/
awesome /ˈɔːsəm/
awful /ˈɔːfl/
band /bænd/
barbecue /ˈbɑːbɪkjuː/
battery /ˈbætri/
beach hut /ˈbiːtʃ hʌt/
block of flats /ˌblɒk əv ˈflæts/
blog /blɒg/
boring /ˈbɔːrɪŋ/
bungalow /ˈbʌŋgələʊ/
cable /ˈkeɪbl/
caravan /ˈkærəvæn/
castle /ˈkɑːsl/
charge /tʃɑːdʒ/
charger /ˈtʃɑːdʒə/
clever /ˈklevə/
competition /ˌkɒmpəˈtɪʃn/
cool /kuːl/
cottage /ˈkɒtɪdʒ/
cross /krɒs/
dead (battery) /ˌded ˈbætəri/
digital camera /ˌdɪdʒətl ˈkæmərə/
disgusting /dɪsˈgʌstɪŋ/
(dream) lifestyle /ˌdriːm ˈlaɪfstaɪl/
earphones /ˈɪəfəʊnz/
event /ɪˈvent/
exciting /ɪkˈsaɪtɪŋ/
fix /fɪks/
fun /fʌn/
funny /ˈfʌni/
gadget /ˈgædʒɪt/
heavy /ˈhevi/

helmet /ˈhelmɪt/
in the morning/afternoon/evening /ɪn ðə ˈmɔːnɪŋ/ˌɑːftəˈnuːn/ˈiːvnɪŋ/
internet connection /ˈɪntənet kəˌnekʃn/
lovely /ˈlʌvli/
nice /naɪs/
noisy /ˈnɔɪzi/
novel /ˈnɒvl/
old-fashioned /ˌəʊld ˈfæʃnd/
on a schoolday/a weekday/Sunday(s) /ɒn ə ˈskuːldeɪ/ə ˈwiːkdeɪ/ˈsʌndeɪ(z)/
once/twice/three times a day /ˌwʌns/ˌtwaɪs/θriː ˌtaɪmz ə ˈdeɪ/
perfect /ˈpɜːfɪkt/
perform /pəˈfɔːm/
(phone) app /ˈfəʊn æp/
photographers /fəˈtɒgrəfəz/
photography /fəˈtɒgrəfi/
plug /plʌg/
poster /ˈpəʊstə/
report /rɪˈpɔːt/
reporter /rɪˈpɔːtə/
second /ˈsekənd/
selfie stick /ˈselfi stɪk/
skate park /ˈskeɪt pɑːk/
skateboarders /ˈskeɪtˌbɔːdəz/
skyscraper /ˈskaɪˌskreɪpə/
smartphone /ˈsmɑːtfəʊn/
sofa /ˈsəʊfə/
space /speɪs/
speaker /ˈspiːkə/
strange /streɪndʒ/
tablet /ˈtæblət/
take photos /ˌteɪk ˈfəʊtəʊz/
technology /tekˈnɒlədʒi/
terraced house /ˌterəst ˈhaʊs/
terrible /ˈterəbl/
test /test/

tester /ˈtestə/
top /tɒp/
touch screen TV /ˈtʌtʃ skriːn ˌtiː ˈviː/
trick /trɪk/
ugly /ˈʌgli/
unusual /ʌnˈjuːʒuəl/
upside down /ˌʌpsaɪd ˈdaʊn/
useful /ˈjuːsfl/
veranda /vəˈrændə/
view /vjuː/
villa /ˈvɪlə/

WORD FRIENDS

using gadgets
chat with friends
download songs
go online
listen to music
make/film a video
play games
read e-books
send/get instant messages
share photos
text friends/parents
upload pictures
watch music videos

describing objects
it's made of metal/wood/plastic/cotton/paper
it's like a/an (+ noun)
it looks (+ adjective)
it looks like a/an (+ noun)
it works like a/an (+ noun)
you can (+ verb)
you can use it like a (noun)
you can use it to (+ infinitive) / for (+ –ing)

VOCABULARY IN ACTION

1 Use the wordlist to find:
   1 three people
   2 three types of houses
   3 three positive adjectives
   4 three types of materials
   5 three gadgets

2 Use the wordlist to find adjectives that describe:
   - the town you live in *exciting*
   - your school
   - your favourite band
   - your school bag
   - your phone or computer

3 Use the wordlist to complete the sentences. In pairs, tell your partner if the sentences are true for you.
   1 I always *listen* to music on my phone when I walk to school.
   2 I relax when I _____ games on the computer.
   3 I like to sing along when I _____ music videos.
   4 My friends usually _____ me instant messages.
   5 I always _____ my parents when I'm late.
   6 I only _____ online when I don't have any homework.

4 🔊 **1.29** **PRONUNCIATION** Listen and decide how *s* is pronounced in each word. Write the word in the correct column.

| earphones   e-books   gadgets   helmets   hours |
| novels   photos   plugs   reporters   tablets   tricks |

| /s/ | /z/ |
| e-books | plugs |

When do you pronounce /s/ and /z/?

Revision

VOCABULARY

1 Write the correct word for each definition.
1. You put these in your ears to listen to music. **e** _ _ _ _ _ _ _
2. If you use a skateboard, you wear this on your head. **h** _ _ _ _ _ _
3. This means the opposite of brilliant. **t** _ _ _ _ _ _ _
4. A small house in the country. **c** _ _ _ _ _ _
5. You put this inside a gadget to give it energy. **b** _ _ _ _ _ _ _
6. Sixty seconds. **m** _ _ _ _ _ _

2 Complete the quiz with one of the expressions. In pairs, ask and answer the questions.

> in the evening   at the weekend   twice a day
> at mealtimes   on a schoolday   at midnight

QUIZ
1. Do you text your friends …?
2. Do you do sport …?
3. Do you use your phone …?
4. Do you go online …?

A: Do you text your friends at mealtimes?
B: I never text my friends at mealtimes.

3 Tell the class about your partner.

GRAMMAR

4 Complete the sentences with the correct form of the verbs in brackets, then match them with the correct function, A, B or C.

A an action in progress
B a regular action
C a state verb

1. Carla _____ (read) an e-book now.
2. My grandparents _____ (usually/phone) us at the weekend.
3. Jake _____ (not/like) music videos.
4. We _____ (not/often/download) songs.
5. I _____ (know) how to upload photos.
6. Why _____ (you/chat) with friends now? It's very late.

5 Complete the questions with the correct form of the verbs in brackets.
1. Are you planning *to go* (go) online later?
2. Are you good at _____ (fix) things?
3. Do you prefer _____ (live) in a village or a town?
4. Do you want _____ (make) a video of your school?
5. Are you looking forward to _____ (see) your little brother?

SPEAKING

6 Complete the dialogue with the words below.

> about   ~~shall~~   idea   rather
> could   sure   don't   let's

A: ¹*Shall* we go to the cinema?
B: No, I'd ² _____ not. What's on TV tonight?
A: Er, not much … Why ³ _____ we watch *The Simpsons*?
B: I'm not ⁴ _____. What time does it start?
A: 7.30 p.m. … Oh, it's 8 p.m. now.
B: What ⁵ _____ watching football on Channel 3? It starts at 8.
A: Mmm, I don't really like football. I know, ⁶ _____ watch a film online!
B: Yes, great ⁷ _____. We ⁸ _____ watch *Despicable Me 3*.

7 In pairs, decide what to watch together. Use the TV guide to help you.

TV GUIDE

Time	Channel 2	Channel 3
7.30	The Simpsons	basketball
8.00	Friends	football
8.30	This Country's Got Talent	tennis

DICTATION

8 🔊 1.30 Listen, then listen again and write down what you hear.

CULTURE

Do smartphones make you **smarter?**

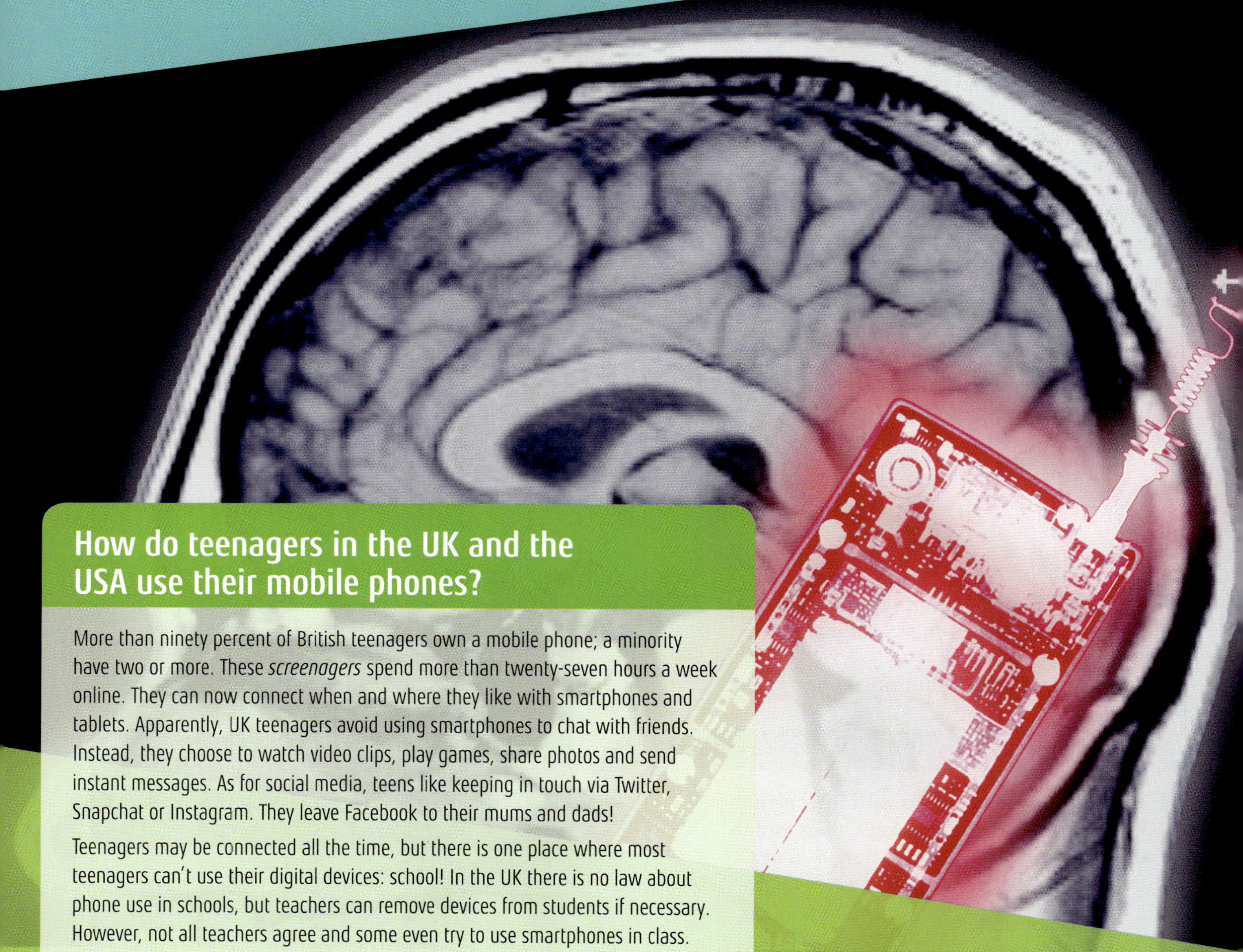

How do teenagers in the UK and the USA use their mobile phones?

More than ninety percent of British teenagers own a mobile phone; a minority have two or more. These *screenagers* spend more than twenty-seven hours a week online. They can now connect when and where they like with smartphones and tablets. Apparently, UK teenagers avoid using smartphones to chat with friends. Instead, they choose to watch video clips, play games, share photos and send instant messages. As for social media, teens like keeping in touch via Twitter, Snapchat or Instagram. They leave Facebook to their mums and dads!

Teenagers may be connected all the time, but there is one place where most teenagers can't use their digital devices: school! In the UK there is no law about phone use in schools, but teachers can remove devices from students if necessary. However, not all teachers agree and some even try to use smartphones in class.

A recent British report said that removing smartphones from schools will give students more time for their education. It said that smartphones are a big distraction, make students less productive and are bad for learning.

However, in the USA some people do not agree. Recently one school in New York decided to allow students to use smartphones at school. They said that smartphones can be an excellent resource for the classroom. We carry a lot of information in our pockets and this information can be really useful. In this New York school, smartphones can definitely make you smarter!

GLOSSARY
device (n) a machine or tool
distraction (n) something that takes your attention away from what you are doing
law (n) a system or rules
minority (n) a small part of a larger group
remove (v) take away

EXPLORE

1 In pairs, ask and answer the questions.
1 What do you do with your phone?
2 Do you think it makes you smarter or less smart? Why?
3 Do many people have smartphones in your country?

2 Correct the sentences about the article.
1 All UK teachers believe smartphones are bad for students.
2 A recent UK report said that using smartphones in school can be positive.
3 All schools in the USA and the UK have similar ideas about smartphone use in schools.

EXPLORE MORE

A

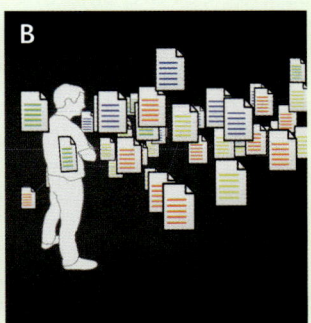
B

C

D

3 1.5 Watch Part 1 of the video and answer the questions.
1 What country can you see in photo A?
2 Why is this country so important in the video?
3 How similar is your country to the one in the report?

4 1.5 Complete the sentences about Korea with the numbers below. Then watch again and check.

eight   a couple of   ~~ten~~   eighteen   four

1 You can download files _ten_ times faster here.
2 Even _____-year-olds spend _____ hours a week online.
3 Some teenagers use the internet for _____ hours a day.
4 Will your country be like this in _____ years from now?

5 What do you think about the issue of internet addiction in Korea? Do you think the same thing could happen in your country in the future?

6 1.6 Watch Part 2 of the video. Match photos B–D with captions 1–3.
1 ☐ Students can interact online to solve problems.
2 ☐ Reading online is not like reading a book.
3 ☐ This is part of a big online conversation.

7 1.6 Watch again. Choose the correct option.
1 Now we *send / receive* information via connections or hyperlinks.
2 You can watch the angry cat and then create your own *clip / text*.
3 Korea is the most *addicted / connected* country in the world.
4 They are regularly at the *top / bottom* of the world's education league tables.

8 Do you think the report is in favour or against the use of the internet? Why? Discuss in pairs.

YOU EXPLORE

9 **CULTURE PROJECT** In groups, prepare a debate based on the question: 'Do smartphones make you smarter?'
1 Prepare a list of points to support your argument.
2 Present your argument to the class.
3 What was the most common point of view among your classmates?

Unit 1   21

2

Wild nature

VOCABULARY
Weather | Temperature | Natural disasters | In the wild

GRAMMAR
Past Simple: regular and irregular verbs | Past Simple and Past Continuous | Adverbs and indefinite pronouns

Grammar: What were you doing while you were away?

Speaking: Why did you do that?

BBC Culture: Severe weather

Workbook p. 28

BBC VOX POPS

2.1 VOCABULARY — Weather and natural disasters

I can talk about the weather and natural disasters.

1 CLASS VOTE What's your favourite season? Why? Compare your ideas.
I like autumn because the trees are different colours.

2 🔊 1.31 Fill in the table with the correct words. Listen and check.

Vocabulary A	Weather	
	Noun	**Adjective**
🌧	rain	rainy
❄		
☀		
🌫🚗		
☁		
💨		
🧊		
⛈		

snow cloud fog wind ice storm sunny foggy cloudy sun icy stormy windy snowy

Watch OUT!
To describe the weather, we use *It's* + adjective:
It's rainy/foggy/windy.
We can use the Present Continuous:
It's raining/snowing. The sun is shining.
When the weather is beginning to change, we use *get* + adjective:
It's getting sunny/foggy/windy/cloudy.

3 In pairs, describe two photos from the website.
In photo 1 it's very windy and in photo 2 it's cold and there's snow on the ground.

22

3 4 5

DID YOU KNOW ... ?

A It isn't always hot and ¹*sunny / sun* in the desert! In January 2015, because of ²*stormy / stormy weather*, there was enough ³*snow / snowing* to build a snowman.

B Less than 1mm of ⁴*rain / raining* falls every year in Arica, in Chile. It would take 100 years to fill a coffee cup.

C The 'zonda' ⁵*windy / wind* in Argentina is a dry wind that often carries dust over the mountains. When it happens, it makes the ⁶*sunny / sun* look brown.

D When it's very ⁷*wind / windy* in hilly places, ⁸*snowy / snow* can move along the ground and make a snowroller.

E A moustache ⁹*cloud / cloudy* forms when a cloud passes over a column of air. But be quick if you want a photo, it doesn't happen very often!

F It's so cold in the Antarctic that in some places the ¹⁰*icy / ice* is more than 4,000 metres thick.

G The Grand Banks are shallow areas of water on the coast of Newfoundland, Canada. They have more than 200 ¹¹*foggy / fog* days every year.

H It can be very ¹²*rain / rainy* in Kerala, India, but in 2001 the ¹³*rain / raining* was red because it was carrying sand from the desert. Strange, isn't it?

4 Read the text. Choose the correct option. Which facts are shown in the photos?

5 🔊 **1.32** Complete gaps 1–6 with the words below. Listen and check.

boiling (hot)   cool   chilly   degrees
freezing (cold)   minus

Vocabulary B	Temperature
1 _____	
hot	
warm	
mild	
2 _____	
cold	
3 _____	
4 _____	
It's 35 ⁵_____ .	
It's ⁶_____ 10 today.	

We can say: *It's boiling hot* or *It's boiling*, *It's freezing cold* or *It's freezing*.

6 🔊 **1.33** Listen to three weather forecasts and complete the gaps below.

New York _____ _____ _____
Rio de Janeiro _____ _____ _____
Krakow _____ _____ _____

7 🔊 **1.34** Match the sentences with the words from the Vocabulary C box. Listen and check.

Vocabulary C	Natural disasters

avalanche   drought   earthquake   flood
hurricane   tsunami

1 The water is going into the houses. People are moving upstairs. _____
2 There's a lot of snow and it's coming down the mountain very quickly. _____
3 People are hungry. They can't grow plants because the ground is dry and hard. _____
4 The building is shaking. _____
5 The beach is empty. People are going into the mountains before the wave arrives. _____
6 It's very windy and it's raining. Everybody is inside and the doors and windows are closed. _____

8 In pairs, choose one of the words from the Vocabulary C box. Describe the problems they can cause in your country.

go outside   grow food   stay indoors
trees fall down   water leaves a (place)
windows break

Unit 2

2.2 GRAMMAR Past Simple: regular and irregular verbs

I can use regular and irregular verbs to talk about the past.

Venezuela's Special Storms

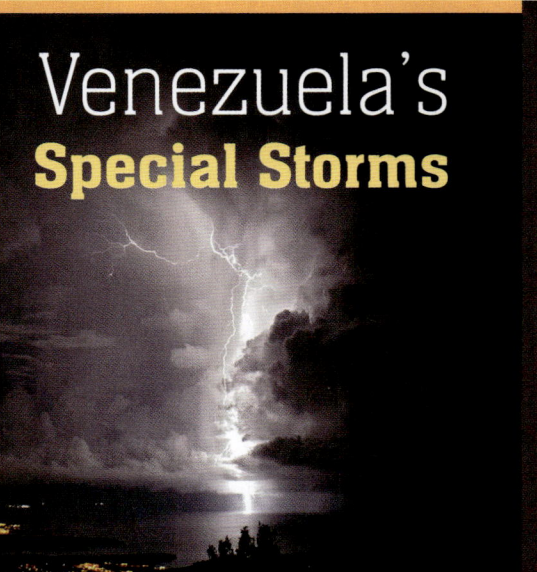

You might find storms fascinating or frightening. But can they be positive? If you live in Venezuela, your answer may be: yes! In 1595 a storm in Venezuela **saved** the country. How **did** that **happen**? Foreign sailors **wanted** to attack but they **saw** strange lightning. It **looked** pinkish-orange, so they **didn't know** what it was. They **felt** scared. In the bright light of the storm, soldiers on land **spotted** the ships.

This **took place** over Lake Maracaibo on the Catatumbo River. It is an area famous for its special storms. Long ago, sailors **used** a storm in the same way as a lighthouse, to help them find their way. The geography of the high mountains by the lake **meant** that storms **didn't move** but **stayed** in the same place. Nowadays Lake Maracaibo holds a Guinness World Record as the place with the most lightning bolts per square kilometre.

1 **CLASS VOTE** Do you enjoy storms? Why? / Why not?

2 🔊 **1.35** Read the text. Find three unusual facts about the colour, place and frequency of the lightning it describes.

3 Study the Grammar box. Find the Past Simple forms of the verbs in the text. Which are regular/irregular? Why do negatives and questions make this difficult to determine?

Grammar	Past Simple
Regular verbs	**Irregular verbs**
It **looked** strange.	We **saw** an unusual storm.
They **didn't** move.	I **didn't know** what to do.
When **did** that **happen**?	**Did** you **take** any photos?
We use the Past Simple with time adverbials. e.g. *yesterday, last week/year; two hours/days/weeks/years ago, in April, in 1595.*	

GRAMMAR TIME > PAGE 119

4 Change the regular verbs to the affirmative (✓) to make true sentences.
1 The Catatumbo storm didn't happen in Venezuela in 1595.
   The Catatumbo storm happened in Venezuela in 1595.
2 The lightning didn't scare the foreign sailors.
3 The storms didn't help many sailors to find their way.
4 The lightning didn't appear in the same place again and again.

5 Change the irregular verbs to the negative (✗) to make true sentences.
1 The sailors saw green lightning.
   The sailors didn't see green lightning.
2 The sailors felt excited about the storm.
3 Sailors thought the Catatumbo storms were normal.
4 The storms took place over the sea.

6 Complete the sentences with a time adverbial, to make them true for you.
1 I saw snow _____.
2 We had really bad weather on our school trip _____.
3 We loved the warm weather on our holiday _____.
4 I went out in the rain without a coat _____.

7 Make questions in the Past Simple.
1 who / Marianna / meet?
   Who did Marianna meet?
2 what / the man / study?
3 when / Marianna / go to Lake Maracaibo?
4 how many storms / she / see?
5 where / she / put / the photos?

8 🔊 **1.36** For each question in Exercise 7, write the beginning of the answers, including the verb. Listen and answer the questions.
1 *Marianna met …*

Unit 2

2.3 READING and VOCABULARY Find out about life in a cold country

I can find specific detail in an article and talk about culture.

Land of Ice and Fire

I love living in Iceland. I hope my diary inspires you to visit my country one day! *Ari*

Wednesday: It's the end of winter now, but it's absolutely freezing this evening, about –10 degrees C. My sister and I did some knitting. Like all children here, we learned to knit at primary school, but we're not very good at it. Mum makes great jumpers for us, though. I helped my dad make some *kakosupa* – it's cocoa soup, like hot chocolate – lovely, thick and really warm!

Thursday: Our maths teacher, Jakob, gave us a very difficult test this morning. By the way, I'm not completely crazy – it's normal here to use your teacher's first name, because most of us don't have a surname, we take our father's name. So, for example, my dad's name is Jón, so my sister is Eva Jónsdottir (Jón's daughter) and I'm Ari Jónsson (Jón's son).

Friday: This evening the news programmes were full of information about the latest volcanic eruptions here. It was really interesting. There were a lot of small earthquakes before the eruptions. Eva downloaded some pictures from the Internet. They are totally amazing!

Saturday: I spent the whole afternoon with my friend's family at a natural thermal pool. We didn't swim, though. We sat in the open air and talked for hours. It's a normal way to relax in Iceland.

Sunday: I took some great photos of the Northern Lights. You can only see them when the sky is dark. Spring and autumn are good times, sometime between 5 p.m. and 2 a.m. when there are no clouds. I waited for ages, and they started at about 10 p.m. It was a brilliant display, and quite long, too – about fifteen minutes.

1 **CLASS VOTE** What do you do when it's cold outside? Vote for the top three ideas.

2 Look at the title, introduction and photo on the blog. What do they tell you about Ari's country?

3 🔊 1.37 Read the text and answer the questions.
1. What did Ari's family do to feel warm?
2. Why do pupils call their teacher by his/her first name?
3. What happened before the volcanic eruptions?
4. Where did Ari go on Saturday?

4 Match the people with the phrases to make true sentences.
1. ☐ Ari
2. ☐ Ari's mum
3. ☐ Ari's father
4. ☐ Ari's sister
5. ☐ People in Iceland

a. is called Jón.
b. likes *kakosupa*.
c. like relaxing in thermal pools.
d. found good photos of volcanoes.
e. is good at knitting.

5 **WORD FRIENDS** Look at the highlighted words in the text. Complete the table with the correct adverb.

adverb + regular adjective	adverb + strong adjective
___ cold	___ freezing
___ good	___ amazing
___ difficult	___ crazy

Watch OUT! You can use *really* and *quite* with both adjective types.

6 Choose the correct option.
1. Wow! The volcano is *absolutely / very* fantastic!
2. These photos are *totally / very* good.
3. Climbing a live volcano is *completely / very* ridiculous!
4. *Kakosupa* is *really / totally* delicious.

7 Use the Word Friends to make sentences about the things below.

> the place where you live   a TV programme
> your favourite hobby   a food or drink

8 Write a blog entry about what you did or saw last week that is typical of life in your country.

2.4 GRAMMAR Past Simple and Past Continuous

I can talk about an event in the past and what was happening around it.

VIDEO — WHAT WERE YOU DOING WHILE YOU WERE AWAY?

Mom: What's that funny smell? Ugh! Dan! You didn't empty your bag last night.
Dan: Oh, sorry, Mum. Skye called while I was doing it. She wanted to know about the Geography trip. We were chatting for ages and then I forgot about my bag.
Mom: These clothes are wet. What were you doing while you were away?
Dan: Most of the time we were studying rocks, but on the last day we had a walk. We were crossing a river when I fell in. Sorry, Mum. It was funny at the time.
Mom: Mmhh. I'm sure it was. Anyway, take these things to the washing machine. You can put them in now.
Dan: Oh, Mum. I've got to go out. Tommo texted while you were talking to me. Can I do it later? Please …

> **OUT of class**
> It was an accident.
> It was (funny) at the time.

1 **CLASS VOTE** What's the first thing you do when you arrive home after a school trip?

  eat something   take a shower   unpack my bag
  talk to friends online   fall asleep

2  2.1 1.38 Watch or listen. What did Dan forget to do when he got home last night?

3 Study the Grammar box. Find examples of the Past Simple and the Past Continuous in the dialogue.

Grammar	Past Simple and Past Continuous
Past Continuous It was raining. We weren't studying Maths. Were you talking?	**Past Simple and Past Continuous** We were walking in the forest when I found a snake. I fell while I was climbing the tree.

GRAMMAR TIME > PAGE 119

4 Choose the correct option.
1. We ate / (were eating) lunch when we were hearing / heard the avalanche.
2. The rain was starting / started while we were swimming / swam in the sea.
3. Emma was walking on the beach while / when she found the money.
4. I was taking / took a lot of photos while I was travelling / travel in Iceland.
5. He was cooking food on the fire when / while he saw the bear.
6. James was falling / fell on the ice while he was skating / skated with friends.

5 Complete the email from Dan's brother with the Past Simple or Past Continuous forms of the verbs in brackets.

Hi Dan,
How was your Geography trip? When I ¹*was doing* (do) Geography at school, we ² _____ (have) a school trip to the Rockies. It was winter and freezing cold.

One day, the weather suddenly ³ _____ (change) while we ⁴ _____ (walk) in the mountains. We soon got lost in the fog! Our teachers had to call for help on their cell phones. While we ⁵ _____ (wait), I ⁶ _____ (hear) a strange noise. It was …

6 What do you think Dan's brother heard?

7 [VOX POPS ▶ 2.2] In pairs, discuss funny things that happened on a school trip or on holiday.

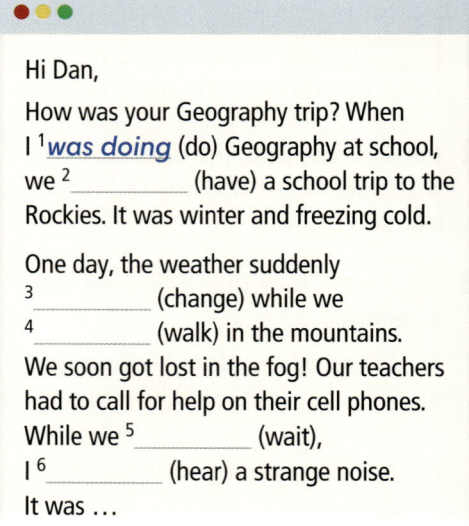

I was skiing down a hill when my phone fell out of my pocket.
We were watching some monkeys when one of them stole my chocolate!

Unit 2

2.5 LISTENING and VOCABULARY In the wild

I can identify specific detail in a conversation and talk about being in the wild.

1 **CLASS VOTE** Do you enjoy being outdoors? Why? / Why not? Compare your ideas with the class.

2 🔊 **1.39** Look at the photos from the *Go Wild!* camp. Decide if sentences 1–3 are true (T) or false (F). Listen and check.
1. ☐ The *Go Wild!* camp is a summer camp.
2. ☐ The *Go Wild!* camp is for families.
3. ☐ The *Go Wild!* camps are in different locations.

3 🔊 **1.40** **WORD FRIENDS** Listen to Abigail telling Max about her experience with *Go Wild.* Choose the correct option.

Word Friends
(make) / build a fire
sit / sleep outside
make / build a shelter
learn about / listen to the wildlife
see / watch the stars
look for / find wild animals
grow / discover unusual plants

4 🔊 **1.40** Listen again. Match the activities from Exercise 3 with the days of the week in Abigail's diary. There are two extra activities.

Monday ...
Tuesday make a fire
Wednesday ...
Thursday ...
Friday ...

5 🔊 **1.40** Listen again and answer the questions.
1. Why didn't Abigail sleep outside in the end?
2. Why didn't Abigail listen to the wildlife?
3. Why weren't there any spiders in the camp?
4. Why do you think Max has a headache?

6 🔊 **1.41** Study the Vocabulary box, using a dictionary. Write the words in the correct category. Listen and check.

Vocabulary In the wild
bat   bear   cave   leaf (leaves)   path   sky
spider   star   sunset   waterfall   wildlife

- elements of landscape: _____ _____ _____ _____ _____ _____
- animals: _____ _____ _____ _____

7 **I KNOW!** Work in groups. Can you add more words to each category in Exercise 6? Each word scores one point. Which group wins?
- elements of landscape: *mountain*, …
- animals: *tiger*, …

8 Choose the correct option.
1. My favorite season is autumn, when the *stars* / (*leaves*) fall off the trees.
2. We walked into the *cave* / *waterfall*, where it was cold and dark.
3. In the distance, there was something big and brown. A *bear* / *spider* was standing and looking at us.
4. At the end of the day, there's an amazing *path* / *sunset* over the lake.
5. The sun was shining and the *sky* / *star* was blue. It was a perfect day to go out on the boat.

9 Choose the correct option to make the sentence true for you. Write a short paragraph.

I'd love/hate to go on a Go Wild! camp because …

Unit 2 27

2.6 SPEAKING Criticising

I can criticise and explain when things go wrong.

VIDEO **WHY DID YOU DO THAT?**

Dan: Phew! I ran all the way here. I'm boiling now.
Skye: But it's so hot today! What were you thinking of? Do you want a drink?
Dan: Oh, yes. Cheers. Thanks.
Skye: Can I introduce you to Basil?
Dan: Who's Basil?
Skye: He's my pet. Close your eyes … Surprise!
Dan: Urgh! What did you do that for? I hate snakes!
Skye: Oh, I didn't realise. I didn't mean to scare you. I brought Basil outside because I was cleaning his tank. He loves the sunshine! Snakes like warm places. Twenty-nine degrees centigrade is just right. But they need a shady place to cool down.
Dan: Me too! Can we go to the pool yet?
Skye: Yes. Alisha texted. She and Tommo are nearly here.
Dan: Great. I brought my water gun for a water fight.
Skye: Brilliant. Get them when they come round the corner … ready?
Gran: Oh! I'm soaking wet! Why did you do that?
Skye: Oh, Gran. I'm so sorry. We thought you were Tommo.
Gran: Well, just be more careful next time!

I'm boiling.   Cheers.   Surprise!   It's just right.

 OUT of class

1 **CLASS VOTE** How do you feel about snakes?

I'm scared of them.   I don't like them.
I'm fine with them.   I think they're great!

2 ▶ 2.3 🔊 1.42 Watch or listen and answer the questions.

1 Why did Dan feel hot?
2 How did Skye scare Dan?
3 Who were Skye and Dan waiting for?
4 What happened to Skye's grandmother?

3 🔊 1.43 Complete the dialogues with the phrases from the Speaking box. Listen and check.

Speaking	Criticising
Criticising	**Explaining**
What did you do that for?	I didn't mean to.
Why did you do that?	I didn't realise.
What were you thinking of?	I really wanted (to) …
Just be more careful next time.	I thought you were / it was …

1 **A:** Hey, why did you push in to the queue? I was here first.
   B: Oh! I _____ to push in. I _____ you were standing in the queue.
2 **A:** I was so angry. I just shouted at the teacher.
   B: _____ for?
   A: I didn't see who it was. I _____ another student!
3 **A:** You did the wrong exercise for homework! What _____ of?
   B: Oh, sorry!
   A: Never mind. Just _____ .

4 In pairs, role play the situations. Follow the instructions.

- I had an argument with a family member.
- I copied my homework from a friend.
- I didn't buy my friend a birthday present.
- I spent a lot of money on a concert/sports ticket.

A: Say what happened and give extra information.
B: Criticise your partner's actions.
A: Explain your reasons.
B: Give your opinion or say if you understand now.

5 [VOX POPS ▶ 2.4] In pairs, tell your partner about a time when you had a problem.

2.7 ENGLISH IN USE — Adverbs and indefinite pronouns

I can use adverbs and indefinite pronouns.

Mum: Perfect weather? I love it when it's sunny and warm. We can do something together like have a picnic…
Dad: …or play basketball, go somewhere for a walk. Rufus loves walks.

Perfect weather? I love it when it's snowy and minus twenty! The school is closed, I don't have to go anywhere and I can do nothing!

Perfect weather? I love it when it's rainy! There's mud everywhere and everybody's happy!

1 Read the cartoon. Who do you agree with most?

2 Study the Language box. Match rules 1–4 with sentences below.

Language	Adverbs and indefinite pronouns	
People	**Things**	**Places**
somebody	something	somewhere
nobody	nothing	nowhere
everybody	everything	everywhere
anybody	anything	anywhere, anyplace

1 We use adverbs and indefinite pronouns with *some-* in positive statements.
   *I want to go **somewhere**.*
2 We use adverbs and indefinite pronouns with *any-* in negative statements and questions.
   *We can't do **anything** because it's raining.*
   *Did you go **anywhere** at the weekend?*
3 We use adverbs and indefinite pronouns with *no-* with positive verbs, but the meaning is negative.
   *There's **nothing** on TV. = There isn't anything on TV.*
4 Pronouns with *every-* are used in both positive and negative statements, and in questions with singular verbs.
   ***Everybody** loves sunny weather.*

A ☐ It was cold outside, so nobody was in the park.
B ☐ Wow, everything looks fantastic!
C ☐ Was there anything about snow in the weather forecast?
D ☐ It's raining today. I don't want to go anywhere.

3 Choose the correct option. Are the sentences true for you?
1 I need some time to stay at home and do *nothing / nowhere*.
2 There is nothing that *everything / everybody* likes.
3 I don't want to go *anywhere / everywhere* now. I just want to sit and relax.
4 It's important to have *nobody / somebody* you can talk to.
5 Do you want *nothing / anything* from the supermarket?

4 🔊 1.44 Complete the text with words from the Language box. Listen and check.

Aunt: Hanna, how was your outdoor survival camp on Crete?
Hanna: It was fun! There was ¹<u>something</u> different to do every day. We made a shelter in the mountains. We went fishing in a river and cooked fish over a fire … It's a long list, but I think we tried ²_____ last week! It was all exciting, so ³_____ was bored and we travelled ⁴_____ on the island. It's an amazing place. People there were very friendly, too. There was always ⁵_____ to talk to.
Aunt: Was there ⁶_____ you didn't try?
Hanna: Well, we didn't go swimming in the lake because there was a storm that day, so it was too dangerous!

5 In pairs, follow the instructions and decide if your partner's answers are for the first or second part of the instruction.

1 Name somewhere you'd like to go to on a hot day and somewhere you'd hate to go to on a hot day.
2 Name somebody you'd like to travel with and somebody you'd like to stay at home with.

A: *Name somewhere you'd like to go to on a hot day and somewhere you'd hate to go to on a hot day.*
B: *Er, a desert and the swimming pool.*
A: *I think on a hot day you'd like to go to the swimming pool and you'd hate to go to the desert.*
B: *Yes, that's right.*

WORDLIST   Weather | Temperature | Natural disasters | In the wild

the Antarctic /æn'tɑːktɪk/
area /'eəriə/
avalanche /'ævəlɑːntʃ/
bat /bæt/
beach /biːtʃ/
bear /beə/
boiling /'bɔɪlɪŋ/
camp /kæmp/
Canada /'kænədə/
cave /keɪv/
chilly /'tʃɪli/
cloud /klaʊd/
cloudy /'klaʊdi/
coast /kəʊst/
cold /kəʊld/
column /'kɒləm/
conditions /kən'dɪʃnz/
cool /kuːl/
create /kri'eɪt/
degrees /dɪ'griːz/
desert /'dezət/
drought /draʊt/
dry /draɪ/
dust /dʌst/
earthquake /'ɜːθkweɪk/
erupt /ɪ'rʌpt/
fire /faɪə/
flood /flʌd/
fog /fɒg/
foggy /'fɒgi/
freezing /'friːzɪŋ/
grow /grəʊ/
geography /dʒi'ɒgrəfi/
ground /graʊnd/
happen /'hæpən/
hilly /'hɪli/
hot /hɒt/

hurricane /'hʌrɪkən/
ice /aɪs/
Iceland /'aɪslənd/
icy /'aɪsi/
India /'ɪndiə/
island /'aɪlənd/
lake /leɪk/
land /lænd/
landscape /'lændskeɪp/
leaf (leaves) /liːf (liːvz)/
light /laɪt/
lighthouse /'laɪthaʊs/
lightning /'laɪtnɪŋ/
lightning bolt /'laɪtnɪŋ bəʊlt/
mild /maɪld/
minus /'maɪnəs/
mountain /'maʊntɪn/
move /muːv/
natural disaster /ˌnætʃrəl dɪ'zɑːstə/
Northern Lights /ˌnɔːðən 'laɪts/
open air /ˌəʊpən 'eə/
outdoor /ˌaʊt'dɔː/
path /pɑːθ/
plants /plɑːnts/
rain /reɪn/
rainy /'reɪni/
river /'rɪvə/
rocks /rɒks/
sailor /'seɪlə/
sand /sænd/
save /seɪv/
season /'siːzn/
shady /'ʃeɪdi/
shallow /'ʃæləʊ/

sky /skaɪ/
snake /sneɪk/
snow /snəʊ/
snowmen /'snəʊmæn/
snowy /'snəʊi/
spider /'spaɪdə/
spot /spɒt/
spring /sprɪŋ/
star /stɑː/
storm /stɔːm/
stormy /'stɔːmi/
summer /'sʌmə/
sun /sʌn/
sunny /'sʌni/
sunset /'sʌnset/
sunshine /'sʌnʃaɪn/
survival /sə'vaɪvl/
temperature /'temprɪtʃə/
thermal pool /ˌθɜːml 'puːl/
thick /θɪk/
thunder /'θʌndə/
tsunami /tsʊ'nɑːmi/
Venezuela /ˌvenə'zweɪlə/
volcanic eruption /vɒlˌkænɪk ɪ'rʌpʃn/
warm /wɔːm/
waterfall /'wɔːtəfɔːl/
water fight /'wɔːtə faɪt/
wave /weɪv/
wet /wet/
wild /waɪld/
wildlife /'waɪldlaɪf/
wind /wɪnd/
windy /'wɪndi/
winter /'wɪntə/

WORD FRIENDS

absolutely freezing
completely crazy
quite long
really interesting
totally amazing
very difficult
soaking wet
weather forecast
make/build a fire
sit/sleep outside
make/build a shelter
learn about / listen to the birds
see/watch the stars
look for / find wild animals
grow/discover unusual plants

VOCABULARY IN ACTION

1 Use the wordlist to find:
1 five weather words
2 three words to describe temperature
3 four natural disasters
4 three things you can do outdoors
5 three countries

2 In pairs, use the wordlist to discuss two things that are:
1 totally amazing
2 completely crazy
3 very difficult
4 absolutely freezing

3 Compare your ideas with the class.

4 In pairs, make sentences with three words and/or phrases from the wordlist.

Student A: *sleep under the stars / absolutely freezing / spider*
Student B: *Last weekend I slept under the stars but it was absolutely freezing and we had a big spider in the tent.*

5 🔊 **1.45** **PRONUNCIATION** Listen and underline the stress in the sentences below. Where does the stress fall when there is just an adjective, and where does it fall when there is an adverb with the adjective?

It was freezing in the park.
It was absolutely freezing in the park.

6 🔊 **1.46** Listen and repeat.

That test was really difficult.
You're completely crazy.
What a totally amazing party!
My hair is soaking wet.
I think he's really interesting.

Revision

VOCABULARY

1 Write the correct word for each definition.
1. A small creature with eight legs. s _ _ _ _ _
2. A very cold area around the South Pole. the A _ _ _ _ _ _ _ _
3. A person who sails on boats or ships, especially as a job. s _ _ _ _ _ _
4. A storm with very strong, fast winds. h _ _ _ _ _ _ _ _
5. Very hot. b _ _ _ _ _ _ _
6. Animals and plants that live in natural conditions. w _ _ _ _ _ _ _ _

2 Look at the pictures and write the words.

1 _____ 2 _____ 3 _____
4 _____ 5 _____ 6 _____

3 Make sentences with as many words as you can from Exercises 1 and 2.

A big bear was looking at us, so we ran away.

GRAMMAR

4 Complete the text with the Past Simple form of the verbs in brackets.

Hi Dan,
Turkey is amazing. Yesterday we ¹*visited* (visit) a thermal pool and ² _____ (sit) in it for ages. In the evening we ³ _____ (watch) the sunset on the beach, and then we ⁴ _____ (make) a fire and ⁵ _____ (eat) sausages, but I ⁶ _____ (not like) them. They ⁷ _____ (be) disgusting! ⁸ _____ (you/enjoy) your trip to London? I ⁹ _____ (not see) your photos online. #hopeitwasok

See you soon,

Anna

5 Complete the sentences with the correct form of the verbs in brackets.
1. It *was snowing* (snow) when I *left* (leave) the house.
2. When I _____ (find) Jack and Emma, they _____ (make) a shelter.
3. We _____ (not see) any bears while we _____ (travel) across Canada.
4. The family _____ (eat) breakfast when the tsunami _____ (happen).
5. When we first _____ (see) the wave, it _____ (not move) very quickly.
6. While we _____ (sleep) outdoors, we _____ (hear) some strange noises.

6 Choose the correct option.
1. We didn't hear *something / anything* before the hurricane started.
2. This drought is very bad. *Nothing / Anything* can grow when there's no water.
3. *Everybody / Somebody* can learn to make a shelter. It's not difficult.
4. We looked *nowhere / everywhere* but we couldn't find the spider.
5. Does *nobody / anybody* know what the temperature is?

SPEAKING

7 Complete the texts with the phrases below.

| I thought it was mine.   What did you do that for?
Just be more careful next time.   I didn't mean to. |

A: Hey, you've written on my notebook. ¹_____ .
B: Sorry, ²_____ because it's the same color.

A: You left your new phone at school!
B: ³_____ But it's OK. Gemma has it.
A: ⁴_____ .

8 In pairs, role play the situations below.
- I borrowed my friend's jacket and now it's dirty.
- I forgot to invite a friend to my party.

DICTATION

9 🔊 **1.47** Listen, then listen again and write down what you hear.

SELF-ASSESSMENT Think about this unit. What did you learn? What do you need help with?

Nice day, innit?

What's the weather like?

If you don't know what to talk about, there's always the weather. In the UK we do this a lot because although the weather is quite mild, it changes a lot.

But American weather systems are very different – they have great extremes. When it's freezing cold in the Midwest, you can barely go outside. In the South East, tropical storms form in the Atlantic. They can build into tornadoes or hurricanes and bring high winds, torrential rain, floods and devastation. The population is prepared for this and there are even storm chasers. They are people who follow tornadoes at high speed to see the damage they cause and to warn local people of the dangers.

In the UK it seems that people are never prepared! When extreme weather comes, it's always a shock. Last year a freak snowstorm brought chaos to transport in the country. British Rail cancelled trains because of 'the wrong kind of snow'! On the night of 15 October 1987 people were going to bed when a terrible storm suddenly hit the country. Trees fell down and the conditions were chaotic. But the weather forecasters didn't predict it at all.

And can the weather affect our moods or character? Well, there is a saying in the UK: 'I feel a bit under the weather'. It means you don't feel very well. People who live in sunny climates seem happier. Those who live with grey skies and little light in winter can be more melancholic. But that's certainly not the whole story. Economic and social factors are more important to people's well-being than whether the sun is out or not.

GLOSSARY
devastation (n) ruin
freak (adj) very unusual
innit? (col) isn't it?
predict (v) to say that something will happen
torrential rain (n) very heavy rain

EXPLORE

1. Do you think the weather can affect you? How? Disuss in pairs.

2. Read the article. Mark the sentences T (true) or F (false). Correct the false sentences.
   1. ☐ Americans are less prepared for bad weather than the British.
   2. ☐ The great storm of 1987 in the UK was a surprise.
   3. ☐ To be *under the weather* means 'to be depressed'.
   4. ☐ The tone of the article is quite serious.

3. Read the article again. Answer the questions.
   1. Does the writer think that the weather can affect mood or character greatly? Do you agree with this opinion?
   2. Think about people from different parts of your country. Are their characters very different depending on the weather where they live?

EXPLORE MORE

4. ▶ 2.5 Watch Part 1 of the video. Match animals 1–6 from the video with photos A–F. Which of these animals live in your country?
   1. ☒ C whale
   2. ☐ penguin
   3. ☐ shark
   4. ☐ seal
   5. ☐ dolphin
   6. ☐ manatee

A

B

C

D

E

F

5. What does the narrator say about the Atlantic Ocean? Choose the best summary.
   A It's very large and mysterious.
   B It's dangerous and beautiful at the same time.
   C It's the most famous ocean in the world.

6. ▶ 2.6 Watch Part 2 of the video. Choose the correct option.
   1. Here *warm / hot* winds from the Sahara Desert have made the sea turn *wild / crazy.*
   2. The waves are *huge / giant* and the conditions are *terrible / difficult.*
   3. *Warm / Cool* air rises from the sea and creates *thick / black* clouds.
   4. *Torrential / Light* rain arrives on land and *frightening / enormous* waves and *heavy / strong* winds cause devastation.

7. What images do you remember of the storm? What most surprised you about it? Discuss in groups.

8. ▶ 2.7 Watch Part 3 of the video. Complete the sentences.
   1. The strong hurricane destroyed …
   2. The young dolphin is in danger because …
   3. The thick vegetation in the mangrove forests is good because it …
   4. The Atlantic can be a heaven or a hell, depending on …

9. Do you have examples of extreme or changeable weather in your country? Where? What kind of weather can you get there?

YOU EXPLORE

10. **CULTURE PROJECT** In groups, prepare a presentation about the weather in your country.
    1. Use the internet or other sources to research different types of weather in your country.
    2. Write a short script and think about images or videos to use in your presentation.
    3. Give your presentation to the class.
    4. Report back: what did you learn from the other presentations?

3

The taste test

3.1 VOCABULARY Food and drink

I can talk about food and drink.

VOCABULARY
Food and drink | Flavours |
Describing food

GRAMMAR
Present Perfect with *ever, never, just, already, yet, for* and *since* |
Present Perfect and Past Simple

Grammar: I've heard it's funny

Speaking: What can I get you?

BBC Culture: Indian food Liverpool style

Workbook p. 40

BBC VOX POPS ▶
EXAM TIME 1 > p. 130
CLIL 2 > p. 140

1 **CLASS VOTE** Which is your favourite meal of the day? Why?

breakfast   lunch   dinner   supper   snack

2 🔊 **1.48** Study the Vocabulary A box. Listen and see if you can find the items you hear in the picture.

Vocabulary A	Food and drink
beef bread rolls cheese chewing gum chilli cream crisps cucumber flour fruit juice garlic grapes honey ice cream lemonade lettuce nuts peach pear pineapple smoothie tuna yoghurt	

3 🔊 **1.49** Match the sentences with the people in the picture. Complete the sentences with words from the Vocabulary A box then listen and check.

1 ___ This person has got a shopping list. She is looking for chilli, cream and some _____ .
2 ___ These people want to buy _____ , honey, yoghurt and _____ .
3 ___ The shop assistant is near the _____ , grapes and _____ .
4 ___ The grandmother wants lettuce, _____ and some _____ .
5 ___ The child is looking at the fruit juice and _____ .
6 ___ The man is buying _____ , beef and _____ .

4 Match the words from the Vocabulary A box with the correct sign.

FRUIT   **VEGETABLES, SALAD AND HERBS**

peach, _____ , _____ , _____   *lettuce*, _____ , _____ , _____

MEAT AND FISH   **DAIRY**   **CEREALS**

beef, _____   *cheese*, _____ , _____   *bread rolls*, _____

SWEETS AND SNACKS   **DRINKS**

ice cream, *chewing gum*, _____ , _____ , _____   *fruit juice*, _____ , _____

34

5 **I KNOW!** Work in groups. How many words can you add to each category in Exercise 4, in one minute? Compare your ideas with the class.

6 🔊 1.50 In pairs, use the words from the Vocabulary B box to discuss the ice cream flavours. Which is your favourite flavour?

Vocabulary B	Flavours

chocolate   coconut   coffee   lemon
melon   mint   strawberry   vanilla

These words can be used as adjectives or nouns.
I like strawberries. [noun]
I like strawberry ice cream. [adjective]

I think the white ice cream is vanilla.
Yes, or maybe it's …

7 🔊 1.51 Complete the text with the words below. Listen and check. Can you think of other kinds of food that makes your mouth feel hot or cold when you eat them?

beef   chilli   coffee   dishes   drink   ~~ice cream~~   mint   taste

Taste and Temperature

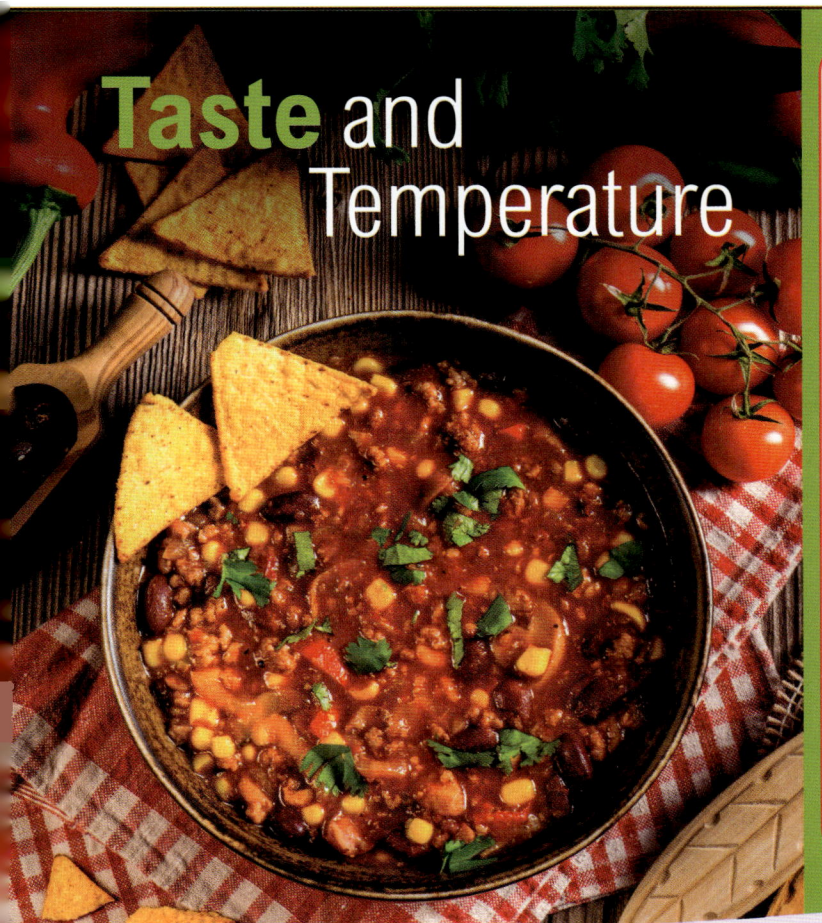

People usually enjoy ¹*ice cream* in the summer because it is cold, in the same way they enjoy hot tea or ² _____ in the winter. But did you notice that some food is not really hot or cold but makes you feel like that? For example, in some hot countries ³ _____ lemonade is very popular. It's a cool, refreshing ⁴ _____ . But does this herb really make your mouth cold?

When you ⁵ _____ mint flavours, your mouth sends a message to your brain: 'Hey, that feels cold!' In fact, it's a 'trick' because the temperature in your mouth doesn't change. Spicy ⁶ _____ do the opposite, they make you feel hot. Take chilli con carne, for example — a famous Mexican dish with meat — usually ⁷ _____ and beans, served with rice. ⁸ _____ doesn't really make you hot. But it makes you FEEL hot.

8 🔊 1.52 Listen to three questions from a food quiz. Did you guess the answers?

9 In pairs, follow the instructions.
- Choose a food that you like.
- Find or think of 2–4 facts about this food.
- Write your facts but DON'T write the answer.
- Swap clues with another pair and guess the food.

And YOU

Unit 3   35

3.2 GRAMMAR   Present Perfect with *ever, never, just, already* and *yet*

I can use the Present Perfect with *ever, never, just, already* and *yet*.

VIDEO — I'VE HEARD IT'S FUNNY

Tommo: I've never seen so much food. Ah, smell that pizza!
Alisha: Yes, I've already had some! This market is great for Chinese food, too. Have you ever eaten noodles?
Tommo: Yes, I have. Dad's cooked them at home.
Alisha: Tommo, look! That's Oliver Jenkins, the famous TV chef. Have you seen his programme?
Tommo: No, but I've heard it's funny.
Alisha: Perhaps he's brought some nice food?
Tommo: Well, he's just opened an ice cream shop. Let's go and see. Perhaps we can try some.
Alisha: Look. There's cheeseburger flavour or chilli or pea-and-mint. He's used weird flavours!
Tommo: You bet!
Alisha: I hate peas, but cheeseburger flavour sounds OK. What about you?
Tommo: I haven't decided yet … What's it like?
Alisha: Yuck! That's disgusting. Hang on, let's try another. Mmhh, chilli. Now, that's the best ice cream I've ever eaten!

OUT of class
You bet!   Yuck!   Hang on.

1 CLASS VOTE Which strange food would you like to try?

  cheeseburger ice cream   pizza with bananas
  cucumber and garlic smoothie

2  3.1 1.53 Watch or listen and answer the questions.
1 Where are Tommo and Alisha?
2 Who is Oliver Jenkins?
3 What type of shop does Oliver Jenkins have?
4 What flavour ice cream does Alisha try first?

3 Study the Grammar box. Find more examples of the Present Perfect in the dialogue.

Grammar	Present Perfect
Have you **ever** tried pizza with banana?
I've **never** eaten so much food.
He's **just** made a new TV programme.
I've **already** tried it.
I **haven't** finished **yet**.
Have you done it **yet**?

GRAMMAR TIME > PAGE 120

4 Complete the sentences and questions with the correct form of the words in brackets.
1 Alisha *has already eaten* (already/eat) some pizza.
2 _____ Tommo _____ (ever/cook) noodles at home?
3 Alisha and Tommo _____ (just/see) Oliver Jenkins.
4 Tommo _____ (never/watch) Oliver Jenkins on TV.
5 Tommo _____ (not have) pea-and-mint ice cream yet.
6 _____ Alisha and Tommo _____ (try) all the ice cream yet?

5 🔊 1.54 Complete the text with the Present Perfect form of the verb in brackets. Listen and check.

Hi Ed,
Sorry I ¹_____ (not call) you. I ²_____ (have) a bad cold and I ³_____ (not speak) to anyone. ⁴_____ (you/decide) about the summer yet? I hope I can come and see you. A new pizza restaurant ⁵_____ (just/open) in town. My friends ⁶_____ (already/try) it. The speciality is pizza with banana on it! I ⁷_____ (never/have) that before but I'd like to try it.
Speak soon,
Dan

6 [VOX POPS ▶ 3.2] Write about a place where you like to eat with friends.
1 What's it called?
2 Who have you been there with?
3 What food have you tried?
It's called Marco's and I've been there with …

Unit 3

3.3 READING and VOCABULARY   A cookery TV show

I can find specific detail in an article and use *make* and *do* accurately.

1 **CLASS VOTE** Do you watch cookery programmes? Where do you watch them: on TV or online?

2 Read the title and the first paragraph of the article. What does the title refer to?
- a Martha's cookery class at school.
- b Martha's experience on a TV show.

3 ▶ 1.55 Read the article. Choose the correct answers.
1. Why can't Martha go out with her friends tonight?
   - a She wants to study at home.
   - b She wants to upload some photos on Twitter.
   - c She wants to bake more cupcakes.
   - d She wants to relax at home.
2. Why has Martha chosen to study Food Technology?
   - a Because she wants to avoid disasters in the kitchen.
   - b Because she loves all kinds of science.
   - c Because she wants to discover what happens when you cook food.
   - d Because it goes well with Maths and Chemistry.
3. What happened during the school cookery competition?
   - a Martha got angry with the other students.
   - b Martha had a disaster with her cake.
   - c The other students left and went home.
   - d Martha's oven gloves caught fire.
4. Why are the people in Martha's family so important?
   - a They go and watch every show.
   - b They can help Martha to stay calm.
   - c They tell her when she's making mistakes.
   - d They help her with her schoolwork.

'I have loved every minute of it!'

She's done her homework but there's no time for 17-year-old Martha to relax with friends tonight. Martha is the youngest contestant in a national cooking competition, *The Great British Bake Off*, and she's got to practise for the next show. Every week she has to impress the judges with different recipes. Next week it's cupcakes. She's already made 24 cakes today, but she hasn't finished yet. Since her first appearance on the show, Martha has posted messages and photos on Twitter. Her profile says: 'I only have friends because I make good cake. Seriously.' So when did this passion begin?

Martha started baking when she was about seven years old. She often made a mess in the kitchen and the results weren't always good. At school she made a decision to study Maths, Chemistry and Food Technology because she says, 'I've always loved food but I've never understood the science behind it.' It hasn't always been easy. Martha has had a few disasters, and once she set her oven gloves on fire during a school cooking competition and the whole building was evacuated. But the judges announced that Martha was one of the winners. She was very happy!

What about Martha's family? Her parents have watched her on TV every week. They know that the competition is getting tough and that Martha is tired. Martha wants to do her best and hates making mistakes so it's important that they keep her calm. Her granddad, James, is incredibly proud that she has made time for both her schoolwork and the TV show. They're all enjoying the competition although, as Martha says with a smile, 'We have all put on a bit of weight!'

4 **WORD BUILDING** Find nouns from the verbs below in the text. In pairs, make sentences with each noun.
1. contest _____
2. compete _____
3. appear _____
4. build _____
5. win _____
6. weigh _____

5 **WORD FRIENDS** Find the phrases in the text. Write *make* or *do* in the correct place in the box.

Word Friends	*make* and *do*
_____ :	a cake (cakes) a decision time a mess mistakes
_____ :	(my/your/his/her) homework my/you/his/her best

6 Read the text again. Answer the questions.
1. Has Martha done her homework?
2. What type of cakes has Martha made today?
3. Where did Martha make a mess when she was a child?
4. What did Martha make a decision to do at school?
5. What has Martha made time for during the competition?

Unit 3   37

3.4 GRAMMAR Present Perfect with *for* and *since*; Present Perfect and Past Simple

I can talk about duration of time, and be general and specific about experiences.

1 **CLASS VOTE** What's your favourite flavour for a fruit juice or smoothie?

2 🔊 **1.56** Read the text. In pairs, answer the questions.

The best drink ever!

We've been in Rio since yesterday afternoon. I'm so excited! My parents are from Brazil but we haven't visited the country many times. The plane tickets are very expensive! We didn't want to go sightseeing yesterday, but we went to the beach. My favourite thing in Rio is the juice bars on every street corner. I've never seen so much fruit!

The owner of one juice bar, Rodrigo, has lived in Rio for many years. His father opened Rio's first juice bar in 1958. Many other juice bars have opened since then. I found out that there are 146 different types of fruit in Brazil! Some of them are very unusual. Have you ever heard of cashew apple? It looks like a red apple, but the cashew nut grows at the top of the fruit. I've just tried it. It's amazing.

Amanda

1 What surprises Amanda about Rio?
2 How many types of fruit are there in Brazil?
3 What drink did Amanda try?

3 Study the Grammar box. Which set of words and phrases do we use with *for*? Which do we use with *since*?

A: two o'clock   yesterday   Monday
last weekend   1958
B: five minutes   a few hours   a long time
two weeks   three years

Grammar | Present Perfect and Past Simple

Present Perfect with *for* and *since*
I've lived in Rio **for** many years. (a period of time)
They've had this bar **since** 1970. (a point in time)

Present Perfect and Past Simple
We**'ve been** to Sao Paolo.
We **went** to Sao Paolo in 2012.
Have you **ever drunk** a mango smoothie?
Did you **like** it?

GRAMMAR TIME > PAGE 120

4 Make sentences in the Present Perfect using *for* or *since*.

1 I / not / have / a chocolate bar / a month.
   I haven't had a chocolate bar for a month.
2 My family / own / this café / 2010.
3 We / not eat / any food / breakfast time.
4 This cookery programme / be / on TV / a few months.
5 Have / you / see / the cookery teacher / last lesson?
6 They / be / at the juice bar / half an hour.

5 Find more examples in the text of the Present Perfect and Past Simple.

6 🔊 **1.57** Complete the dialogue with the Present Perfect and Past Simple forms. Listen and check.

Mia: ¹*Have* you had any fruit juice yet today?
Miguel: No, I ²_____ had any yet, but I'd like some now.
Mia: ³_____ you ever tried sugar apple juice?
Miguel: Yes, I ⁴_____ some yesterday. Sugar apples look like pears! They're very good for you.
Mia: ⁵_____ you like it?
Miguel: Yes, I ⁶_____. Why don't you try some?
Mia: Yeah. I'd love to try it. Where ⁷_____ you buy it?
Miguel: At the juice bar on the beach.

7 Write questions in the Present Perfect and Past Simple. In pairs, ask and answer the questions.

And YOU

Start with a general question with *ever* (Present Perfect):
• Have you ever eaten … ?
• Have you ever drunk … ?

Then ask about details (Past Simple):
• When did you try it?
• Did you like it?
• What was it like?

Unit 3

3.5 LISTENING and VOCABULARY — A dream cake

I can identify specific detail in speech and describe food.

1 **CLASS VOTE** Is it important to have a special cake on your birthday? Compare your ideas with the class. Vote *Yes* or *No*.

2 🔊 1.58 Study the Vocabulary box, using a dictionary. Choose the correct option. Listen and check.

Vocabulary	Describing food
bitter bland delicious dry fresh rich sour spicy stale sweet tasty	

1 I like chilli popcorn because it's so *spicy / stale*.
2 These cupcakes aren't very tasty, they're quite *sweet / bland*.
3 I love this fruit juice, it's really *dry / delicious*.
4 This cake has icing and a filling with butter, so it's very *rich / bitter*.
5 This milk has been in the sun too long, it tastes *sour / fresh*.
6 This bread is old, I think it's *stale / bitter*.

3 🔊 1.59 Listen to Gianni talking about a very special cake. Mark the sentences T (true) or F (false).
1 ☐ Gianni saw the cake in New York.
2 ☐ The cake took a week to make.
3 ☐ The baker didn't make the cake in his shop.
4 ☐ The cake weighed around 70 kilos.
5 ☐ Gianni didn't like the cake at all.

4 Look at the text. In pairs, decide what kind of information is missing from gaps 1–6: words or numbers?

Is it a car? Is it a robot? No … it's a cake!

5 🔊 1.60 Listen to information about how to enter the competition. Complete the text in Exercise 4.

6 [VOX POPS ▶ 3.3] In pairs, describe the best cake you've ever had. Ask and answer the questions:
- What did it look like?
- What did it taste like?
- What flavour was it?
- Who made it?

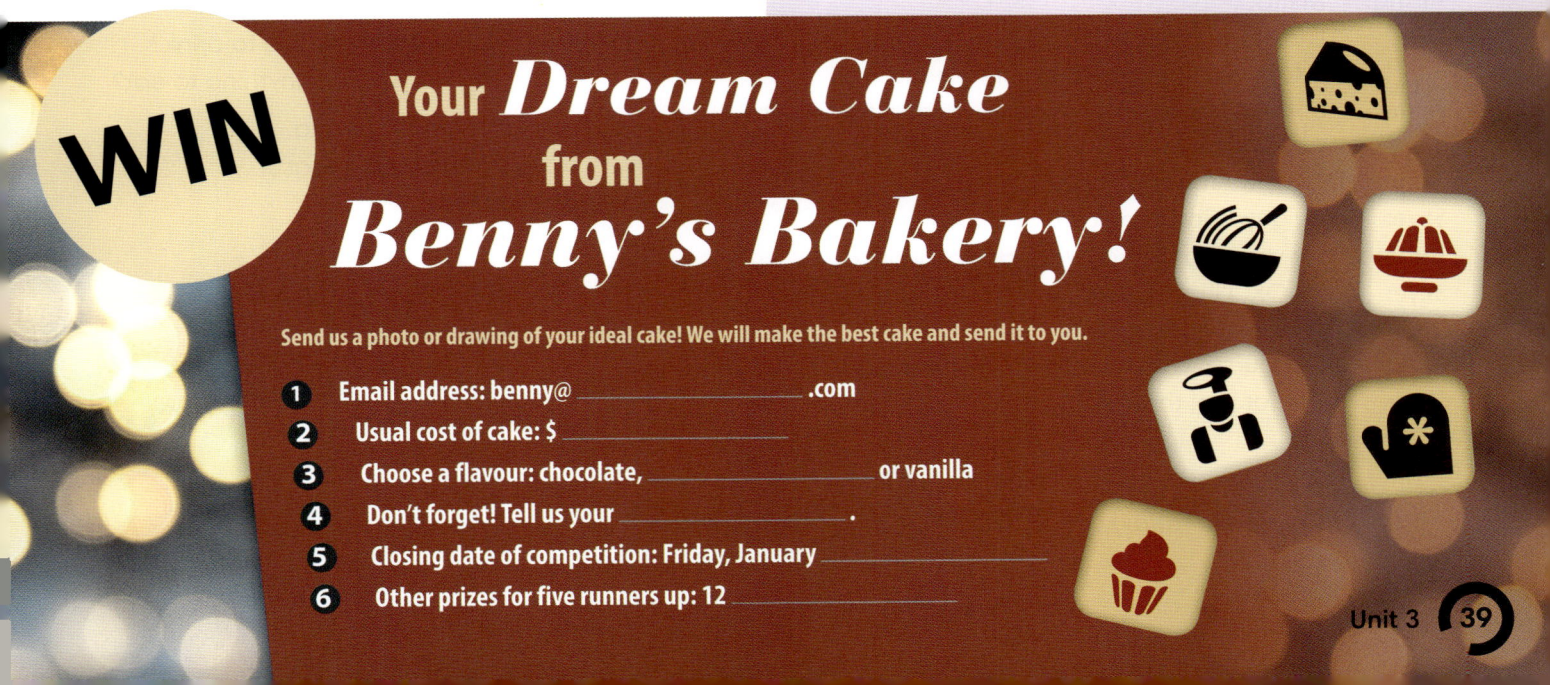

And YOU?

WIN Your *Dream Cake* from *Benny's Bakery!*

Send us a photo or drawing of your ideal cake! We will make the best cake and send it to you.

1 Email address: benny@ _____ .com
2 Usual cost of cake: $ _____
3 Choose a flavour: chocolate, _____ or vanilla
4 Don't forget! Tell us your _____ .
5 Closing date of competition: Friday, January _____
6 Other prizes for five runners up: 12 _____

Unit 3 39

3.6 SPEAKING Ordering food

I can order food in a café or restaurant.

Annie's Café
eat in or take away!

Homemade tomato soup and roll
Toasted cheese sandwich
Salad with tuna or cheese
Chocolate cupcakes
A selection of biscuits

Today's speciality: green cake!
ALSO Why not try a smoothie?
Melon-and-mango or
banana-and-strawberry
OR our homemade lemonade!

1 **CLASS VOTE** What would you like from the menu?

2 🎬 3.4 🔊 1.61 In pairs, discuss what you think green cake is. Watch or listen and check.

3 🔊 1.61 Read and listen to the dialogue. What do Dan, Alisha, Tommo and Skye order?

VIDEO **WHAT CAN I GET YOU?**

Annie: Hi! Take a seat and I'll get you the menus. Here you are. Now what can I get you to drink?
Alisha: I'll have an apple juice, please.
Dan: Just water for me, thanks.
Tommo: Could I have a melon-and-mango smoothie, please?
Annie: Of course. Are you ready to order?
Alisha: Nearly. That green cake looks interesting. What's in it?
Annie: Green tea and yoghurt. It's quite sweet.
Tommo: Mmhh. I'd like that, please.
Alisha: Me too.
Dan: Um, I don't fancy cake today. I'll have a toasted cheese sandwich, please.
Annie: So that's one toasted sandwich and two slices of cake.
Tommo, Dan and Alisha: Thanks.
Skye: Hi, guys. Sorry I'm late.
Tommo: We've just ordered. What do you want?
Skye: It's OK. I'll get it. Excuse me. Can I have a hot chocolate, please?
Annie: Of course. Would you like anything to eat?
Skye: Not for me, thanks.

OUT of class
Hi, guys. I'll get it!
I don't fancy (cake today).

4 Study the Speaking box. Match questions 1–5 with answers a–e.

Speaking Ordering food

Customer
I'll have … / I'd like a … / a slice of …
Excuse me, can/could I have …
Just … for me, please.
Not for me, thanks.

Waiter
Take a seat and I'll get you the menu.
What would you like to drink?
Are you ready to order?
Would you like anything to eat?
Can I get you something?
Here you are.

1 ☐ Are you ready to order?
2 ☐ What's in it?
3 ☐ What soup do you have?
4 ☐ What can I get you to drink?
5 ☐ Would you like anything to eat?

a Homemade tomato.
b I'll have a cola, please.
c Nearly.
d Not for me, thanks.
e It's just fruit and yoghurt.

5 **And YOU** In pairs or small groups, use the Speaking box to order food from the menu in Exercise 1.

Unit 3

3.7 WRITING An email to a friend

I can write an email to a friend.

1 **CLASS VOTE** What food would you have at a party with friends?

2 🔊 **1.62** Study the Vocabulary box, using a dictionary. Match the words with the pictures.

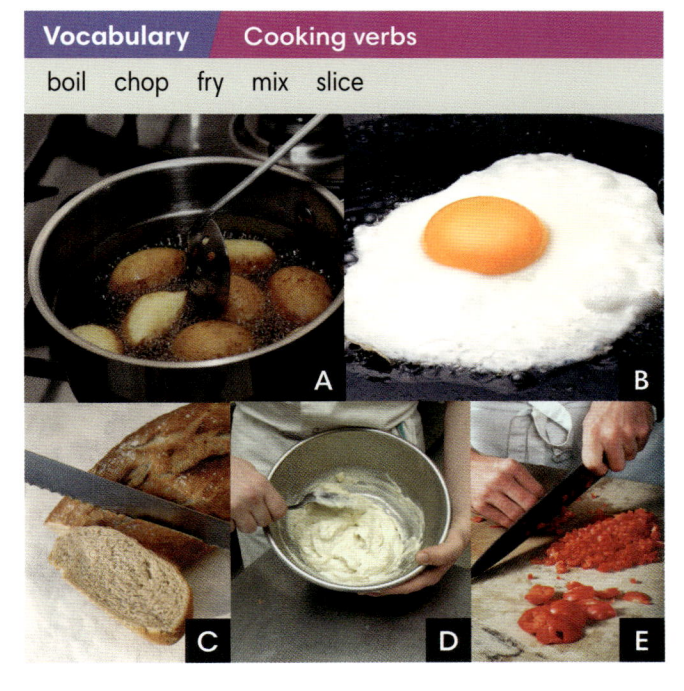

Vocabulary	Cooking verbs
boil chop fry mix slice	

A B C D E

3 Use the words in the Vocabulary box to make sentences about two types of food.

You can boil potatoes and peas.

4 Read Alisha's email. Does it mention your ideas from Exercise 1?

PARTY TIME

Hi,

Thanks for getting in touch. It was great to hear about your school trip. The photos were awesome.

Tommo and I have just finished our exams and we've decided to have a party tomorrow on his boat! He's bought lots of yummy food, including sausages and cheese. I'm making my famous chicken salad. It's really easy. First, I fry the chicken and boil some eggs. Then I slice them. After that, I chop tomatoes into small pieces and mix everything together with some mayonnaise. I can't tell you how good it is!

Anyway, I was wondering if you'd like to come. We're asking everybody to bring some fruit or some juice because we want to make smoothies of different flavours.

Let me know if you can make it.

Alisha

5 Read the text again. Order the information as it appears in the text.

a ☐ Alisha talks about what's happening in her life now.
b ☐ Alisha invites her friend and asks her friend to do something.
c ☐ 1 Alisha thanks her friend and comments on her friend's news.
d ☐ Alisha asks her friend to reply to the invitation.

6 Look at the Writing box. Underline the sentences that are in the text in Exercise 4.

Writing	Email to a friend

Starting your email
How are things?
Great to hear from you.
Thanks for getting in touch.

Responding to news
It was great to hear about your school trip.
I can't wait to hear more about it.

Giving your news
Tommo and I have just finished our exams.
We've decided to have a party.
I'm making a cake for the party.

Explain why you're writing
Anyway / By the way, I was wondering if you'd like to come.
I'm writing to ask if you'd like to come to the party.

Ending your email
Let me know if you can make it.
See you soon.
Bye for now.

Writing Time

7 Write an email to a friend. Follow the instructions below:

1 thank your friend for his/her email and comment on his/her news
2 explain that you're having a party and describe what food you're making
3 invite your friend and suggest something he/she can make for it

TIPS
- It's important to use the correct style when you write to a friend.
- Use different tenses and don't forget contractions. They make your email sound friendly and informal.

Unit 3 41

WORDLIST Food and drink | Flavours | *make* and *do* | Describing food

appearance /əˈpɪərəns/
baker /ˈbeɪkə/
beef /biːf/
bitter /ˈbɪtə/
bland /blænd/
boil /bɔɪl/
bread roll /ˈbred rəʊl/
breakfast /ˈbrekfəst/
building /ˈbɪldɪŋ/
cheese /tʃiːz/
chef /ʃef/
chewing gum /ˈtʃuːɪŋ ɡʌm/
chicken /ˈtʃɪkɪn/
chilli /ˈtʃɪli/
chocolate /ˈtʃɒklɪt/
chop /tʃɒp/
coconut /ˈkəʊkənʌt/
coffee /ˈkɒfi/
competition /ˌkɒmpəˈtɪʃn/
contestant /kənˈtestənt/
cook /kʊk/
cookery class /ˈkʊkəri klɑːs/
cookery teacher /ˈkʊkəri ˌtiːtʃə/
cream /kriːm/
crisps /krɪsps/
cucumber /ˈkjuːkʌmbə/
cupcake /ˈkʌpkeɪk/
dairy /ˈdeəri/
delicious /dɪˈlɪʃəs/
dinner /ˈdɪnə/
dish /dɪʃ/
dry /draɪ/
egg /eg/
enter /ˈentə/
filling /ˈfɪlɪŋ/
fish /fɪʃ/
flavour /ˈfleɪvə/

flour /flaʊə/
Food Technology /ˈfuːd tekˌnɒlədʒi/
fresh /freʃ/
fruit /fruːt/
fruit juice /ˈfruːt dʒuːs/
fry /fraɪ/
garlic /ˈɡɑːlɪk/
grapes /ɡreɪps/
herbs /hɜːbz/
homemade /ˌhəʊmˈmeɪd/
honey /ˈhʌni/
ice cream /ˌaɪs ˈkriːm/
icing /ˈaɪsɪŋ/
lemon /ˈlemən/
lemonade /ˌleməˈneɪd/
lettuce /ˈletɪs/
lunch /lʌntʃ/
mango /ˈmæŋɡəʊ/
mayonnaise /ˌmeɪəˈneɪz/
meal /miːl/
meat /miːt/
melon /ˈmelən/
mint /mɪnt/
mix /mɪks/
noodles /ˈnuːdlz/
nuts /nʌts/
order /ˈɔːdə/
oven gloves /ˈʌvən ɡlʌvz/
pea /piː/
peach /piːtʃ/
pear /peə/
pineapple /ˈpaɪnæpl/
popcorn /ˈpɒpkɔːn/
recipe /ˈresəpi/
refreshing /rɪˈfreʃɪŋ/
rice /raɪs/
rich /rɪtʃ/

salad /ˈsæləd/
sausage /ˈsɒsɪdʒ/
serve /sɜːv/
shopping list /ˈʃɒpɪŋ lɪst/
slice /slaɪs/
smoothie /ˈsmuːði/
snack /snæk/
soup /suːp/
sour /saʊə/
speciality /ˌspeʃiˈæləti/
spicy /ˈspaɪsi/
stale /steɪl/
strawberry /ˈstrɔːbəri/
supper /ˈsʌpə/
sweet /swiːt/
sweets /swiːts/
taste /teɪst/
tasty /ˈteɪsti/
tea /tiː/
try /traɪ/
tuna /ˈtjuːnə/
vanilla /vəˈnɪlə/
vegetables /ˈvedʒtəblz/
waiter /ˈweɪtə/
weight /weɪt/
winner /ˈwɪnə/
yoghurt /ˈjɒɡət/

WORD FRIENDS

make a cake (cakes)
make a decision
make a mess
make mistakes
make time
do my/your/his/her homework
do my/your/his/her best
put on weight

VOCABULARY IN ACTION

1 Use the wordlist to find:
  1 four drinks: *fruit juice*, …
  2 four types of main meal or small meal: *breakfast*, …
  3 ten adjectives to describe food: *bitter*, …
  4 four actions you do when you're cooking: *boil*, …
  5 four people: *contestant*, …

2 Use the wordlist to find the opposites of the words below.
  1 disgusting *delicious*
  2 loser _____
  3 sweet _____
  4 spicy _____
  5 fresh _____

3 In pairs, ask your partner about the spelling of one word in each category in Exercise 1 or 2.

How do you spell tasty?   It's T–A–S–T–Y.

4 🔊 1.63 **PRONUNCIATION** Listen to the underlined vowels in each word and repeat.

/ə/
vanill<u>a</u> cucumb<u>e</u>r breakf<u>a</u>st may<u>o</u>nnaise
flav<u>our</u> comp<u>e</u>tition

5 In pairs, find more words in the wordlist with the /ə/ sound.

Revision

VOCABULARY

1 Write the correct word for each definition.

1. This person takes part in a competition. **c o n t e s t a n t**
2. This is a type of meat. **b _ _ _ _**
3. This is a synonym for tasty. **d _ _ _ _ _ _ _ _**
4. These are small, round fruit and can be green, red, or black. **g _ _ _ _ _ _**
5. You do this to cook food in very hot water. **b _ _ _**

2 In pairs, complete the questions. Then ask and answer the questions in pairs. Make your own food quiz.

QUIZ — Favourite foods beginning with 's'

1. Some people like garlic and chilli with everything! Do you like s<u>picy</u> food?
2. You have two slices of bread and butter and you want to make a s_____. What filling do you like?
3. You're buying a s_____ in a juice bar. What flavour do you choose?
4. You'd love something s_____ to eat, like cake. What do you want?
5. Your family is having a nice, healthy, green s_____ for dinner. What do you put in it?

3 Complete the sentences with *make* or *do*.

1. I often *make* cakes for my friends.
2. I never _____ mistakes in English lessons.
3. I listen to music when I _____ my homework.
4. I always tidy up when I _____ a mess.
5. I _____ my best to eat healthy food.

GRAMMAR

4 Complete the dialogue with the words below.

already   ~~yet~~   just   for   since

Ana: Hi, Mum! Have you made my birthday cake ¹<u>yet</u>?
Mum: Yes, I've ²_____ taken it out of the oven. It's still warm.
Ana: Brilliant! We haven't had cake ³_____ ages! It looks amazing. What about the rest of the food? Is there any pizza?
Mum: Yes, everything's ready for the party. Go and look.
Ana: Oh, you've ⁴_____ put all the food on the table. Thanks, Mum.
Mum: I'm glad you like it. I've been in the kitchen ⁵_____ midday!

5 Write five questions using one word or phrase from each column.

Have/Has Did	your mum/dad	ever been in a competition?
	you	go to the supermarket last weekend?
	your brother/sister	ever made a cake?
	your friends	cook dinner yesterday?
	your teacher	ever had a picnic or a barbecue outside?
	your parents	take the family to a restaurant last year?
	your grandparents	ever eaten too much at a party?

Did you cook dinner yesterday?

6 In pairs, ask and answer your questions from Exercise 5.

Did you cook dinner yesterday?
No, I didn't cook yesterday, but I've cooked dinner a few times.

SPEAKING

7 In pairs, role play the situation. Follow the instructions.

Student A, you are a waiter. Ask the customer
- to take a seat, and offer to get the menu.
- if he/she is ready to order food.
- what he/she would like to drink.

Student B, you are a customer. Make your order from the menu on page 144.

DICTATION

8 🔊 1.64 Listen, then listen again and write down what you hear.

SELF-ASSESSMENT Think about this unit. What did you learn? What do you need help with?

What do the British really eat?

Popular food in the UK

Most people think that food in Britain is all about fish and chips, chip butties or afternoon tea, but that's not the whole story. There are so many different cultures in the UK that you have a huge choice of flavours and cuisines to choose from.

1. Indian food has been the country's favourite for years. Every town has at least one Indian restaurant. People even say that the national dish is now *chicken tikka masala*, a spicy curry usually served with rice or Indian bread called naan. It's delicious!

2. American food is everywhere. There's not only McDonald's now, but new gourmet burger restaurants like Five Guys. American food is popular because the recipes are very familiar to British people – hot dogs, fried chicken, pepperoni pizza, nachos and BBQ ribs are all big favourites.

3. People have a passion for fresh and healthy food these days and that's why Japanese food is popular. It's also easy to eat as a takeaway meal. Young people now prefer to eat sushi at lunchtime to the traditional British sandwich, although some still have problems with chopsticks!

Do you want to try more international food? Then check out the amazing Zaza Bazaar in Bristol! It opened in 2011 and has become one of the most popular places to eat in the city. It's also the biggest restaurant; they can serve over 1,000 people and have food from everywhere – Vietnam, Italy, China, Thailand, as well as Britain's three favourites, of course!

GLOSSARY
chopstick (n) a pair of thin sticks used for eating in China and Japan
cuisine (n) style of cooking typical of a country or region
gourmet (adj) (of food) high quality

EXPLORE

1 In pairs, ask and answer the questions.
1. What do people like eating in your country?
2. What are your favourite dishes?
3. What do you think British people really eat?

2 Read the article. Mark the sentences T (true) or F (false). Then check your answers to question 3 in Exercise 1.
1. ☐ People have the wrong idea about food in the UK.
2. ☐ It's easy to find an Indian restaurant in the UK.
3. ☐ American food is not very varied.
4. ☐ A lot of people eat sushi for their evening meal.
5. ☐ Zaza Bazaar doesn't serve Indian food.

3 According to the article, why is each food particularly popular? Match types of food 1–3 with adjectives a–c.
1. American   a practical
2. Japanese   b tasty
3. Indian   c familiar

EXPLORE MORE

4 ▶ 3.5 Watch Part 1 of the video and answer the questions.
1. Who are Anjum and Lynn?
2. What type of food are they cooking?

5 ▶ 3.5 Watch again. Choose the correct option.
1. Kerala is in *northern / southern* India.
2. Anjum and Lynn go to the market to *raise money for charity / help the community*.
3. Keralan food is *heavy and spicy / light and healthy*.
4. It's *easy / difficult* to find the ingredients for Keralan dishes in Liverpool.

6 Tick the three dishes that Anjum and Lynn are going to make.
1. ☐ coconut curry with pepper
2. ☐ coconut chicken with ginger
3. ☐ spicy salmon wraps
4. ☐ rice and salmon wraps
5. ☐ rice noodles
6. ☐ vegetable noodles

7 Which of the three dishes would you like to try? Why?
I'd like to try the first dish because I love coconut.

8 ▶ 3.6 Watch Part 2 of the video. Answer the questions.
1. Does Anjum like Lynn's cooking?
2. How many people visit Liverpool's farmers' market?
3. Do the people at the market buy Lynn's food immediately?
4. Do they sell all the food?

9 Have you ever cooked for a lot of people? Or have you ever helped out in the kitchen? What did you do?
I once helped my mum cook dinner for six.

YOU EXPLORE

10 **CULTURE PROJECT** In groups, prepare a survey based on the question: 'What do people really eat in your town?'
1. Prepare a questionnaire. Include local and international dishes (e.g. pizza, burgers).
2. Give the questionnaire to friends and family. Then collect the results.
3. Report your results to the class.

4

Curtain up!

VOCABULARY
Types of films | Film and TV | Compound nouns

GRAMMAR
Comparatives and superlatives | Quantifiers | Adverbs of manner

Grammar: How many bangles are you wearing?

Speaking: Do you want to try it?

BBC Culture: London celebrates

Workbook p. 52

BBC VOX POPS ▶

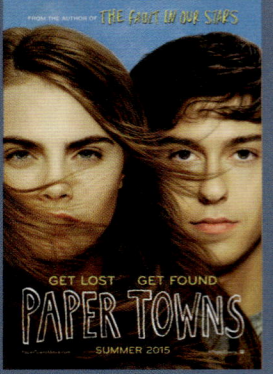

4.1 VOCABULARY Film and TV

I can talk about films and television.

1 🔊 **2.01** Study the Vocabulary A box. Use the words to describe the films in the posters. Sometimes more than one word is possible.

Vocabulary A	Types of films
action film cartoon comedy documentary fairy tale fantasy romantic film sci-fi thriller	

I think Arctic Tale is a documentary.

2 **I KNOW!** Can you add more film types to the Vocabulary A box?

3 🔊 **2.02** Match speakers 1–6 to films in the Vocabulary A box.

1 <u>documentary</u> 3 _____ 5 _____
2 _____ 4 _____ 6 _____

4 In pairs, talk about your favourite film or TV programme.

A: *My favourite film is Minions. It's a cartoon.*
B: *What's it about?*
A: *It's about some minions. They're small, yellow creatures.*
B: *What's it like?*
A: *It's very funny.*

Speaking	Talking about a film or TV programme
My favourite film is … It's a (*comedy, an action film etc*). What's it about? It's about (*a group of friends*). Who's in it? … is/are the main actor(s). What's it like? It's + adjective (*exciting/scary/strange/dramatic*).	

46

MINIONS!

5 **WORD BUILDING** Study the table. Complete the sentences.

Verb	Noun	Person
act	action	actor
entertain	entertainment	entertainer
produce	production	producer
perform	performance	performer

TEENLINK:
film and TV news by you for you!

☹ I'm not sure about the new *Mission Impossible*. Tom Cruise is a good ¹**a**ctor but I didn't like the story.

☺ I'd love to know how they ²**p**_____ the special effects in *The Avengers*. They're really cool.

☺ The costumes and the make-up were brilliant in the film. I don't know how they can ³**a**_____ with all that stuff on their faces.

☺ Yes, we all watched *Minions* in our house. My dad said it was great family ⁴**e**_____.

😐 Before making the film *Bears*, the ⁵**p**_____ had to learn a lot about them.

☺ I liked the *Mamma Mia* film much better than the musical ⁶**p**_____ it was based on!

★★★★★

6 Read the website. Choose the correct option.

Dr Who

1 *Dr Who* is *a new / an old* TV programme.
2 The Tardis is a *type of car / time machine*.

7 🔊 **2.03** Study the Vocabulary B box, using a dictionary. Complete the text with the words. Listen and check.

Vocabulary B	Film and TV

audience   character   episode   hit
reviews   ~~screen(s)~~   series   special effects

He's 900 years old and we love him!

The first *Doctor Who* appeared on our TV ¹*screens* in 1963. The producers wanted a family adventure ²_____ for Saturday evenings. It was an instant ³_____ and received great ⁴_____ from people of all ages. Although it was in black and white, the TV ⁵_____ liked the ⁶_____ which were difficult to produce in those days. In the first ⁷_____, two school teachers follow one of their pupils home. They discover that she lives with her grandfather, and that's when we meet the amazing ⁸_____ of the Doctor! He owns the Tardis, a time machine that can transport people through time. When the teachers enter the Tardis, they go back in time ...

8 In pairs, discuss the topics below.
- a popular TV series at the moment
- your favourite character from a film or from TV
- an example of a special effect
- a song that was a big hit last year
- a film that had bad reviews

9 🔊 **2.04** Listen to the dialogue. Complete the table.

	Emma	Max	You
Favourite TV series			
Type of programme			
What's it like?			
Best special effect/scene			

10 [VOX POPS ▶ 4.1] Think about a TV series you like, and complete the table to make it true for you. In pairs, discuss your ideas.

And YOU

Unit 4

4.2 GRAMMAR — Comparatives and superlatives

I can compare different things.

Curtain Up! ★★★★★

Your seat moves, you feel water on your face and you can smell something. It's the latest 4D cinema experience. The screens are bigger and the seats are in the most comfortable position for your eyes and neck. But, is it fun? 'It's more exciting than 3D,' said 15-year-old Adam, 'because it's brighter and louder.' His friend Jessica agrees. 'The most exciting scene was in the car. I felt like I was driving but I wasn't going fast enough.' For others, the experience isn't as good as 3D, and you can feel dizzy. 'The moving seats were worse than the sound,' said Alice. 'I was too uncomfortable. Some special effects are also scarier in 4D. Of course, the tickets are also more expensive, but it seems some people are happy to pay for "the best feeling" in the world!'

1 **CLASS VOTE** Do you prefer watching films at home or at the cinema?

2 🔊 2.05 Read the text quickly. Choose the correct option.
1. Adam has just watched a film in *3D / 4D*.
2. They watched the film *in a theatre / at the cinema*.

3 Study the Grammar box. Find more examples of comparatives and superlatives in the text.

Grammar — Comparatives and superlatives

Comparative
The new screens are **brighter**.
It's **more interesting than** the theatre.

Superlative
It's **the latest** sci-fi film.
The most exciting part was at the end.
It's **the best** cinema in the town.

too / (not) enough
I was **too** hot.
I felt like I was walking but I was**n't** going fast **enough**.

(not) as … as
However, others say the film is**n't as** good **as** the book.

GRAMMAR TIME > PAGE 121

---

4 Complete the sentences with the correct form of the words in brackets.
1. *Doctor Who* is the **best** (good) series ever!
2. It's _____ (cheap) to watch films at home than at the cinema and it's _____ (relaxing).
3. *Top Gear* is the _____ (funny) programme on TV.
4. The book is _____ (interesting) than the film.
5. The _____ (expensive) cinema ticket is £20.
6. The _____ (bad) thing is when people keep talking in the cinema.

5 Complete the second sentence so that it means the same as the first one.
1. In the film, the adults aren't as good as the children.
   In the film, the children are **better than** the adults.
2. Our town isn't big enough to have a good theatre.
   Our town is _____ to have a good theatre.
3. The film is funnier than the book.
   The book isn't _____ the film.
4. The main character in the fairy tale is too old.
   The main character in the fairy tale isn't _____.
5. The French thriller isn't as scary as the Danish thriller.
   The Danish thriller is _____ the French thriller.

6 [VOX POPS ▶ 4.2] What's your opinion? Write two sentences for each comparison. **And YOU**
1. the theatre / the cinema
   The cinema is cheaper than the theatre.
   The theatre isn't as exciting as the cinema.
2. comedies / documentaries
3. films / books
4. sci-fi films / fairy tales

4.3 READING and VOCABULARY A theatre evening

I can understand the main points of an article and talk about entertainment.

1 **CLASS VOTE** Does your school have enough trips to the theatre?

2 Study the words below, using a dictionary. Use the words to describe the pictures in the *High Five Entertainment Guide*.

> circus   costume   lights   make-up   mime
> puppet   stage

3 🔊 **2.06** Read the text. Why is Nathan going to the theatre?

> Hi Kate, Elena and Luke,
> Mum's getting some theatre tickets for my birthday and I can take three friends. I don't know which show to choose because they all look good. Send me a text telling me what you like most.
> Nathan

4 🔊 **2.07** Read the texts and *The High Five Entertainment Guide*. Match each person with the best show for them. There is one extra option.

> **Katie** ☐
> Brilliant idea! You know I love anything with music, and I prefer funny stories. I want to have fun! By the way, I have to be home before 9 p.m.

> **Elena** ☐
> I'm not keen on funny plays. I like stories that make me think about the world and things in my life. I also love watching good actors perform, so the cast is very important for me!

> **Luke** ☐
> Hi, Nathan, thanks. I'm not really into comedies or musicals. They're too childish. I prefer dramas and classical plays. I like new and fresh interpretations of classical plays, as well.

5 Which show would you choose? Why?

6 🔊 **2.08** Look at the highlighted phrases in the text and complete the sentences. Listen and check.

1 He's been an actor for a long time but he's always nervous when he *goes* on stage.
2 The producer is very happy when the show _____ good reviews.
3 There was a lot of noise during the show, and I didn't enjoy _____ the performance.
4 Jake wants to learn robotic dancing so he's _____ a workshop.
5 The film _____ the sad story of a boy who loses his dog.
6 She's always wanted to be famous, and now she's _____ in a film in Hollywood.

The High Five Entertainment Guide

FIND OUT WHAT'S ON NEAR YOU

A LOOK, NO STRINGS!
Puppets aren't just for kids! Join the Look, No Strings puppet show for a weekend of serious Shakespeare. Our youth theatre makes its own puppets and writes the stories. This weekend it's Macbeth. Come and be surprised, and stay for a class on puppet making (Saturday only).

B NO WORDS, LOTS OF FUN!
Words can't describe how much fun we have on stage. That's why we don't use them! Don't miss the excitement and drama of our new mime show. It combines a fantastic mix of movement and music. If you would like to learn more, do our hands-on workshop after the show at 9.30 p.m.

C ENJOY INDIAN ENERGY!
Welcome to Dance Bollywood, for one day only. This happy musical experience brings Indian energy and fun to the stage. It's getting good reviews, so come and enjoy great dancing and amazing costumes! You can also go on stage after the show for your first Bollywood dance class. The class ends at 8 p.m.

D THE SAD STORY OF EDWARD
Johnny Depp starred in the film and now the musical is here! Meet Edward Scissorhands, and watch a brilliant performance as he tries to find friendship, family and love. There are no spoken words, but music, dance and songs tell this sad story. Tickets are selling fast, so hurry!

Unit 4   49

4.4 GRAMMAR — Quantifiers: *some, any, much, many, (a) few, (a) little, a lot of, lots of*

I can talk about quantities of countable and uncountable nouns.

VIDEO: HOW MANY BANGLES ARE YOU WEARING?

Tommo: Cool music. You look great! Thanks for letting me take a few photos for the school magazine.
Alisha: No problem. Come in.
Tommo: Let's stand near the window. So, when do you wear these clothes?
Alisha: Mostly at weddings and *Diwali*, the festival of light. I've got lots of cousins, and we dance too … Like this.
Tommo: Cool, but stand still. This is awesome material. Is it from India?
Alisha: No, we get some material at the market here. There aren't many shops, and there's very little choice, so we mostly buy online.
Tommo: Don't move your hands. Wow, how many bangles are you wearing?
Alisha: Lots! We always wear a lot of jewellery. I've got some anklets too …
Tommo: This is perfect. How much time does it take to paint your hands?
Alisha: Ages! My gran does them, but she doesn't have much patience!
Tommo: Awesome! But stand still, please. I haven't got any photos of the whole outfit.

OUT of class: Like this. Lots! Ages!

1 CLASS VOTE Do you sometimes wear a traditional costume? Why? / Why not?

2 ▶ 4.3 🔊 2.09 Look at the photo. Why do you think Alisha is wearing her traditional costume? Watch or listen and check.

3 Study the Grammar box. Find more examples of quantifiers in the dialogue.

Grammar — Quantifiers

Countable nouns	Uncountable nouns
We learn **a lot of / lots of** songs.	I've got **a lot of / lots of** money.
How **many** bracelets are you wearing?	How **much** luggage has she got?
There aren't **many** markets near here.	We have**n't** got **much** furniture.
We've got **some** DVDs.	I've got **some** orange juice.
I have**n't** got **any** bracelets.	I have**n't** got **any** water.
Have you got **any** pictures?	Have you got **any** sugar?
Thanks for letting us take **a few** magazines.	I've got **a little** money.
There are very **few** people.	There's very **little** information.

GRAMMAR TIME > PAGE 121

4 Find four countable nouns and four uncountable nouns in the dialogue.

5 Choose the correct option.

teenfestblog

In ¹*a lot of / much* countries, there aren't ²*many / much* days when you can wear a traditional costume. However, for ³*some / any* lucky teenagers in Seville in Spain there are ⁴*a few / any* days in April, during the April Fair, when they can put on costumes, dance and enjoy ⁵*much / some* hot chocolate with *churros*.

6 Complete the sentences with one word in each gap.
1 I'd like to buy _some_ new shoes today.
2 How _____ material do you need?
3 I've got a _____ of cousins.
4 We haven't got _____ time to make a costume. It isn't possible in ten minutes!
5 She's got a _____ text messages from him.

7 And YOU In pairs, ask and answer questions. Use *How much … ? / How many … ?* and the words below.

jewellery / wear   hours / study at night
music / buy   sport / do   classes / do

50 Unit 4

4.5 LISTENING and VOCABULARY The Junino festival

I can identify specific detail in an interview and talk about festivals.

1 CLASS VOTE What's your favourite festival?

2 🔊 **2.10** Listen to the first part of an interview with Santiago. Where does he live?

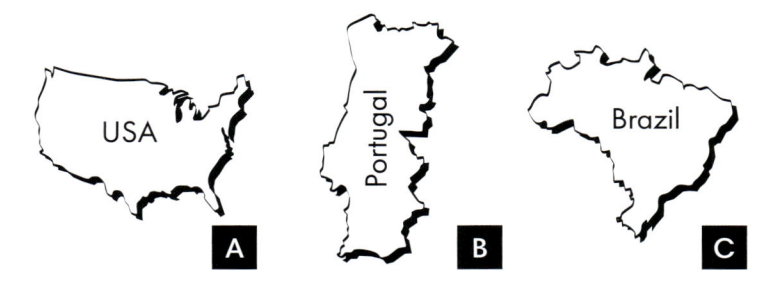

A USA   B Portugal   C Brazil

3 🔊 **2.11** Listen to the second part of the interview. Choose the correct answers.

1 Why is the festival special for Santiago?
   a He doesn't have to go to school.
   b He enjoys the winter in Brazil.
   c He likes being with his family.

2 How are the costumes different now?
   a The girls wear the same type of clothes as the boys.
   b The boys don't wear checked shirts any more.
   c They don't paint their faces now.

3 What happens in the toilet paper game?
   a People run with the paper in their hand.
   b One person wraps another person in toilet paper.
   c People write secret messages on the paper.

4 What does the music celebrate?
   a Old and young people.
   b Country life.
   c Carnival tradition.

5 What is Santiago's favourite food at the festival?
   a Corn cake.
   b Popcorn.
   c Corn pudding.

4 🔊 **2.12** In groups, complete the compound nouns in the Vocabulary box with the words below. Compare your ideas with the class. Which group has the most compound nouns? Listen and check.

cake   clothes   dance   dress   hat
music   party   vacation

Vocabulary	Compound nouns
Noun +	**noun**
family	*party, vacation*
summer	_____
country	_____
straw	_____
party	_____
carnival	_____
square	_____

5 How many more compound nouns can you remember from Exercise 3?

6 In pairs, discuss what you think makes a good festival. Compare your ideas with the class.

✗ (not important) ✓ (quite important)
✓✓ (important) ✓✓✓ (very important)

good entertainment   tasty food
friendly people   sunny weather
cheap tickets   fun games
carnival music

We think fun games for all the family are very important.
We don't think sunny weather is important.

Unit 4 **51**

4.6 SPEAKING Talking about preferences

I can ask about, express and explain preferences.

VIDEO DO YOU WANT TO TRY IT?

Dan: How was the African dance class, Skye?
Skye: Good, but it was hot. Do you want to try it?
Dan: No, thanks, I'm not mad about dancing. I'd prefer to watch something.
Skye: Well, there are two activities this afternoon. There's the outdoor cinema that's showing a comedy, or a puppet show. What would you prefer to see?
Dan: Definitely the comedy. It sounds very funny. Let's go together.
Skye: OK. We should take some food with us. I'd rather eat outside in this weather.
Dan: Great! How about a pizza?
Skye: Mmhh. I'd prefer to get something different. After all, it is an international festival.
Dan: OK. What would you rather have?
Skye: I think I'd prefer a Mexican dish. Maybe the chilli with rice.
Dan: OK. Cool! Let's see what we can find.

> I'm not mad about (dancing).
> It sounds (very funny).

OUT of class

1 CLASS VOTE What do you like doing with your friends?

- do music/dance classes   eat out
- go to music events   play instrument(s)
- watch films or shows

2 4.4 2.13 Study the Speaking box. Watch or listen. Find examples of talking about preferences in the text.

Speaking Talking about preferences

Asking about and expressing preferences
(What) would you rather + *verb*?
(What) would you prefer to + *verb*?

I'd rather + *verb*   I'd prefer to + *verb*

Giving reasons
It sounds very funny/great/boring …
It looks good.   It's healthier.

3 Make questions with the words below. Ask and answer them. Use the ideas in brackets to help you.

1 you / rather / do / tonight? (stay in / go out)
  What would you rather do tonight?
  I'd rather stay in.
2 you / prefer / to watch / at the cinema? (a horror / spy film)
3 you / rather / have for dinner? (Chinese food / Indian food)
4 you rather / learn? (the drums / the electric guitar)
5 you / prefer / dance to? (salsa / hip hop)

4 Study the poster. In pairs, discuss which activities you'd prefer to do.

Would you rather listen to … or … ?
I'd rather … because …

> 'Don't miss the fun!… comedy shows, outdoor cinema, live music, puppet shows, dance and drama classes, games, tasty food… and more!'

Unit 4

4.7 ENGLISH IN USE Adverbs of manner

I can describe how people do things.

Panel 1: Now, listen carefully, Benny. Breathe deeply and relax. If you think positively, you can do it easily.
I can't do it, Davina. Look at me!

Panel 2: BENDY BENNY the world's greatest escape artist
Ladies and Gentlemen, I'm sorry we're running late. Thanks for waiting patiently. Now, please welcome Bendy Benny!
About time! Boo!

Panel 3: Breathe deeply? Impossible!

1 Read the cartoon. Why is Bendy Benny scared?

2 Find examples of adverbs in the cartoon. Match them with the correct rule below.

Language — Adverbs of manner

To form adverbs from adjectives, add **-ly**.
bad – bad**ly**   beautiful – beautifu**lly**

For adjectives that end in -y, change -y to **-ily**.
angry – ang**rily**   happy – happ**ily**

Some adjectives are irregular: **good – well**

Some adjectives don't change: **early, hard, straight**

We use adverbs to describe how we do something. They *usually* come after the direct object OR (if there is no object) after the verb.

He arrived **late**.
She ate the cake **slowly**.

Comparatives and superlatives of adverbs of manner are formed like adjectives.
fast – **faster** – **the fastest**
slowly – **more slowly** – **the most slowly**

3 Rewrite the sentences with the correct form of the words in brackets.
1 Anna performed on TV last night. (brilliant)
   Anna performed brilliantly on TV last night.
2 The other singers weren't very good. She won the competition. (easy)
3 They were sitting during the mime show. (quiet)
4 Everyone clapped at the end. (loud)
5 Please text him. (quick)
6 The performer worked to perfect her act. (hard)

4 Read the text. Choose the correct answers.

Star review ...

I've just seen the play *War Horse*. It's about a young man, Albert, who ¹_____ on his dad's farm. Albert has a horse called Joey that he loves, but his dad sells him. He decides to go and look for Joey. In the play, the horse changes the lives of everyone he meets. The stage model of the horse was amazing. The actors moved it ²_____ across the stage. Although the film ³_____ when Albert finds Joey, a few people in the audience were crying ⁴_____ because the story was so moving.

1 a works harder
   b works hardest
   c hardly works
   d works hard
2 a beautiful
   b more beautifully
   c beautifully
   d most beautiful
3 a ends happy
   b ends happier
   c ends happily
   d happily ends
4 a quietly
   b quiet
   c quieter
   d more quietly

Unit 4 53

WORDLIST Types of films | Film and TV | Compound nouns

act /ækt/
action /ˈækʃn/
actor /ˈæktə/
angrily /ˈæŋgrəli/
anklets /ˈæŋkləts/
artist /ˈɑːtɪst/
audience /ˈɔːdiəns/
badly /ˈbædli/
bangles /ˈbæŋglz/
beautifully /ˈbjuːtəfli/
black and white film /ˌblæk ənd ˌwaɪt ˈfɪlm/
brilliantly /ˈbrɪljəntli/
carefully /ˈkeəfli/
carelessly /ˈkeələsli/
carnival /ˈkɑːnɪvl/
carnival clothes/dress/music/dance /ˌkɑːnɪvl ˈkləʊðz/ˈdres/ˈmjuːzɪk/ˈdɑːns/
cartoon /kɑːˈtuːn/
cast /kɑːst/
character /ˈkærəktə/
checked /tʃekt/
childish /ˈtʃaɪldɪʃ/
circus /ˈsɜːkəs/
clap /klæp/
classical /ˈklæsɪkl/
clearly /ˈklɪəli/
comedy /ˈkɒmədi/
corn cake/pudding /ˈkɔːn keɪk/ˌpʊdɪŋ/
costume /ˈkɒstjuːm/
country clothes/music/dance /ˌkʌntri ˈkləʊðz/ˈmjuːzɪk/ˈdɑːns/
dancing /ˈdɑːnsɪŋ/
deeply /ˈdiːpli/
dizzy /ˈdɪzi/
documentary /ˌdɒkjuˈmentəri/
dramatic /drəˈmætɪk/
early /ˈɜːli/
easily /ˈiːzɪli/
entertain /ˌentəˈteɪn/
entertainer /ˌentəˈteɪnə/

entertainment /ˌentəˈteɪnmənt/
episode /ˈepɪsəʊd/
escape /ɪˈskeɪp/
excitement /ɪkˈsaɪtmənt/
exciting /ɪkˈsaɪtɪŋ/
experience /ɪkˈspɪəriəns/
fairy tale /ˈfeəri teɪl/
family party/vacation /ˌfæmli ˈpɑːti/vəˈkeɪʃn/
fantasy /ˈfæntəsi/
fast /fɑːst/
festival /ˈfestɪvl/
freckles /ˈfreklz/
hands-on /ˌhændz ˈɒn/
happily /ˈhæpɪli/
hard /hɑːd/
hip-hop /ˈhɪp hɒp/
hit /hɪt/
international /ˌɪntəˈnæʃnl/
interpretation /ɪnˌtɜːprɪˈteɪʃn/
jewellery /ˈdʒuːəlri/
late /leɪt/
lights /laɪts/
loudly /ˈlaʊdli/
make-up /ˈmeɪk ʌp/
material /məˈtɪəriəl/
mime /maɪm/
movement /ˈmuːvmənt/
musical /ˈmjuːzɪkl/
outdoor /ˌaʊtˈdɔː/
party clothes/hat/dress/music /ˌpɑːti ˈkləʊðz/ˈhæt/ˈdres/ˈmjuːzɪk/
patiently /ˈpeɪʃntli/
perform /pəˈfɔːm/
performance /pəˈfɔːməns/
performer /pəˈfɔːmə/
play (n) /pleɪ/
politely /pəˈlaɪtli/
positively /ˈpɒzətɪvli/
poster /ˈpəʊstə/
produce /prəˈdjuːs/
producer /prəˈdjuːsə/

production /prəˈdʌkʃn/
puppet /ˈpʌpɪt/
quickly /ˈkwɪkli/
quietly /ˈkwaɪətli/
review /rɪˈvjuː/
romantic /rəʊˈmæntɪk/
safely /ˈseɪfli/
salsa /ˈsælsə/
scary /ˈskeəri/
scene /siːn/
sci-fi /ˈsaɪ faɪ/
screen(s) /skriːn(z)/
series /ˈsɪəriːz/
serious /ˈsɪəriəs/
show /ʃəʊ/
special effects /ˌspeʃl əˈfekts/
square hat/dance/cake /ˌskweə ˈhæt/ˈskweə dɑːns/ˌskweə ˈkeɪk/
stage /steɪdʒ/
star /stɑː/
straight /streɪt/
strange /streɪndʒ/
straw hat /ˌstrɔː ˈhæt/
theatre /ˈθɪətə/
thriller /ˈθrɪlə/
toilet paper /ˈtɔɪlət ˌpeɪpə/
traditional /trəˈdɪʃnəl/
well /wel/
workshop /ˈwɜːkʃɒp/

WORD FRIENDS

do a/the workshop
do music/dance classes
eat out
get good reviews
go on stage
go to music events
play instrument(s)
star in a/the film
tell a (sad/happy) story
watch a/the performance
watch films or shows

VOCABULARY IN ACTION

1 Use the wordlist to find:
1. four people who work in the theatre or in films
2. three adverbs that are the same as the adjective
3. four types of music and dance
4. five types of film
5. two items of jewellery
6. four adjectives that describe a film/play

2 Use the wordlist to complete the sentences.
1. I don't like cooking at home. I prefer to _____ out.
2. I'd like to learn to _____ an instrument but I'm not very patient.
3. I enjoy _____ workshops where I can learn with other people.
4. If a film _____ a bad review, I don't go and watch it.
5. I'd like to _____ in a film or a TV show one day.
6. When somebody _____ me a sad story, I often cry.

3 In pairs, tell your partner if the sentences in Exercise 2 are true for you.

I like cooking at home. It's fun.

4 🔊 2.14 PRONUNCIATION
Listen to the words and decide if the stress is on the first or the last syllable.

actor   artist   cartoon
costume   escape   outdoor
patient   perform   produce
puppet   review

First syllable   **Last syllable**
actor

Revision

VOCABULARY

1 Write the correct word for each definition.
1. The place in a theatre where people perform.
   s _ _ _ _ _
2. A meeting where people learn something new.
   w _ _ _ _ _ _ _ _
3. A performance with movement but no words.
   m _ _ _
4. A film with characters that an artist has drawn.
   c _ _ _ _ _ _
5. One of the parts of a TV or radio story.
   e _ _ _ _ _ _
6. A person who makes a film. p _ _ _ _ _ _ _ _
7. The clothes that an actor wears in a play or film.
   c _ _ _ _ _ _
8. An exciting film, programme or book about a crime. t _ _ _ _ _ _ _

2 Complete the text with the words below.

> comedy   country music   music events
> outdoor cinema   performance   reviews
> ~~summer vacation~~

Harry,
Hope you're OK. I've just come back from ¹**summer vacation** in Turkey. My dad is really into music and he loves going to ² _____ . On our last night we watched a ³ _____ by local belly dancers. Mum and I tried it but we were awful … How was the festival in your village? Did you listen to ⁴ _____ , or was it more carnival music? I love dancing in the street. Maybe we can go to the ⁵ _____ in the park on Saturday. It's good weather for it. There's a ⁶ _____ on with Steve Martin in it. It's got great ⁷ _____ and everybody says it's funny.
Speak soon,
Elli

GRAMMAR

3 Order the words to make sentences.
1. are / for / festival tickets / students / most / expensive / too
2. isn't / good / the old one / the new TV series / as / as
3. singing / the performance / the worst part / the / was / of
4. find / at the market / you / cheapest / the / costumes / can
5. concerts / relaxing / than / music festivals / more / are / pop

4 Choose the correct option.

How ¹many / **much** free time have you got this weekend? If you've got ²a few / some extra hours, come to one of our weekend workshops. We offer ³any / lots of activities. In our workshops you can make basic puppets with ⁴some / much wood, help paint the stage (we've got ⁵a lot of / a few black paint!), or learn how to make costumes with ⁶any / some old material.

We don't think there are ⁷many / much theatres that offer this range of activities and you don't need ⁸some / any experience … so what are you waiting for?

5 In pairs, tell your partner about two things you can do:
- fast   *I can get dressed fast in the morning.*
- brilliantly
- patiently

SPEAKING

6 Complete the dialogues.

> Would you prefer   Would you rather
> I'd prefer   I'd rather

A _____ do dance classes or play an instrument?
B _____ learn to play an instrument because I want to be in a band.
A _____ to have a summer vacation in your country or somewhere else?
B _____ to stay here because it's beautiful.

7 Work in pairs. Use the prompts to ask about, express and explain preferences.

Student A
wear a traditional costume to school / wear your own clothes?
go to the theatre / go to the circus?

Student B
watch a documentary about lions / watch a sci-fi film?
perform on stage / help behind the stage?

DICTATION

8 2.15 Listen, then listen again and write down what you hear.

SELF-ASSESSMENT Think about this unit. What did you learn? What do you need help with?

CULTURE

How do you like to celebrate?

Multicultural festivals in London

The eighteenth-century writer Samuel Johnson said, 'If you're tired of London, you're tired of life.' Looking at the city's annual calendar of cultural events, it's easy to agree with him!

There is such a mixture! There are traditional festivities that have existed for generations and new events which highlight the city's varied population. If you're looking for tradition, why not head for **Trooping the Colour** in June? It's a summer military parade which celebrates the Queen's official birthday.

For something more international, a big favourite is the five-day Hindu Festival of Lights, called **Diwali**. It is held in the autumn and celebrates the victory of good over evil. Head for Trafalgar Square to see the best contemporary Asian music and dance, and the most beautiful costumes. You also have the chance to taste delicious Indian food.

Don't forget the **Chinese New Year**, usually held in February. There's a parade in Chinatown, which changes each year to celebrate a different animal – the horse, the monkey, the cow, the dragon, etc. There's also a great atmosphere in the streets and restaurants nearby.

Finally, if it's Caribbean culture you're after, go to Europe's biggest summer street festival – the **Notting Hill Carnival**. You'll find live reggae, calypso and soul sounds, costume parades and the most amazing party atmosphere in the streets!

GLOSSARY
highlight (v) if you highlight something, you say it is very important
head for (phr) go towards
parade (n) an event in which people walk through the streets and play music

EXPLORE

1 What events do you celebrate in your country?

2 Read the text. Complete the sentences with the words below.

> ~~multicultural~~   parade   animal   traditional

1. A lot of London's new festivals are *multicultural*.
2. One of the most _____ festivals is linked to the Royal Family.
3. Many of the festivals in the text have a _____.
4. The Chinese New Year features a different _____ each year.

3 Match festivals 1–4 with descriptions a–d.

1. [b] Trooping the Colour
2. [ ] Diwali
3. [ ] Chinese New Year
4. [ ] Notting Hill Carnival

a. It lasts for a few days.
b. It happens on the same day every year.
c. There are lots of types of music.
d. It's a little different every year.

4 Which of the festivals from the text would you most like to go to? Why?

EXPLORE MORE

5 ▶ 4.5 Watch Part 1 of the video and answer the questions.
1. Where is the Chinese man from?
2. What does the woman like about Chinese New Year in London?
3. How many people attend the celebrations?

6 ▶ 4.5 Watch again. Choose the correct option.
1. The Chinese New Year is usually celebrated in *December / February*.
2. It's a great opportunity for Chinese businesses to make *contacts / money*.
3. Chinatown is *near to / far from* the celebrations in Trafalgar Square.

7 ▶ 4.6 Watch Part 2 of the video. Tick the things you see.
1. ☐ sunny weather
2. ☐ a man with a blue T-shirt
3. ☐ a lot of people in the street
4. ☐ man with green face make-up
5. ☐ people playing steel pan drums
6. ☐ people celebrating on a train

8 ▶ 4.6 Watch again. Complete the text with the words below. There are four extra words.

> police   costumes   parties   weather
> million   Caribbean   ages   happiest
> ~~fifty~~   much   biggest   British

The Notting Hill Carnival is ¹*fifty* years old. It celebrates ² _____ culture. It's famous for its colourful ³ _____ and great live music and performances. It's now the ⁴ _____ street festival in Europe, with more than a ⁵ _____ people coming to the party! There are people of all ⁶ _____ here – both young and old. 7,000 ⁷ _____ officers are at the Carnival to help keep everybody safe. The only problem is the London ⁸ _____ !

9 Have you ever been to a festival like the ones in the video? What were the differences and similarities?

YOU EXPLORE

10 **CULTURE PROJECT** In groups, prepare a survey based on the question: 'How do you like to celebrate?'

1. Prepare a questionnaire about festivities. Ask about favourite forms of entertainment and types of festivals.
2. Give the questionnaire to friends and family. Collect the results.
3. Report your results to the class. Are there differences or similarities? What are the most popular festivals? Why?

Unit 4

5
The big match!

VOCABULARY
Sports | Sporting events
Phrasal verbs with *up*

GRAMMAR
The future: *will* / *going to* / Present Continuous | First Conditional + *if*/*unless*

Grammar: We're having a competition

Speaking: What are you up to?

BBC Culture: The Highland Games

Workbook p. 64

BBC VOX POPS ▶
CLIL 3 > p. 141

MAYFIELD SUMMER SPORTS CAMPS
Click on an icon to find out more.

[Icons numbered 1–16]

5.1 VOCABULARY Sports and sporting events

I can talk about sports and sports events.

1 **CLASS VOTE** In groups, suggest the names of three sportswomen and three sportsmen for 'sports person of the year' in your country. Compare your ideas with the class, and vote for top sportswoman and top sportsman.

2 🔊 **2.16** Study the Vocabulary A box. Listen and match the pictures with the names of sports.

Vocabulary A	Sports						
badminton	☐	basketball	☐	climbing	☐	diving	☐
gymnastics	☐	handball	☐	horse-riding	☐	ice hockey	☐
ice-skating	☐	kayaking	☐	skateboarding	☐	snowboarding	☐
surfing	☐	table tennis	☐	volleyball	☐	yoga	☐

3 🔊 **2.17** Listen to people taking part in the Mayfield sports camp. Complete the gaps with the names of sports.

1 Katia _____
2 Max and Heather _____
3 The red and blue teams _____
4 The green team _____
5 Alexia _____
6 Leo _____

4 **I KNOW!** Work in pairs. How many words can you add to the Vocabulary A box, in two minutes? Use the notes to give yourselves a score.

Score:
- *one point for each item*
- *two points if you are the only team to think of that sport!*

5 Use the Vocabulary A box and the words from Exercise 4 to give three examples of each type of sport.

indoor sports   team sports   water sports
outdoor sports   individual sports   winter sports

6 🔊 2.18 **WORD FRIENDS** Complete the gaps with the words below. Listen and check.

> a sport (x2)   ball games or competitive games
> ~~football lessons~~   karate, yoga, gymnastics
> swimming, walking, climbing, skiing

1 have *football lessons*
2 do _____
3 play _____
4 go _____
5 practise _____
6 take up _____

7 Which sports from the Vocabulary A box (or your own list) …
- do you play or do in your PE classes?
- do you practise outside school?
- do you watch on TV?
- would you like to take up in the future?

8 🔊 2.19 Study the Vocabulary B box. Listen and match as many words as you can to the pictures.

Vocabulary B	Sporting events
changing rooms   fans   goal   kit   mascot   match
pitch   score   scoreboard   seats   stadium   team

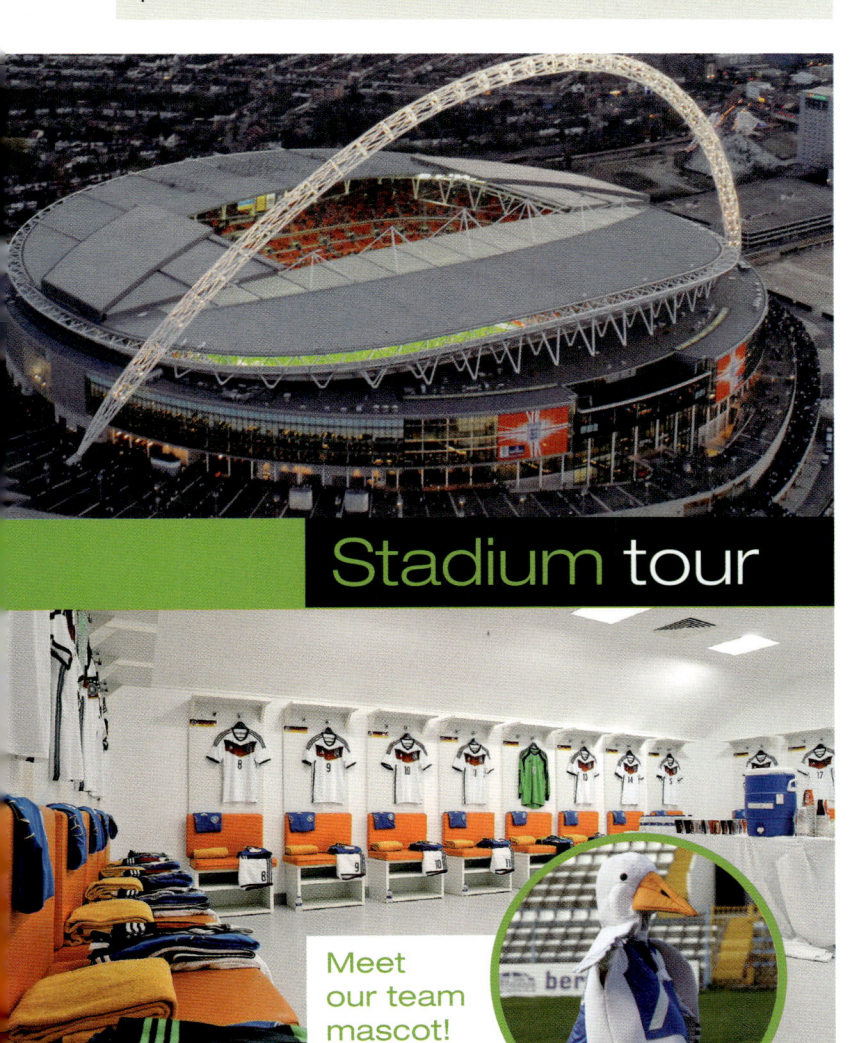

Stadium tour

Meet our team mascot!

9 🔊 2.20 Complete the text with words from the Vocabulary B box. Listen and check.

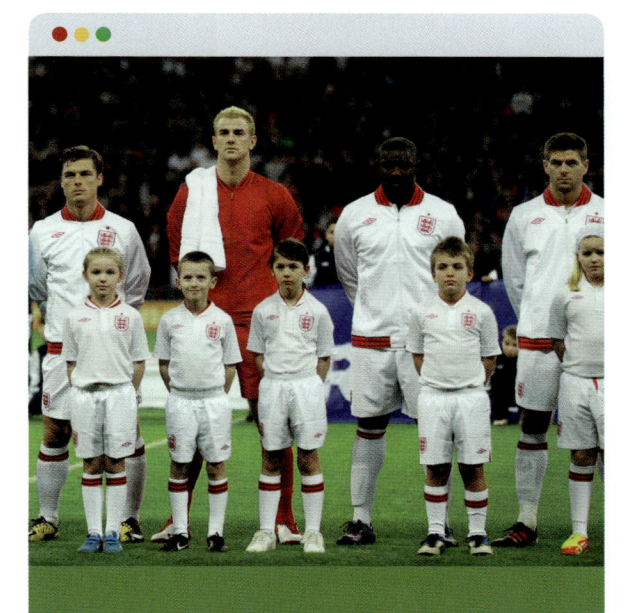

Mascot for the day!

Yesterday afternoon I was a team mascot for the English football ¹*team*. There were twelve of us mascots, boys and girls, and we had a tour of the famous Wembley ² _____ in London in the morning. Before the match, we went to get ready in the ³ _____. I was very excited because they gave each of us a present, a new white-and-red ⁴ _____ to wear!

Finally, we walked along the tunnel in pairs, with each mascot next to a player. Then we came into the stadium, and we stood on the beautiful green ⁵ _____. The crowd made a lot of noise because there were thousands of ⁶ _____. When the match started, we sat in special ⁷ _____ at the front. By the end of the match, the score on the big ⁸ _____ was 2–1. Our team won!

10 Would you like to be a team mascot? Why? / Why not? What sport and what team would you choose?

I'd like to be a team mascot because I'm a big sports fan. I'd be a football mascot for my favourite team, FC Barcelona.

And YOU

Unit 5

5.2 GRAMMAR The future: *will* / *going to* / Present Continuous

I can talk about plans, predictions, arrangements and timetables.

Skye: Oh, you got weights. Cool!
Tommo: Yeah, we're having a competition at the kayak club next month. I'll be one of the youngest, so I'm going to train well for it.
Skye: They aren't very heavy!
Tommo: They don't have to be heavy. The important thing is to use them every day.
Skye: You won't have much free time then.
Tommo: Yes, I will. It doesn't take long. Look, I'll show you. You lift your arms like this, and repeat about ten times.
Skye: Here, let me have a quick go. Hey, my swimming training starts next week. These exercises will help.
Tommo: Why don't you stay and do some more?
Skye: Sorry, Tommo, I can't. Oh, I'm going to be late and I'm meeting Dan for a run.
Tommo: Oh, OK, but don't forget. You have to use them every day.
Skye: I know.

VIDEO WE'RE HAVING A COMPETITION

OUT of class
The (important) thing is (to use them every day).
It doesn't take long.   Let me have a (quick) go.

1 **CLASS VOTE** Do you regularly go to a gym or do exercise at home?

2 ▶ 5.1 🔊 2.21 Watch or listen. What sports do Tommo and Skye mention?

3 Study the Grammar box. Find more examples of talking about the future in the dialogue.

Grammar   The future

Predictions or decisions made at the moment of speaking
You**'ll be** one of the fittest.

Plans and predictions based on what we know now
She**'s going to** train for it.

Arrangements
We**'re having** a sports day at school on Tuesday.

Timetables
The judo classes for beginners **start** next month.

GRAMMAR TIME > PAGE 122

4 Complete the sentences with the future form of the verbs in brackets.
1 Next year, the football club *is going to have* (have) new changing rooms. GOING TO
2 The fans _____ (not be) happy with the result. WILL
3 The basketball match _____ (start) in ten minutes. PRESENT SIMPLE
4 We _____ (go) to Nick's house after the match. PRESENT CONTINOUS
5 _____ (you/buy) your tickets for the match online? GOING TO

5 🔊 2.22 Complete the text with the words below. Listen and check.

> are offering   ~~are you doing~~
> begins   is going to help
> will be   will need   won't have

What ¹*are you doing* this summer?
If you don't have any plans, join us at your local park. *Fitness in the Park* is a new idea that ²_____ you to get fit and make friends. The fun ³_____ on June 22 with a special yoga class for beginners. All you ⁴_____ is a good pair of trainers and a bottle of water. Each day for four weeks we ⁵_____ a different activity for you to try. We think it ⁶_____ the best summer ever so don't miss out. Call us now to register. But hurry! We ⁷_____ enough places for everyone.

6 Complete the sentences to make them true for you.   **And YOU**
1 This evening I'm going to …
2 Tomorrow the weather will be …
3 On my birthday I'm not going to …
4 In two years everybody in this class will …
5 In 2050 I will …
6 When I'm 50, I won't …

Unit 5

5.3 READING and VOCABULARY   Why don't you volunteer at *Force4Sport* festival?

I can identify specific detail in an article and talk about volunteering at a sports event.

Force4Sport

You're not into sport but you like watching it. Why not take up a new hobby as a volunteer at the Force4Sport summer sports festival? You decide how many hours you want to volunteer and what kind of job you'd like to do. Our volunteers do lots of different things, from helping competitors to tidying up the stadium. Click on our case studies now, and find out more about our volunteers.

1 **CLASS VOTE** Do you regularly go to sports events? What is the most popular event?

2 🔊 2.23 Read the website. When is the Force4Sport festival?

3 🔊 2.24 Read the text. Complete gaps 1–6 below.

Hi, my name's Danielle Marley and I'm 16 years old. My cousins volunteered two years ago, and talked non-stop about it. I ended up applying to volunteer this year, and I'm really excited. I'm going to help at an international gymnastics competition at our local sports stadium. I did gymnastics when I was younger, but gave up a couple of years ago because I didn't have enough time. The event starts on 17 July and it lasts for two weeks. I'm only doing the first week, from Monday to Friday. I can't do the weekend. On the first day I'm going to help set up the spectators' area. After that I'm going to take photographs for the local newspaper and for the website. They've offered me a digital camera to take action shots and some team photos. I'm picking it up this afternoon so that I can practise with it. I've already won photography competitions, so I think I'll do a good job. In the future I'd like to study photography, so this could be very useful. I'm excited about volunteering because I enjoy watching sport. I don't think there'll be much chance to do that though, because I'll be too busy!

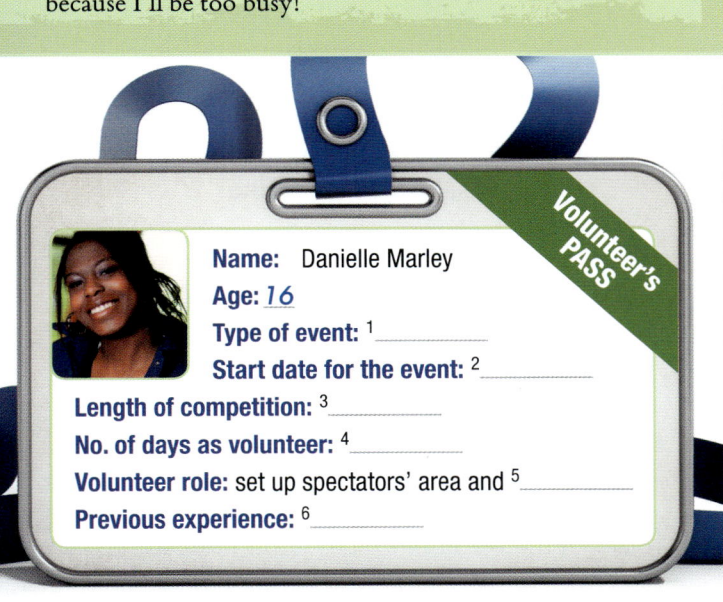

---

4 **PHRASAL VERBS** Use the phrasal verbs to complete the sentences.

Vocabulary	Phrasal verbs with *up*
end up give up pick up	
~~set up~~ take up tidy up	

1. Let's *set up* a gym in the garage and we can train there.
2. I don't want to _____ horse-riding but it is very expensive.
3. The team isn't doing well. They could _____ losing the game.
4. Emma loves trying new sports. She's just decided to _____ karate.
5. I've got to _____ the tickets. I paid online and they're at the ticket office.
6. There are clothes all over the floor. I want everybody to _____ the changing room.

Volunteer's PASS

Name: Danielle Marley
Age: *16*
Type of event: [1] _____
Start date for the event: [2] _____
Length of competition: [3] _____
No. of days as volunteer: [4] _____
Volunteer role: set up spectators' area and [5] _____
Previous experience: [6] _____

---

5 [VOX POPS ▶ 5.2] Would you like to be a volunteer at a sports event? Use the ideas below to make true sentences. **And YOU**

I would/wouldn't like to be a volunteer because …

watch/learn about different sports …
get free tickets …
take great photos …
crowds at the stadium …
not earn anything for hard work …

Unit 5

5.4 GRAMMAR First Conditional

I can talk about possible future situations.

1 Look at the photo. Describe what the girl is doing.

walk   fall   balance   rope

2 CLASS VOTE   Do you think you can do this activity? Yes or No?

3 🔊 2.25 Read the poster. What is a slackline?

SLACKLINING CLUB

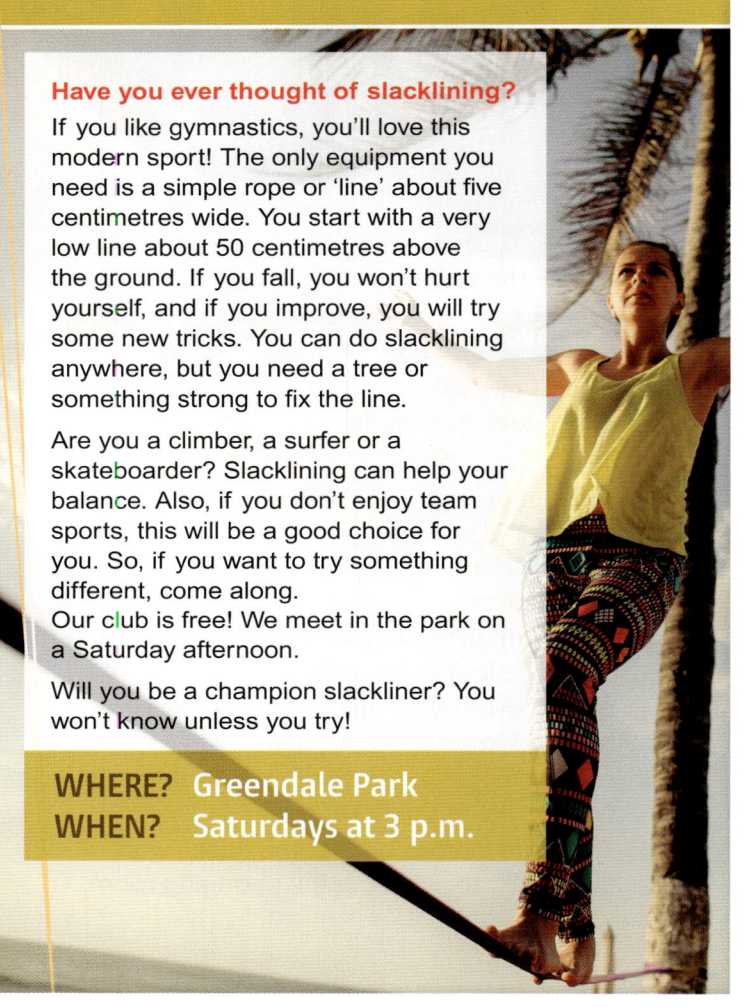

Have you ever thought of slacklining?
If you like gymnastics, you'll love this modern sport! The only equipment you need is a simple rope or 'line' about five centimetres wide. You start with a very low line about 50 centimetres above the ground. If you fall, you won't hurt yourself, and if you improve, you will try some new tricks. You can do slacklining anywhere, but you need a tree or something strong to fix the line.

Are you a climber, a surfer or a skateboarder? Slacklining can help your balance. Also, if you don't enjoy team sports, this will be a good choice for you. So, if you want to try something different, come along.
Our club is free! We meet in the park on a Saturday afternoon.
Will you be a champion slackliner? You won't know unless you try!

WHERE? Greendale Park
WHEN? Saturdays at 3 p.m.

4 Study the Grammar box. Find more examples of the First Conditional in the poster.

Grammar	First Conditional + if/unless

You **won't know if** you **don't try**!
You **won't know unless** you **try**!

Time clauses with *when* are constructed similarly.
When I'm back home, **I'll watch** some slacklining videos.

GRAMMAR TIME > PAGE 122

5 Match phrases 1–4 with phrases a–d to make sentences.

1 ☐ If you do slacklining, …
2 ☐ You won't do any special tricks …
3 ☐ I won't go to the slacklining club …
4 ☐ You'll see people slacklining …

a   unless you're very good.
b   if you go to the park on Saturday.
c   you will improve your balance.
d   unless a friend comes too.

6 🔊 2.26 Read and complete the sentences with the correct form of the verbs in brackets. Listen and check.

Goodbye to the Sports Centre!

The old Riverside Sports Centre will close next week. The new sports centre, with a large pool, tennis courts and a modern gym, won't be ready until next year.

1 If they **close** (close) the sports centre, we **won't play** (not play) handball for ages!
2 I _____ (not stop) playing badminton if they close it.
3 We _____ (not have) karate lessons unless the teacher _____ (find) a new classroom.
4 I _____ (go) swimming every week if they _____ (build) a pool at the new centre.
5 If there _____ (be) tennis courts, I _____ (take up) tennis.
6 We _____ (join) the new gym if it _____ (not be) too expensive.

7 [VOX POPS ▶ 5.3] Finish the sentences to make them true for you. In pairs, discuss your ideas.

And YOU

What will you do if there's a new sports centre in town?

I'll take up tennis.

1 If there's a new sports centre in town, …
2 If my friends are free this evening, …
3 If I get some money for my birthday, …
4 If the weather's nice at the weekend, …

5.5 LISTENING and VOCABULARY   A Norwegian footballer

I can identify specific detail in a conversation and talk about sports training.

1 **CLASS VOTE** Should a 16-year-old play sport professionally or wait until he or she is older? Why?

2 🔊 **2.27** Listen to the sports news. Choose the correct answers

1 What number football shirt did Martin first play football in?

A 19   B 76   C 36

2 What does Ødegaard like to do in football?

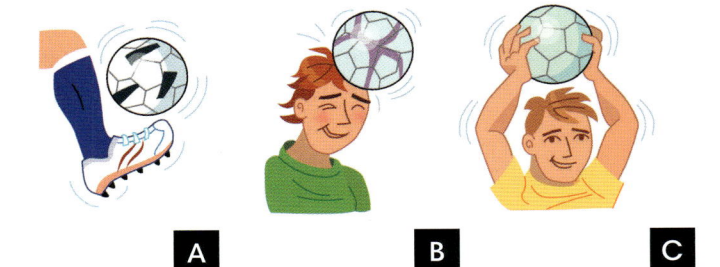

A   B   C

3 🔊 **2.28** Listen to a dialogue. Mark the sentences T (true) or F (false). Correct the false sentences.

1 ☐ Ben would be afraid to live in a different country.
2 ☐ Avril thinks Martin will learn Spanish quickly because he'll do a language course.
3 ☐ Martin will have lots of free time when he finishes training.
4 ☐ Ben thinks it will be difficult for Martin to be without his family.
5 ☐ Martin Ødegaard's uncle is going to be his coach.
6 ☐ Ben says Martin will be rich if he plays well.

4 In pairs, tell your partner what you can remember about Martin Ødegaard. Use Exercises 2 and 3 to help you.

Martin joined Real Madrid. He's only 16.

5 **WORD BUILDING** Study the table. Decide if the word underlined is a verb, noun (action) or noun (person).

1 Jack was too tired to finish the race.
2 Four nil! Do you know who scored the goals?
3 There's no football practice today.
4 The team are training very hard.
5 Their coach doesn't look very happy.
6 He's useless! He can't kick the ball at all.

Verb	Noun (action)	Noun (person)
train	training	trainer
run	running	runner
play	–	player
practise	practice	–
coach	–	coach
race	race	–
score	score	–
kick	kick	–

6 Complete the text with one word in each gap. Use Word Building to help you.

Interschool Handball Victory 28–33

Well done to all handball ¹p*layers* who joined us on Saturday! It was a great match and a fantastic ²s_____. Handball ³p_____ will be on Tuesday next week. As you know, Ms Ennis will ⁴c_____ the team from now on. She would also like to offer extra ⁵t_____ on Saturdays for anybody who is interested.

7 Would you like to train for your favourite sport in a different country? Discuss in pairs. Use the ideas below to help you.

family and friends
earn money
the weather
meet other teams/players
learn another language

I wouldn't want to …
It would be nice to …

Unit 5

5.6 SPEAKING Talking about plans

I can ask and talk about plans.

VIDEO — WHAT ARE YOU UP TO?

Alisha: So, is this the Wild Run course you organised?
Dan: Yep. Well, a lot of people helped, of course.
Alisha: Well done! But why is it called a Wild Run? I hope there aren't any wild animals?
Dan: Don't be daft! It's just a fun run! What are you up to before it starts?
Alisha: Nothing much.
Dan: Well, if you come with me, I'll explain it all. Over two hundred people are running here later, so I need to check everything. First, they're going under a net.
Alisha: Seriously? It's very muddy!
Dan: Yeah. Try it! Yeah, that's it.
Alisha: Well, if they don't like dirt, they won't enjoy this run!
Dan: Come on. Then they're crossing a stream and running up a hill.
Alisha: Oh no! It's fun, but I'm tired already! Have you got any plans for after the run?
Dan: Yes. When you all finish, we'll give you a medal. Then we're going to have a barbecue.
Alisha: Great. I'll need a medal. Wish me luck!

OUT of class
Don't be daft! Seriously? Wish me luck.

1 In pairs, look at the photo. What do you think is happening?

2 ▶ 5.4 🔊 2.29 Watch or listen and check your answer to Exercise 1. Mark the sentences T (true) or F (false).
1. ☐ Dan is going to run.
2. ☐ The event isn't a competition.
3. ☐ There will be two hundred volunteers.

3 🔊 2.30 Study the Speaking box. Order the sentences. Listen and check.

Speaking	Talking about plans

Asking
What are you up to today / at the weekend?
Have you got any plans for this evening / after the run?
What are you doing on Sunday / next Monday?

Answering and following up
I'm visiting my grandma / going to the cinema.
First (of all) I'm going to / I'm seeing ...
Then ... / After that ... / Later ...
I don't have any plans. / I don't know yet.
What about you? / And you? / What are your plans?

a ☐ Sam: Yes, OK. I'll probably see you on Sunday, then.
b ☒1 Sam: What are you up to this weekend?
c ☐ Tara: We'll get home late, so I'm definitely going to have a lie-in on Sunday ... Then I'll probably do some homework. We could go to the cinema after that, if you like?
d ☐ Tara: Well, first I'm visiting my grandparents on Saturday morning. Then we're going to go to a basketball match together. It starts at 4 p.m.
e ☐ Sam: That's nice. Have you got any plans after that?

4 In pairs, ask and answer about your plans for the weekend. Use the ideas below to help you. **And YOU**

sports and activities   shopping
family and friends   relaxation
homework   entertainment
trips   special events

5 Tell the class about some of your partner's plans.

Linda is going to see her grandparents on Saturday afternoon. Then they're going to the cinema in the evening.

Unit 5

5.7 WRITING Notes, making a request

I can write notes and make requests.

1 **CLASS VOTE** How do you and your friends usually send messages to each other? How long does it usually take you to reply?

> a text message   an email   a postcard
> an instant message   a message on paper
> a message on Facebook or social media

2 Read the messages. What types of messages are they?

> Hey Thkq 4 your help on Saturday. I had a gr8 time at the race but it was fast! Glad I trained 4 it. Left my trainers in the changing rooms :(Would u mind keeping them at your house? If it's OK with u, I'll pick them up at the weekend. Skye

GROUP CHAT

Hi,

Just a quick note to thank you all for competing on Saturday. More than 200 runners entered the race and we think everybody enjoyed themselves. We're now planning another race, which will take place in Northfield Park next month. Details will be on our website soon.
I've also got some great photos of the event. If you'd like a photo of you with your medal, could you please email me before June 30?

All the best,

Dan

2 mins ...

3 Read the messages again and answer the questions. Underline where in the messages you found your answers.
1 What does Dan want the runners to do?
2 What does Skye want Dan to do?

4 Order the information in Skye's message.
- [ ] Skye asks Dan to do something.
- [ ] Skye introduces the topic of the race.
- [ ] Skye thanks Dan.

5 Study the Writing box. Find the phrases from the Writing box in the texts in Exercise 2.

| Writing | Notes, making a request |

Greeting
Hi ... / Hi, there / Hiya / Hey ...

Thank the other person
Thanks for your note/message/present ...
Thanks for inviting me/writing/sending/coming ...
Just a quick note to thank you for ...

Introduce the topic
I had a great time at the race, although ...
I really enjoyed meeting the ...

Making a request
If you'd like ..., could you please ... ?
Would you mind ... ?
If it's OK with you, could we ... ?
Would it be possible to ... ?
Let me know if that's OK.

Ending
Bye! / Cheers! / All the best. / See you later.

6 Match phrases 1–5 with phrases a–e to make requests.
1 ☐ If you'd like to join the kayak club,
2 ☐ Would you mind
3 ☐ If it's OK with you,
4 ☐ Would it be possible
5 ☐ I could start at 8 p.m.

a could we meet at the tennis club at 7 p.m.?
b Let me know if that's OK.
c to train on Friday instead of Tuesday?
d helping with the sports day?
e please email us with your name and address.

7 You were a runner at the Wild Run. Write a note to Dan. Follow the instructions below:
1 thank him for his message
2 describe what you did at the race
3 ask Dan to do something for you

WORDLIST Sports | Sporting events | Phrasal verbs with *up*

badminton /ˈbædmɪntən/
balance /ˈbæləns/
basketball /ˈbɑːskɪtbɔːl/
changing rooms /ˈtʃeɪndʒɪŋ ruːmz/
climber /ˈklaɪmə/
climbing /ˈklaɪmɪŋ/
coach (v) /kəʊtʃ/
compete /kəmˈpiːt/
competition /ˌkɒmpəˈtɪʃn/
competitor /kəmˈpetɪtə/
crowd /kraʊd/
diving /ˈdaɪvɪŋ/
end up /ˌend ˈʌp/
equipment /ɪˈkwɪpmənt/
event /ɪˈvent/
exercises /ˈeksəsaɪzɪz/
fall /fɔːl/
fan /fæn/
fitness /ˈfɪtnəs/
football shirt /ˈfʊtbɔːl ʃɜːt/
footballer /ˈfʊtbɔːlə/
game /ɡeɪm/
get fit /ˌɡet ˈfɪt/
give up /ˌɡɪv ˈʌp/
goal /ɡəʊl/
gym /dʒɪm/
gymnastics /dʒɪmˈnæstɪks/
handball /ˈhændbɔːl/
head a ball /ˌhed ə ˈbɔːl/
horse-riding /ˈhɔːs ˌraɪdɪŋ/
ice hockey /ˈaɪs ˌhɒki/
ice-skating /ˈaɪs ˌskeɪtɪŋ/
improve /ɪmˈpruːv/
individual sports /ˌɪndəˈvɪdʒuəl spɔːts/
indoor sports /ˈɪndɔː spɔːts/
judo /ˈdʒuːdəʊ/
karate /kəˈrɑːti/
kayaking /ˈkaɪækɪŋ/
kick (v/n) /kɪk/

kit /kɪt/
lead (in the lead) /liːd (ˌɪn ðə ˈliːd)/
lift (v) /lɪft/
lose /luːz/
mascot /ˈmæskət/
match /mætʃ/
medal /ˈmedl/
net /net/
outdoor sports /ˌaʊtˈdɔː spɔːts/
PE /ˌpiː ˈiː/
pick up /ˌpɪk ˈʌp/
pitch /pɪtʃ/
play /pleɪ/
player /ˈpleɪə/
pool /puːl/
practice (n) /ˈpræktəs/
practise (v) /ˈpræktəs/
race (v/n) /reɪs/
register /ˈredʒɪstə/
rope /rəʊp/
run (v/n) /rʌn/
runner /ˈrʌnə/
running /ˈrʌnɪŋ/
score (v/n) /skɔː/
scoreboard /ˈskɔːbɔːd/
screen /skriːn/
seat /siːt/
set up /ˌset ˈʌp/
skateboarder /ˈskeɪtbɔːdə/
skateboarding /ˈskeɪtbɔːdɪŋ/
skiing /ˈskiːɪŋ/
slackline /ˈslæklaɪn/
slackliner /ˈslæklaɪnə/
snowboarding /ˈsnəʊbɔːdɪŋ/
spectator /spekˈteɪtə/
sports camp /ˈspɔːts kæmp/
sports centre /ˈspɔːts ˌsentə/
sports festival /ˈspɔːts ˌfestɪvl/

sportsperson / sportsman
sportswoman / sportspeople
/ˈspɔːtsˌpɜːsn/ˈspɔːtsmən/
ˈspɔːtsˌwʊmən/ˈspɔːtsˌpiːpl/
stadium /ˈsteɪdiəm/
surfer /ˈsɜːfə/
surfing /ˈsɜːfɪŋ/
swimming /ˈswɪmɪŋ/
table tennis /ˈteɪbl ˌtenəs/
take up /ˌteɪk ˈʌp/
team /tiːm/
team sports /ˈtiːm spɔːts/
tennis court /ˈtenəs kɔːt/
ticket /ˈtɪkɪt/
tidy up /ˌtaɪdi ˈʌp/
train /treɪn/
trainer /ˈtreɪnə/
trainers /ˈtreɪnəz/
training /ˈtreɪnɪŋ/
tricks /trɪks/
volleyball /ˈvɒlibɔːl/
volunteer /ˌvɒlənˈtɪə/
walking /ˈwɔːkɪŋ/
water sports /ˈwɔːtə spɔːts/
weights /weɪts/
whistle /ˈwɪsl/
win /wɪn/
winter sports /ˈwɪntə spɔːts/
yoga /ˈjəʊɡə/

WORD FRIENDS

do karate, yoga, gymnastics
go swimming, walking, climbing, skiing
have (a sport) lessons
play ball games or competitive games
practise (a sport)
take up (a sport)

VOCABULARY IN ACTION

1 Use the wordlist to find:
1. five places where you can do sport
2. six different people
3. three sports for which you need a ball
4. two pieces of sports equipment
5. two things you wear to do sports
6. three types of sports
7. three verbs that are the same as nouns

2 In pairs, ask your partner about the spelling of one word in each category in Exercise 1.

> How do you spell 'weights'?

> It's W-E-I-G-H-T-S.

3 Choose the correct option. Use the wordlist to check your answers. In pairs, say if the sentences are true for you.
1. I often (go) / play swimming.
2. I never *take up* / *have* any new sports.
3. I sometimes *go* / *play* basketball at school.
4. I'd like to *do* / *have* karate.
5. I *go* / *have* PE lessons twice a week.

4 🔊 **2.31** **PRONUNCIATION** Look at the underlined vowels in each word. Do you think we say them as one syllable or two? Listen and check.

c**oa**ch   g**oa**l   tr**ai**ner   w**ei**ght   s**ea**t   t**ea**m

5 🔊 **2.32** In pairs, say these words. Listen and check.

Revision

VOCABULARY

1 Write the correct word for each definition.
1. This person helps at events but isn't paid any money. v _ _ _ _ _ _ _ _ _
2. You can sit on this in a stadium, cinema or theatre. s _ _ _ _
3. If you want to be good at a sport, you must do this: p _ _ _ _ _ _ _ _
4. This is the object which shows spectators how each person or team is doing. s _ _ _ _ _ _ _ _ _ _ _
5. If you win a race, you might get this. m _ _ _ _ _

2 Read the word groups. Choose the odd one out. Give a reason for your decision. In pairs, make your own quiz questions.

1	player	competitor	coach	score
2	karate	tennis	volleyball	football
3	do karate	practise judo	play volleyball	give up tennis
4	kayaking	horse-riding	diving	swimming
5	net	race	kit	ball

GRAMMAR

3 Complete the sentences with the future form of the verbs in brackets. Match the sentences with their function below.
1. ☐ I *won't get* (not get) a medal, but I hope to do well. (WILL)
2. ☐ My favourite team _____ (play) at the stadium on Saturday. (GOING TO)
3. ☐ The karate class _____ (finish) at 8 p.m. (PRESENT SIMPLE)
4. ☐ _____ (come) to the cup final next week? (PRESENT CONTINUOUS)
5. ☐ Thank you! I'll be happy to come. I _____ (get) the tickets for us all, then. (WILL)

a plan
b decision at the moment of speaking
c prediction
d arrangement
e timetable

4 Complete the questions with the correct forms of the verbs in brackets.
1. What new sport will you try if you _____ (go) to summer sports camp?
2. Will you meet me when school _____ (finish)?
3. If you _____ (have) some free time in winter, where will you go?
4. What will you do if someone _____ (give) you some money for your birthday?

5 Choose the correct option.

A: What are you doing for Sports Day tomorrow?
B: ¹*First* / *Then* I'm watching the races. ²*Then* / *Later* I'm taking part in football. After that I'm going to try karate, I think. What about you?
A: ³*Then* / *First* I'm taking part in the street dance display. ⁴*First* / *After that* I'm not sure. I'll probably watch the volleyball competition ⁵*later* / *then*.
B: What are your plans for the evening?
A: I'm definitely going to take part in the sports quiz. And you?
B: I'm playing live music with one of the bands. ⁶*First* / *Then* I'll probably go to the barbecue, too.

6 In pairs, make your own dialogue. Use the sports day programme.

School sports day

Time	Events	Display
3 p.m.	football competition	skateboard display
4 p.m.	volleyball competition	gymnastics display
5 p.m.	try-it-yourself sessions: karate slacklining yoga skateboarding	
Evening 6 p.m. – 8 p.m.	live music with school bands barbecue sports quiz (teams of four–six people)	

DICTATION

7 🔊 **2.33** Listen, then listen again and write down what you hear.

SELF-ASSESSMENT Think about this unit. What did you learn? What do you need help with?

CULTURE

Where do they toss the caber?

Aussie Rules

If you think the most popular sport in Australia is rugby or cricket, think again. It's a sport that you have probably never heard of, called Australian Rules Football. Commonly known as 'Aussie Rules', big matches attract huge crowds, especially in the large stadiums of Sydney or Melbourne.

So what is Aussie Rules? Well, it's very different from the football that you and I know. The game is played between two teams of eighteen players and the field is oval-shaped. Though called football, it is more similar to rugby. For example, the ball is oval and you score points by kicking it between two goalposts, just like in rugby.

However, players can be anywhere on the field and they can use any part of their bodies to move the ball. Running with the ball is fine, but you have to bounce it or touch it on the ground at the same time. Throwing the ball is not allowed. Aussie Rules includes a lot of physical contact and can be dangerous. Players can tackle each other using their hands or even their whole body!

The sport was invented in the 1850s in Melbourne, but amazingly, a national competition didn't take place until the 1980s. It is equally popular among men and women, although there isn't a women's league yet. Because it is purely Australian, it is rich in cultural history and references. Australians identify with it greatly. They are very proud to have a sport that they can call their own.

It is only really played in Australia, but it has fans worldwide. Who knows? Perhaps one day it will become very popular in the UK too!

GLOSSARY
bounce (v) (of a ball) hit the ground and go up
goalpost (n) one of the two posts of a goal in games such as football
league (n) a group of sports teams or players who compete against each other
oval (adj) shaped like an egg
tackle (v) to try to take the ball from another player

EXPLORE

1 In pairs, ask and answer the questions.
1. What sports do you practise? Who do you play with? Why do you play them?
2. What is the national sport in your country?
3. What role do sports have in your country?

2 Read the article and answer the questions.
1. In what ways is Aussie Rules culturally important for Australia?
2. Do you think many sports have this cultural role? Why? / Why not?

EXPLORE MORE

3 ▶ 5.5 Watch Part 1 of the video with no sound. Order the actions as they appear in the video.
a ☐ men running a race
b ☐ spectators watching the sports
c ☑ 1 a man throwing a large piece of wood (the 'caber')
d ☐ men playing bagpipes and drums
e ☐ a man throwing a hammer
f ☐ two men wrestling
g ☐ two girls dancing

4 ▶ 5.5 Watch Part 1 of the video with sound. Complete the sentences with the words below.

> Olympics   parks   ~~tradition~~
> celebration   disappeared

1. The Highland Games are a very old _tradition_.
2. They include the colours and symbols of a culture that almost _____.
3. The Highland Games are a meeting place of strength, speed and _____.
4. Today the Games are played on sports grounds, farmers' fields and city _____.
5. For Scottish people, the Highland Games are Scotland's _____.

5 ▶ 5.5 Watch again. Answer the questions.
1. What do the Games capture?
2. Why are the Games in the village of Ceres important?
3. At what time of the year do they hold the Highland Games?
4. For many Scots, the Highland Games are as important as which other events?

6 ▶ 5.6 Watch Part 2 of the video. Tick (✓) six sports you hear or see.
1. ☐ cycling
2. ☐ horse-riding
3. ☐ climbing
4. ☐ tossing the caber
5. ☐ running
6. ☐ wrestling
7. ☐ hammer throw
8. ☐ handball
9. ☐ stone shot
10. ☐ hockey

7 ▶ 5.6 Watch again. Choose the correct option.
1. The Highland Games are a unique blend of sport and *fantasy* / *culture*.
2. The Games usually include athletics and *sometimes* / *always* heavy events.
3. The caber is six metres long and weighs *fifteen* / *fifty-five* kilos.
4. There are more Highland Games celebrated *in* / *outside* Scotland.
5. The Games are about competing and also making time for old *traditions* / *friends*.

8 In pairs or groups, ask and answer the questions.
1. Would you like to attend the Highland Games? Why? / Why not?
2. Which part of the Highland Games would you enjoy the most: the music and dancing or the sports? Why?

YOU EXPLORE

9 **CULTURE PROJECT** In pairs or groups, prepare a presentation about a national sport in other countries.
1. Research national sports of other countries.
2. Write a short script and think about images or videos to use in your presentation.
3. Give your presentation to the class.

Unit 5

6 See the world!

VOCABULARY
Types of holidays | At the hotel |
Equipment | Travel: confusing words

GRAMMAR
Obligation and prohibition | Modal verbs for speculation | Time clauses

Grammar: You mustn't do that!

Speaking: I didn't catch that

BBC Culture: Adventures of a lifetime

Workbook p. 76

BBC VOX POPS ▶
EXAM TIME 2 > p. 133

My Trips

6.1 VOCABULARY Travel

I can talk about holidays and travelling.

1 **I KNOW!** How do you prefer to travel? Look at the pictures below. How many types of transport can you name for each?

by sea   by road   by rail   by air

Watch OUT! We say *by sea/road/rail/air* and *by boat/car/bus/train/plane* but *on foot*.

2 Match questions 1–5 with responses a–e. In pairs, ask and answer the questions with your books closed.

Speaking	Travelling phrases
1 ☐	Excuse me, is the bus/train station near here?
2 ☐	What time does the bus/train arrive/leave?
3 ☐	What platform does the train arrive at / leave from?
4 ☐	Excuse me, how do I get to the airport?
5 ☐	I'd like a bus/train ticket to Paris, please.

a Single or return?
b At 9.15 a.m.
c There's a bus service every half hour.
d Platform 6.
e Yes, it's at the end of the road.

3 Do you ever write a diary when you're on holiday? Why? / Why not? What sort of information can you include?

4 🔊 2.34 Study the Vocabulary A box. Match the words with photos 1–7.

Vocabulary A	Types of holidays
☐ activity camp ☐ backpacking holiday ☐ beach holiday
☐ camping trip ☐ city break ☐ cruise ☐ sightseeing holiday

70

5 🔊 **2.35** Listen and match dialogues 1–5 with the types of holidays in the Vocabulary A box.

1 _____ 2 _____ 3 _____
4 _____ 5 _____

6 In pairs, describe:
1 three things to do at an activity camp.
2 four countries to visit on a cruise.
3 three things to see on a sightseeing holiday.
4 three things to do on a backpacking holiday.
5 two places to stay during a city break.

7 🔊 **2.36** Study the Vocabulary B box. Use the words to complete the text. Listen and check.

Vocabulary B	At the hotel

check in/out   double room(s)   facilities   floor   guests
pool   ~~reception~~   reservation   single room(s)   view

Diary

We arrived late last night at the hotel. Nobody was working in ¹*reception* so we couldn't ² _____ to our rooms. In the end, Mum phoned the hotel from her mobile! The manager arrived, but there was a problem with our ³ _____ . We needed two ⁴ _____ because there are four of us, but the hotel only had two ⁵ _____ .

In the end, the manager found us another hotel and here we are, in a better hotel! We're on the top ⁶ _____ and there's a brilliant ⁷ _____ of the city. It's got great ⁸ _____ and I can't wait to use the ⁹ _____ and the gym. There are lots of ¹⁰ _____ and they're all speaking different languages … I'm very excited to be here!

8 In pairs, discuss the last time you travelled. Use the questions below to help you.
- Where did you go?
- Where did you stay?
- What facilities were there?

I went to Austria with the school and we stayed in a big hotel. We had a view of the mountains but we didn't have a pool.

9 🔊 **2.37** Study the Vocabulary C box, using a dictionary. In pairs, describe the words.

Vocabulary C	Equipment

guidebook   map   passport
rucksack/backpack   sleeping bag
suitcase   sun cream   sunglasses   tent
torch   trunks/swimsuit

A: This has your personal information and a photograph, and you must bring it when you travel to another country …
B: It's a passport!

10 [VOX POPS ▶ 6.1] Choose a holiday from the list below. In pairs, make a list of things you should take with you. Compare your ideas with the class.
- a backpacking holiday with friends
- a city break in Ireland
- a cruise around the Mediterranean
- an activity camp in the mountains

Unit 6   71

6.2 GRAMMAR Modal verbs for obligation, prohibition and advice: *must*, *have to*, *ought to*, *should*

I can talk about obligation, prohibition and advice.

Gran: Skye, can you come down? Your mum's calling soon about our visit. We ought to have a quick chat first … Oh, you look lovely, dear.
Skye: Thanks. It's my party outfit. Have you got the tickets yet?
Gran: No, I'll get them soon, but I must know the exact date you finish school.
Skye: Our exams finish on June 16th, but I have to be here for Sue's birthday party on July 29th.
Gran: Yes. You mustn't miss that! Should we go the first week of July, then?
Skye: Perfect. Do Mum and Dad have to work in July?
Gran: They don't have to work every day. It rains quite a lot in July, so they ought to have some free time to be with us.
Skye: Hang on. What do you mean, it rains? I wanted a beach holiday.
Gran: Sorry, Skye. In July it's winter in New Zealand.
Skye: In that case, Mum and Dad should come here.
Gran: Then I think you have to ask them, Skye.

VIDEO YOU MUSTN'T MISS THAT!

OUT of class
What do you mean, (it rains)?
In that case, (they should come here).

1 CLASS VOTE How important is good weather on holiday?

2 6.2 2.38 Watch or listen. Why is Skye disappointed?

3 Study the Grammar box. Find more examples in the dialogue of obligation and prohibition.

Grammar Obligation and prohibition

obligation and prohibition
You **must** visit us in Paris.
You'll **have to** take warm clothes.
You **mustn't** be late for the flight.

advice
We **ought to** ask them about their plans.
You **shouldn't** take too much luggage.

lack of obligation
They **don't have to** go by car.

GRAMMAR TIME > PAGE 123

4 Choose the correct option.
1 I'm going to China soon. I *must* / *don't have to* buy a guidebook.
2 You can never find your passport. You *should* / *shouldn't* put it in a safe place.
3 *Do we have to* / *Should we* get a visa for the USA?
4 The plane leaves at 9 a.m., but we *mustn't* / *don't have to* be there until 7 a.m.
5 I *shouldn't* / *ought to* pack my bags. We leave in an hour.
6 It's going to be very hot at the beach. We *must* / *mustn't* forget the sun cream.

5 2.39 Complete the text with the words below. Listen and check.

don't have to   have to   must
mustn't   ~~ought~~   should

Mountain fun

Are you looking for adventure this summer? Then you [1]**ought** to try our mountain activity camp. You [2]_____ bring any special equipment because we provide everything. You [3]_____ be between 13 and 17 years old and have your parents' permission. All you [4]_____ bring are enough clothes for a week of camping, hiking and climbing and, of course, you [5]_____ forget a warm coat for evenings around the camp fire. Reserve a place now and you [6]_____ hear from us before the end of the month.

6 [VOX POPS ▶ 6.3] Finish the sentences to make them true for you. Compare your ideas with the class.

1 When you're on a beach holiday, you should …
When you're on a beach holiday, you should use sun cream.
2 In a plane, people mustn't …
3 When I'm on holiday with my parents, I don't have to …
4 On an activity camp, you have to …

6.3 READING and VOCABULARY
Live life outside

I can find specific detail in an article and talk about travelling.

1 **CLASS VOTE** Do you agree that travel is important? Why? / Why not?

2 In pairs, describe the main photo.

3 🔊 2.40 Read the text quickly. Order photos A–D as you find them in the article.

1 ☐ 2 ☐ 3 ☐ 4 ☐

Live life outside

Most travellers know that learning a new language can make a holiday more fun. But what about *frontside, lipslide, kickflip*? What sort of language is this?

It's the international language of the skateboarding world, and a language that teens like Booker Mitchell from New York know well. It has helped him to explore different places around the world and meet local people in different countries. Booker knows he's lucky to have parents who have always travelled with him. He's made videos of his trips since he was young. With the help of his mum, who's a film-maker, Booker has made videos that share an experience of skateboarding and surfing with the rest of the world.

Booker loves travelling and enjoys the feeling of adventure that goes with it. He doesn't think you should travel with a lot of luggage, and says the most important thing is to feel comfortable wherever you are. His favourite place to sleep is in a hammock, even if he's at home in New York! Of course, like the rest of us, there are some things Booker has to travel with. In his case, it's a skateboard or surfboard, a video camera and a notebook.

Does Booker sometimes go on holiday at the last minute? No way! Planning a trip is really important. Before every trip, he makes a list of where he wants to go sightseeing and why. He learns about the culture, food, music and scenery. He thinks that's the best way to enjoy somewhere.

Back at home, Booker rides his skateboard to school. He never takes the same route, and always listens to a different song on his iPod. He likes to see the different things that are happening around him. 'Life is fascinating, no matter where you live', he says. 'You just have to look at it the right way.'

---

4 Read the text again. Answer the questions.
1 What has skateboarding language helped Booker to do?
2 Why does Booker think he's lucky?
3 What does Booker like about travelling?
4 What does Booker always travel with?
5 How does Booker get to school?

5 Complete the sentences with one word in each gap.
1 Booker's *mother* has helped him with his skateboarding and surfing videos.
2 Booker doesn't think it's right to take much _____ when you travel.
3 When he's travelling, or at home, Booker prefers to _____ in a hammock.
4 It's important for Booker to _____ where he wants to go on a trip.
5 At home, Booker always uses a different _____ to get to school.
6 Booker thinks that if you look at life in the right way, it's _____.

6 **WORD FRIENDS** Find the words in the text and complete the Word Friends. Use the words in the correct form.

Word Friends	Travel phrases
learn a new language	
_____ different places	
_____ local people	
_____ an experience	
_____ a trip	
_____ on holiday / sightseeing	

7 Booker doesn't think people should travel with a lot of luggage. What about you?

And YOU

I take a huge suitcase. I always pack too many clothes.
I don't take much, and I often forget things. Last year I forgot my swimsuit!

6.4 GRAMMAR Modal verbs for speculation: *must, could, might/may, can't*

I can speculate about the present.

1 CLASS VOTE Look at the photo. Is this a fun place to sleep? Why? / Why not?

2 🔊 2.41 Read the text. What are the advantages and disadvantages of hanging tents?

My camping blog

TENTS

Hi Guys,
Welcome to my camping blog, the best place for all the latest camping news. This month I've discovered these amazing tree tents. It might be difficult to find them in the shops at the moment, but I think they're going to be popular. They're warm and comfortable, and great fun. I slept in one last weekend, in the middle of a forest, and it was awesome! Have a look and let me know what you think.

JO123 6.30 p.m. They don't look very big. It can't be easy to stand up in them if you're tall.

TENTFAN 7.10 p.m. It might be fun to sleep up in the air, but it must be difficult to go to the loo in the middle of the night!

TIMABC 8.00 p.m. They are cool! But they must be expensive because I haven't seen many of them.

CAMPER 8.30 p.m. They may look cool, but I think they could be really uncomfortable because they move around with the wind.

3 Study the Grammar box. Find more examples of speculating in the text.

Grammar | Modal verbs for speculation

must + infinitive
It *must be* cold outside. People are in jackets.

could/might/may + infinitive
It *might be* difficult to travel with the suitcase because it's very big.

can't + infinitive
That *can't be* our tent. It's the wrong colour.

GRAMMAR TIME > PAGE 123

4 Choose the correct option.
A: That's a strange tent? It looks like a balloon.
B: Oh, that ¹*must* / *can't* be the new tree tent. I've seen them on the internet.
A: I'd love to get one. Are they expensive?
B: They ²*can't* / *could* be expensive because my uncle's got one, and he hasn't got much money.
A: Is there a campsite near here?
B: I'm not sure. There ³*might* / *must* be one near the lake. I've seen people there in summer. Why?
A: I'd love to try a tree tent. Can we ask your uncle if we can borrow it?
B: OK, but today ⁴*could* / *can't* be a bad time. He's going on holiday with it!

5 Rewrite the sentences, using the verbs from the Grammar box. Sometimes more than one answer is possible.
1 I'm sure this is Ellie's tent. That's her rucksack.
   This *must* be Ellie's tent. That's her rucksack.
2 They're very quiet. Perhaps they're sleeping.
   They _____ be sleeping.
3 I'm sure this isn't the same campsite.
   This _____ be the same campsite.
4 Dad thinks this is your ticket, but your ticket is in your hand.
   This _____ be your ticket because your ticket is in your hand.
5 I'm sure the map is on the table. I put it there.
   The map _____ be on the table. I put it there.
6 Here's a guidebook, but perhaps it's the wrong one.
   Here's a guidebook, but it _____ be the wrong one.

6 What do you think of these ideas for unusual holiday accommodation? Use the Grammar box to help you.
- a canal boat in Holland
- a tree house in a forest
- an ice hotel in Sweden
- a castle on an island

It could be noisy in a tree house in a forest because of all the animals.

And Y?U

6.5 LISTENING and VOCABULARY Jess lives the dream!

I can identify specific detail in a conversation and talk about trips and excursions.

1 In pairs, describe the photo. What do you think is happening?

They're on a boat.
It might be a sailing holiday.

2 🔊 **2.42** Listen to the first part of the interview. What does Nick do?

3 🔊 **2.43** Listen to the second part of the interview. Mark the sentences T (true) or F (false).
1. ☐ Nick was working in South America when he met a girl who couldn't see.
2. ☐ The girl was on holiday with her family.
3. ☐ Special bikes are popular with kids who don't usually cycle.
4. ☐ Nick thinks the journey is more important than the holiday.
5. ☐ Hotel staff don't always realise how difficult it is for blind guests.
6. ☐ The winter holidays are the most popular.

4 🔊 **2.43** Work in groups of three. Listen again. Write down:
- four activities mentioned in the interview
- three kinds of holidays
- three problems that blind people might have

5 🔊 **2.44** Listen to Jess's story. Answer the questions.
1. How old is Jess and where does she come from?
2. What type of holiday did she go on?
3. What did Jess want to do during the trip?

6 In pairs, discuss why this sort of holiday is important for people like Jess. Compare your ideas with the class.

It's an adventure.
It might help them to meet people.

7 🔊 **2.45** Use a dictionary to check the words in the Vocabulary box and choose the correct option. Listen and check.

Vocabulary	Travel: confusing words
excursion journey travel (noun) travel (verb) trip voyage	

1. It was a three-hour car *journey* / *excursion* to the beach.
2. The *trip* / *voyage* across the Atlantic took two months and the cabins were comfortable.
3. Air *travel* / *journey* is very expensive at the moment.
4. The school is organising a two-day *travel* / *trip* to London.
5. Let's get tickets for the afternoon *journey* / *excursion* to the castle.
6. I'd love to *travel* / *voyage* to the North Pole one day.

8 **And YOU** Imagine your school has invited some students from another country. In pairs, discuss the best trips and excursions in your area. Compare your ideas with the class.

They could go on an excursion to the waterpark.
They could visit the capital city, but it's a long journey.

Unit 6

6.6 SPEAKING — Understanding a conversation

I can clarify what I have said and ask for clarification.

VIDEO | I DIDN'T CATCH THAT

Dan: Tickets, yes. Passport, yes … Hi, Ed. I'm just in the middle of packing for New York, but I can't see you. The camera's not working.
Ed: It doesn't matter. I can see you. What time …?
Dan: Sorry, I didn't catch that. You're breaking up.
Ed: What I said was, what time does your plane leave?
Dan: At seven, but I've got to be at the airport for four in the morning. Now, what should I pack?
Ed: You just need lots of sports clothes and …
Dan: Hang on, this is really annoying. Mum, I'm trying to talk to Ed. I didn't get the last part, Ed. What did you say?
Ed: I was just saying that you should bring things for the beach.
Dan: OK. How about these?
Ed: You must be joking. Dan, promise me …
Dan: Sorry, can you say that again?
Ed: Don't bring those smelly sneakers.
Dan: What was that?
Ed: Forget it, Dan. Thanks. See you tomorrow …

OUT of class
Forget it. You're breaking up. This is really annoying.

1 CLASS VOTE Do you like packing when you go on holiday? Do you prefer somebody else to do it for you? Why? / Why not?

I like doing it because I know I'll pack the right things.

2 Look at the photo. Would you take these things on holiday?

3 ▶ 6.4 🔊 2.46 Watch or listen and answer the questions.
1 What's Dan packing for?
2 What time does Dan have to be at the airport?
3 What type of clothes should Dan take?
4 What doesn't Ed want Dan to take?

Speaking | Understanding a conversation

Asking for clarification
Sorry, I didn't catch that.
Sorry, can you say that again?
What was that?
Sorry, I didn't get the first/last part.
Could you speak louder / more slowly?

Clarifying
What I said/asked was …
I said that …
I was just saying …
I just wanted to ask you about …

---

4 Complete the dialogues with the phrases from the Speaking box. In pairs, say the dialogues.

1 **A:** Hi, Maria! There's a school trip to Venice this year.
   B: _____ ?
   A: _____ there's a trip to Venice this year.
2 **A:** I think we need a visa for our holiday.
   A: _____ ?
   B: _____ we need a visa for our holiday.

5 In pairs, role play the situations. Follow the instructions. **And YOU**

A You're at the train station and your train is late. Call your friend and explain what's happening.

B Your friend calls from the station but it's noisy. You want to know what time she is arriving.

A: Hi, it's me. I'm at …

Unit 6

6.7 ENGLISH IN USE   Time clauses

I can use time clauses.

Boy: Are we nearly there? I'm starving!
Mum: Not long now. We'll eat as soon as we arrive.

Mum: I think we're lost.
Dad: You're right. It'll be dark when we get there.

Dad: Oh no! I've forgotten the tent pegs.
Mum: Look, I've got an idea. I'll find a hotel while you get some food.
Boy and Girl: Yay! We always wanted to stay in a hotel!

1 Read the cartoon and answer the questions.
   1 What type of holiday is the family planning to have?
   2 How are the teenagers feeling in the car?

2 Find examples of time clauses in the cartoon.

> **Language   Time clauses**
>
> **When** I'm at the station, I'll buy the tickets.
>
> What are you going to do **while** you're waiting for the bus?
>
> I will have a party **after** I finish my exams.
>
> **Before** we go hiking, we'll look at the map.
>
> We'll wait here **until** the ticket office opens.
>
> I'll call you **as soon as** I arrive.
>
> We use the Present Simple in future time clauses with *when, while, before, until, as soon as*.
>
> Put a comma after the time clause if it comes first in a sentence.

3 Complete the sentences with the correct form of the verbs in brackets.
   1 We'll wait until she _____ . (come)
   2 Jack will drive us to the party as soon as you _____ ready. (be)
   3 Write to me when you _____ on holiday? (go)
   4 Alice and Ben will leave after they _____ breakfast. (have)
   5 Before you _____ (sunbathe), put on some sun cream.

4 Choose the correct answers.

Interrail

I love the idea of travelling by train, but it could be a disaster. Has anybody got any advice or ideas?

tedyy 10:52 Just enjoy it! Interrail is simply the best choice! I'm sure you'll agree as soon ¹*after/when/so/as* your journey begins.

Ella 11:06 The interrail company will help you plan your journey before you ²*leave/leaves/left/will leave*. It's really easy.

Mark 12:41 It was easy to buy the tickets online. I'm waiting for them to arrive, but I won't relax ³*after/as soon as/until/while* I get them.

Tom12 12:53 Go for it! As soon as you ⁴*'ll get/get/gets/'re getting* on the train, you'll meet lots of people.

Mike 12:55 You'll travel through amazing scenery ⁵*while/after/before/until* you're on the train, and the trains are comfortable.

WORDLIST Types of holidays | At the hotel | Equipment | Travel: confusing words

accommodation /əˌkɒməˈdeɪʃn/
activity camp /ækˈtɪvəti kæmp/
adventure /ədˈventʃə/
airport /ˈeəpɔːt/
annoying /əˈnɔɪɪŋ/
arrive at /əˈraɪv ət/
the Atlantic /ði ətˈlæntɪk/
backpack /ˈbækpæk/
backpacking holiday /ˈbækˌpækɪŋ ˌhɒlədeɪ/
balloon /bəˈluːn/
beach holiday /ˈbiːtʃ ˌhɒlədeɪ/
blind /blaɪnd/
break up /ˌbreɪk ˈʌp/
bus service /ˈbʌs ˌsɜːvəs/
bus station /ˈbʌs ˌsteɪʃn/
cabin /ˈkæbɪn/
camera /ˈkæmərə/
camping /ˈkæmpɪŋ/
camping trip /ˈkæmpɪŋ trɪp/
campsite /ˈkæmpsaɪt/
castle /ˈkɑːsl/
check in /ˌtʃek ˈɪn/
check out /ˌtʃek ˈaʊt/
city /ˈsɪti/
city break /ˈsɪti breɪk/
climbing /ˈklaɪmɪŋ/
country /ˈkʌntri/
cruise /kruːz/
culture /ˈkʌltʃə/

diary /ˈdaɪəri/
double room /ˌdʌbl ˈruːm/
excursion /ɪkˈskɜːʃn/
facilities /fəˈsɪlətiz/
fascinating /ˈfæsɪneɪtɪŋ/
film-maker /ˈfɪlmmeɪkə/
floor /flɔː/
forest /ˈfɒrɪst/
guest /gest/
guidebook /ˈgaɪdbʊk/
hammock /ˈhæmək/
hanging tent /ˌhæŋɪŋ ˈtent/
hiking /ˈhaɪkɪŋ/
hotel /həʊˈtel/
ice hotel /ˈaɪs həʊˌtel/
island /ˈaɪlənd/
journey /ˈdʒɜːni/
key /kiː/
leave from /ˈliːv frəm/
loo /luː/
luggage /ˈlʌgɪdʒ/
manager /ˈmænɪdʒə/
map /mæp/
mast /mɑːst/
the Mediterranean /ðə ˌmedɪtəˈreɪniən/
noisy /ˈnɔɪzi/
the North Pole /ðə ˌnɔːθ ˈpəʊl/
notebook /ˈnəʊtbʊk/
organisation /ˌɔːgənaɪˈzeɪʃn/
pack /pæk/
passport /ˈpɑːspɔːt/

platform /ˈplætfɔːm/
pool /puːl/
popular /ˈpɒpjʊlə/
provide /prəˈvaɪd/
reception /rɪˈsepʃn/
reservation /ˌrezəˈveɪʃn/
reserve /rɪˈzɜːv/
return ticket /rɪˈtɜːn ˌtɪkət/
Rome /rəʊm/
route /ruːt/
rucksack /ˈrʌksæk/
safe (n) /seɪf/
sailing holiday /ˈseɪlɪŋ ˌhɒlədeɪ/
scenery /ˈsiːnəri/
school trip /ˈskuːl trɪp/
ship /ʃɪp/
sightseeing holiday /ˈsaɪtˌsiːɪŋ ˌhɒlədeɪ/
single ticket /ˌsɪŋgl ˈtɪkət/
single room /ˌsɪŋgl ˈruːm/
sleeping bag /ˈsliːpɪŋ bæg/
smelly /ˈsmeli/
suitcase /ˈsuːtkeɪs/
summer holidays /ˌsʌmə ˈhɒlədeɪz/
sun cream /ˈsʌn kriːm/
sunglasses /ˈsʌnˌglɑːsɪz/
swimsuit /ˈswɪmsuːt/
tent /tent/
tent peg /ˈtent peg/
ticket /ˈtɪkɪt/
ticket office /ˈtɪkɪt ˌɒfəs/

top /tɒp/
torch /tɔːtʃ/
train station /ˈtreɪn ˌsteɪʃn/
transport /ˈtrænspɔːt/
travel (n,v) /ˈtrævl/
traveller /ˈtrævlə/
tree house /ˈtriː haʊs/
tree tent /ˈtriː tent/
trip /trɪp/
trunks /trʌŋks/
view /vjuː/
visa /ˈviːzə/
visit /ˈvɪzɪt/
voyage /ˈvɔɪɪdʒ/
winter holidays /ˌwɪntə ˈhɒlədeɪz/

WORD FRIENDS

learn a new language
explore different places
meet local people
share an experience
plan a trip
go on holiday
go sightseeing
on foot
by sea/road/rail/air
by boat/car/plane/train/bus

VOCABULARY IN ACTION

1 Use the wordlist to find:
1 five different means of transport
2 five things that you would take on holiday
3 three things that you could do on holiday
4 two facilities you might have at a hotel

2 In pairs, discuss the differences between the words below.
1 a voyage / a cruise
2 a visa / a passport
3 a sightseeing holiday / a city break
4 a camping holiday / a backpacking holiday
5 a single ticket / a return ticket

3 Use the wordlist to complete the sentences. Use the words in the correct form. In pairs, say if the sentences are true for you.
1 You don't have to _____ a trip but it can be exciting.
2 You need a lot of money to _____ sightseeing.
3 It's best to _____ different places by bus.
4 An activity camp is a good place to _____ an experience.
5 It's easy to _____ a new language when you have to use it every day.

4 🔊 **2.47** **PRONUNCIATION** Sentence stress falls on the important information in a sentence. Underline the important words in the sentences. Listen, check and repeat.
1 The children enjoyed the activity camp, but the weather was terrible.
2 I'd love to sail across the Atlantic in the future.
3 We stayed on a campsite near the river.
4 They were waiting at the bus station for two hours.
5 We can leave the luggage in the hotel reception.
6 Don't forget to take the map and the guidebook with you.

Revision

VOCABULARY

1 Write the correct word for each definition.
1. The area you see from a place. **v** _ _ _ _
2. This helps you to see things in the dark. **t** _ _ _ _ _
3. A big bag you put things in for your holiday. **s** _ _ _ _ _ _ _ _
4. The place where you wait to get on a train. **p** _ _ _ _ _ _ _ _
5. Put things in bags ready for a journey. **p** _ _ _
6. A place where you stay on holiday, e.g. a hotel. **a** _ _ _ _ _ _ _ _ _ _ _ _

2 Complete the text with the words below.

> travel   learn   meet   go   pack   plan

HOW MUCH OF A TRAVELLER ARE YOU?
Do you like exploring new places or would you rather stay closer to home?

1. What's the first thing you _____ in your bag when you're getting ready to travel?
2. Would you try to _____ a new language before visiting a different country?
3. What's the best way to _____ local people when you're on holiday?
4. When you _____ sightseeing, do you always take photos?
5. What type of trip would you like to _____ for this summer?
6. Who would you rather _____ to another country with, family or friends? Why?

3 In pairs, ask and answer the questions. Tell the class about your partner.

The first thing Anna packs is her make-up!

GRAMMAR

4 Choose the correct option.
1. When you're on holiday, you *must / ought* to buy food in local shops.
2. On a hot sunny day, you *don't have to / must* put on lots of sun cream.
3. When you visit a new country, you *should / mustn't* try to learn the language.
4. You *don't have to / have to* go to a travel agency. You can buy your tickets online.
5. It's a long train journey. We *must / mustn't* forget to take lots of food and water.

5 Match sentences 1–6 with sentences a–f.
1. ☐ I've just had a postcard from Julia.
2. ☐ That can't be my rucksack.
3. ☐ It's a bit cloudy to go to the beach.
4. ☐ The maps might be in reception.
5. ☐ It's a very long journey for the children.
6. ☐ Let's have a camping holiday.

a. It's the wrong colour.
b. Hotels often put them there.
c. It could be too cold to swim.
d. They must be very bored.
e. It could be fun in a tent.
f. She's on holiday.

6 In pairs, speculate about the situations below.
1. Your friends have arrived at the airport but can't find a taxi.
2. You're going on holiday tomorrow but you can't find your tickets.
3. You arrive at your hotel but there aren't any rooms.

SPEAKING

7 In pairs, role play the situations. You and your partner meet in a noisy café at a train station. Follow the instructions.

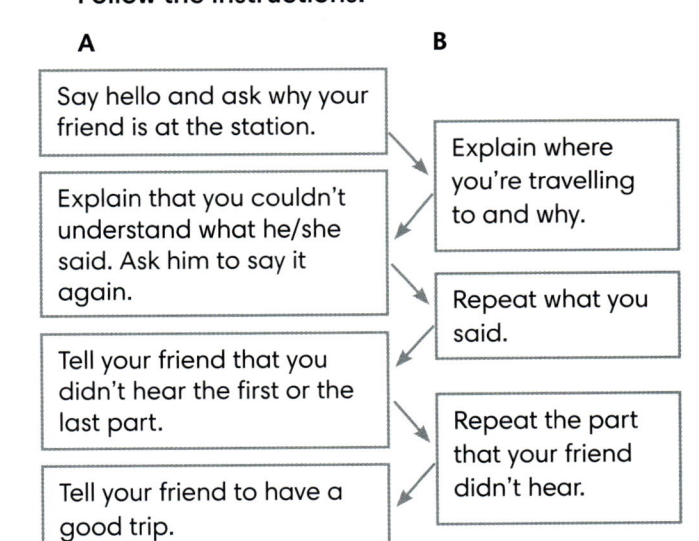

A
- Say hello and ask why your friend is at the station.
- Explain that you couldn't understand what he/she said. Ask him to say it again.
- Tell your friend that you didn't hear the first or the last part.
- Tell your friend to have a good trip.

B
- Explain where you're travelling to and why.
- Repeat what you said.
- Repeat the part that your friend didn't hear.

DICTATION

8 🔊 **2.48** Listen, then listen again and write down what you hear.

SELF-ASSESSMENT Think about this unit. What did you learn? What do you need help with?

Can ironing make holidays exciting?

The Brits on holiday

It could be because their weather is so unpredictable, but British people – the Brits – love to go abroad. They even invented the concept of budget airlines. In fact, these cheap airlines have allowed more people to travel to more destinations for less money. So, what kind of holiday do they prefer and what activities do they like most?

Unsurprisingly, even though extreme ironing was invented in 1997 in the UK, it is not the most popular sport among the British. Not many people fancy ironing and even fewer doing it in remote locations. Beach holidays are still their preferred option and sunbathing their favourite occupation. After the beach, sightseeing remains very popular and city breaks are the way many Brits like to sightsee. Some wonderful destinations are just a short flight away, so people go there for a long weekend. Some lazy Brits love a cruise holiday, while more dynamic travellers choose activity holidays which involve outdoor sports, trekking or camping.

So, what city could combine all of these holiday types? It's easy: Barcelona in Spain! It's unique because it combines the beach and sightseeing. And as an important port, Barcelona also attracts cruises, especially in summer. You can even have an adventure holiday in the Pyrenees mountains nearby. Its football team, Barça, is also a great attraction.

But it's not just Barcelona. Spain has been the Brits' clear favourite since 1994. More than twelve million Brits visit every year. Obviously, the weather is a key factor. Sun is guaranteed most of the year round in most places. There are large ex-pat communities along the coast, so speaking English is not a problem. Spanish people also have a friendly reputation and the food is popular, especially the tapas. It's a surprise that the Brits haven't taken over completely!

GLOSSARY
abroad (adv) to a different country
budget (adj) here: cheap
lazy (adj) a lazy person doesn't like to work
occupation (n) a way of spending your time
unpredictable (adj) changing a lot so it is impossible to know what will happen

EXPLORE

1 In pairs, ask and answer the questions.
1. What type of holiday do you prefer? Do you like to:
   - relax?
   - try something new?
   - do lots of activities?
2. Where is your favourite holiday destination?
3. Would you like to go on an adventure holiday? Why? / Why not?
4. Would you like to try extreme ironing?

2 Read the article. Answer the questions.
1. Why do the British love to go abroad?
2. Why can more people travel by plane now than in the past?
3. Why is it easy for the Brits to sightsee abroad?
4. Why are cruises and activity holidays opposites?
5. Why is Barcelona such a popular city with tourists?

EXPLORE MORE

3 ▶ 6.5 Watch Part 1 of the video. Mark the sentences T (true) or F (false). Correct the false sentences.
1. ☐ The Maldives is a luxury holiday destination.
2. ☐ Kirstie really wants to do jet skiing from the beginning.
3. ☐ Doing jet skiing is quite cheap.

4 ▶ 6.6 Watch Part 2 of the video. Choose the correct option.
1. To do snowmobiling in Iceland, you need special protective *clothing* / *vehicles*.
2. You should follow your guide's advice because the sport can be *difficult* / *dangerous*.
3. Icelandic landscapes look like the surface of *Mars* / *the Moon*.

5 ▶ 6.7 Watch Part 3 of the video. Complete the sentences with one word in each gap.
1. The hot-air ballooning option is a much more _____ choice.
2. The great thing about this sport is the total _____ when you're up there.
3. You see the landscapes below from such a different _____.

6 ▶ 6.5–6.7 Watch the three parts of the video again. Match sports a–c with sentences 1–9 used to describe them.
a. jet skiing (the Maldives)
b. snowmobiling (Iceland)
c. hot-air ballooning (Morocco)

1. You can also do other less energetic sports there.
2. The vehicle is specially prepared.
3. The landscapes are unique there.
4. You can do the sport with many others.
5. Some people get annoyed by this sport.
6. You can only do this at a certain time of day.
7. You have to hold on tight when you do this sport.
8. The views are particularly special.
9. It's the best possible way to relax.

7 Which of these three sports would you most like to do? What rules and regulations do you have to follow to do each one? How would you imagine doing each sport? Discuss in pairs.

YOU EXPLORE

8 CULTURE PROJECT In groups, prepare a presentation about an adventure sport.
1. Use the internet or other sources to research an adventure sport.
2. Write a short script and think about images or videos to use in your presentation.
3. Give your presentation to the class.

7 Getting to know you

VOCABULARY
Phrasal verbs | Talking about friends

GRAMMAR
Second Conditional | Defining and non-defining relative clauses

Grammar: I'd come if I was free

Speaking: Who's the guy at the back?

BBC Culture: On the move

Workbook p. 88

BBC VOX POPS ▶
CLIL 4 > p. 142

'Miss Baker, I've got something to tell you about my project. My dad helped me a bit. Any mistakes are his.'

A

7.1 VOCABULARY Family and friends

I can talk about relationships with family and friends.

1 CLASS VOTE Who would you like to spend a day with?

grandfather   grandmother   teacher   neighbour   aunt   uncle   cousin

2 WORD BUILDING Read the texts. Use the words in bold to complete the definitions (1–3).

> My **great**-grandmother, Julia, is ninety and she's my **grand**mother's mother. Julia was adopted.

> I've got a little **half**-brother. He's my father's son from his second marriage.

> I really like my **step**sister. Some people say we are similar, although we aren't really related by blood.

1 The prefix _____ describes a family relative who is two generations away from you. Add an extra _____ for each extra generation.
2 The prefix _____ describes a brother, sister or parent who is related to you by marriage but not by blood.
3 The prefix _____ describes a brother or sister who is related to you through one shared parent.

3 🔊 **2.49** Look at the cartoons. Guess the relationships between the people. Give reasons. Listen and check.

parent, stepparent and neighbour
parent, child and teacher
great-grandparent and great-grandchild

Oh, they're not all our children! These are my nieces, Clara and Sara. This is David's son, Max, and these are Max's friends, Tom and Tara.

When I was your age, things were very different. We only had ONE screen, and the whole family gathered around to spend a lovely evening all together!

B

C

4 🔊 **2.50** Listen and check you understand the words in the Vocabulary box. Complete the personality test.

Vocabulary	Phrasal verbs
deal with (a problem)	go out
fall out with	hang out with
get on with	put up with
go ahead	laugh at

5 In pairs, discuss your answers. What have you got in common? Tell the class about your partner.

Both of us like/dislike …
I think I'm quite similar to/different from …

6 🔊 **2.51** **WORD FRIENDS** Choose the correct option. Listen and check. Who do you agree with? Jessica or Mark?

Should friends have a lot in common?

JESSICA: Yes! My friend Sarah and I ¹share/get loads of interests. We both like horse-riding and cinema. We ²have/get the same sense of humour, too. We ³share/spend a lot of time together and we're like sisters. My singing can ⁴share/get on her nerves sometimes, but we never ⁵see/have arguments.

MARK: I disagree. I'm completely different from my friend Mike, but we ⁶enjoy/see each other's company. When I ⁷enjoy/get to know people, I find them more interesting if they ⁸come/have from different backgrounds. Mike loves to ⁹spend/see time on his own, so we don't ¹⁰have/see each other often, but when we meet, we have fun.

PERSONALITY TEST

1 Can you put up with being on your own?
a Yes
b No
c It's OK

2 Do you like to go out and meet new people?
a I find it difficult
b I love it
c I like it

3 Do you ever fall out with other people?
a Never
b Sometimes
c Not often

4 Do you get on well with big groups of people?
a I find it difficult
b I love it
c I like it

5 Are you good at dealing with friendship problems?
a No
b Yes
c Not always

6 Do you like to hang out with just a small group of friends?
a Yes
b No
c It's OK

7 Are you the first one in your group to go ahead and try new things?
a Never
b Yes, I hate things to be boring!
c Sometimes

8 Is it important for you and your friends to laugh at the same things?
a Yes, I like my friends to be similar to me
b No, but they must be fun to be with
c No, I get on with everyone

Go to page 144 to read about your answers.

7 Should friends share interests? In pairs, discuss your opinions.

And YOU

Unit 7

7.2 GRAMMAR Second Conditional

I can talk about imaginary situations.

VIDEO I'D COME IF I WAS FREE

Damian: Alisha? I can't tie this bow tie. If mum wasn't busy, she'd help, but …

Alisha: I can do it. There you go. The bow tie's smart, but you look like a waiter! And your hair's a mess. It would look much better if you had some gel in it. Here.

Damian: Get off! Stop bothering me. Anyway, you look like a giant cream cake.

Alisha: *(mobile rings)* Skye! Swimming? Oh! I'd come if I was free, but we've got a family wedding. My auntie's getting married and I'm her bridesmaid. I can't talk now, I'm getting ready. Sorry. Bye!

Mum: Damian! Alisha! Hurry up. We're going in five minutes.

Alisha: Nooo! I'm not ready yet! *(sneezes)* Hold this a sec.

Damian: What's up? Your eyes are really red.

Alisha: I know! I'm allergic to these flowers. *(sneezes)* I keep sneezing!

Damian: If I were you, I'd take some tissues. Loads of tissues!

Alisha: Agh! What a nightmare.

OUT of class
There you go.   Stop bothering me.
Get off!   Hold this a sec.

1 **CLASS VOTE** Which of these family events do you prefer? What do you like/dislike about them?

☐ a meal   ☐ a wedding   ☐ a short visit / holiday

2 ▶ 7.1 🔊 2.52 Watch or listen. Why does Alisha need to take tissues?

3 Study the Grammar box. Find more examples of the Second Conditional in the dialogue.

Grammar	Second Conditional
I'd come if I was free. (but I'm not free) What would you do if you were me?	

GRAMMAR TIME > PAGE 124

4 🔊 2.53 Complete the sentences with the Second Conditional form of the verbs in brackets. Listen and check.

1 If she _____ (have) enough time, she _____ (help) him.
  If she had enough time, she would help him.
2 If you _____ (listen) carefully, you _____ (understand) the lesson.
3 _____ (you/go) to the beach if _____ (you/be) free today?
4 He _____ (not be) here if he _____ (not want) to.
5 What _____ (you/do) if _____ (you/win) a lot of money?
6 I _____ (phone) your mum if I _____ (be) you.

5 [VOX POPS ▶ 7.2] In pairs, finish the sentences to make them true for you. **And YOU**

1 If my friend phoned when I was busy, …
2 If I didn't like my clothes, …
3 If there was a big wedding in our family, …
4 If I was late for a family meal, my parents …
5 I'd be very worried if …
6 It would be a nightmare for me if …

If my friend phoned when I was busy, I'd probably talk to her. What about you?

Unit 7

7.3 READING and VOCABULARY — Friendship day

I can find specific detail in an article and talk about friends.

Friendship Day

The idea of a special friendship day has several origins. An American woman, Joyce Hall, owned a greetings card company. In 1930 she planned a Friendship Day to create more business. She thought, 'If people had a new celebration, they would buy more cards.' The first Friendship Day in the USA was on 2 August. Many Americans sent cards, but then this tradition died out after a few years.

However, a different idea of Friendship Day has been celebrated in some South American countries since 1958. It began with a group of friends in Puerto Pinasco, Paraguay. They decided to celebrate friendship and understanding on 30 July every year. One man in the group, Ramon Artemio Bracho, wanted to do more. He wanted to turn strangers into friends. He worked hard to start celebrations in other countries. Thanks to Ramon's work, people in India and China also took up the idea. Friendship Day was growing.

Finally, in 2011, the celebration became International Friendship Day when the United Nations agreed to support it. They saw it as a good way to encourage peace by getting different cultures to communicate more. They set up activities for children and teenagers of mixed nationalities, such as fun runs or friendly games. The hope is that these kinds of events help people to respect one another's culture and to make new friends.

In some countries, people have a meal, phone friends or use social media to send messages. In Paraguay, the 'Invisible Friend' game is played one week before the special day. All names of schoolmates or workmates are written on pieces of paper and put in a box. Then everybody takes one card with a name and buys a small present for that person, wraps it and writes the name on it. When you get your gift on Friendship Day, you don't know who bought it! However, if I wanted to do something for my buddies, I would give them friendship bands because they are so popular.

Jyoti Singh, age 15, India

---

1 CLASS VOTE Is it important to have a special day to celebrate friendship? Why? / Why not?

2 🔊 2.54 Read the text. Mark the sentences T (true) or F (false).
1. ☐ Joyce Hall owned a company in the UK.
2. ☐ In the USA in 1930s, people celebrated by giving cards.
3. ☐ The decision to spread the celebration to more countries was made in Paraguay.
4. ☐ Asian countries are not keen on Friendship Day.
5. ☐ The United Nations encourage younger people to take part.
6. ☐ The 'Invisible Friend' game involves writing a message to your friends.

3 🔊 2.55 Study the Vocabulary box. Find more examples in the text.

Vocabulary	Talking about friends
synonyms for *friends*	
mates classmates best friends	
_____ _____ _____	
antonyms for *friends*	
enemy _____	
phrases with *friends*	
have a friend be friends _____	

4 Complete the sentences with the words from the Vocabulary box.
1. At first I felt like a *stranger* here. Nobody knew me.
2. Of all my friends, Ezra is my _____ because he understands me.
3. She was nervous about the new school but it was easy to _____.
4. My dad sometimes plays tennis with his _____ from the office.
5. He started secondary school early, so his _____ are older than him.

5 What would you like to do with your friends to celebrate Friendship Day?

And YOU

7.4 GRAMMAR Defining and non-defining relative clauses

I can be specific about people, things and places.

PARK STREET PUZZLE
Who lives in these houses?

1 Lucy lives in one of the flats above the café.
2 One of Lucy's friends lives in a house which has a big tree in the garden.
3 In front of another friend's house, there is a small space where he leaves his bike.
4 Mr and Mrs Morris, who are Lucy's grandparents, live next door to her.
5 Mrs Morris loves colourful flowers, which she grows in window boxes.
6 Paddy lives in a house which is next to the bus stop.
7 Lucy doesn't know the man who has just moved to the house with a pink roof.
8 The man's cat loves the balcony, where it can watch the birds.

☐ Lucy ☐ Molly ☐ Paddy ☐ Frank Jones ☐ Mr and Mrs Morris

1 🔊 2.56 Who lives in each house? Read the puzzle and write the house numbers next to each name. Which is the house where nobody lives?

2 Study the Grammar box. Find examples of defining and non-defining relative clauses in the puzzle.

> **Grammar | Defining and non-defining relative clauses**
>
> **Defining relative clauses**
> The man **who** (that) moved to Park Street is Frank.
> Molly lives in a house **which** (that) is a hundred years old.
> That's the cafe **where** the children often buy ice cream.
>
> **Non-defining relative clauses = extra information**
> Frank, **who** moved to Park Street, has a cat.
> Molly's house, **which** has a tree in the garden, is very old.
> There's a café in the street, **where** we buy ice cream.
>
> **Be careful!**
> The woman that/who grows flowers is Mrs Morris.
> Mrs Morris, ~~that~~/who grows flowers, is Lucy's grandma.
>
> GRAMMAR TIME > PAGE 124

3 Choose the correct option. Which pronouns can be replaced with *that*?

1 The children *who / which* are in the park live nearby.
2 Here's the office *where / which* my mum works.
3 I live in a flat *which / who* is in the town centre.
4 Frank Jones's cat, *which / who* is five years old, loves hunting.

4 Combine the sentences with relative pronouns.

1 Lucy has a good friend. **She** lives near Park Street.
   Lucy has a good friend who lives near Park Street.
2 In Molly's garden there's a tree. **It**'s 100 years old.
3 That's the café. Lucy sometimes meets her friends **there**.
4 There's a park. The children play **in it**.

5 Rewrite the sentences, using non-defining relative clauses.

1 Mrs Morris is sixty-seven. (who/be/Lucy's grandmother)
   Mrs Morris, who is Lucy's grandmother, is sixty-seven.
2 Paddy uses his bike every day. (which/be/new)
3 Number 24 is a beautiful house. (where/Molly/live)
4 Frank has a cat. (who/used to work/at the hospital)

6 Make one true and one false sentence about your house, street or town. In pairs, say if your partner's sentences are true or false.

Unit 7

7.5 LISTENING and VOCABULARY — A friend in need …

I can identify specific information in a monologue and talk about pets.

1 **CLASS VOTE** Can animals be your friend or part of your family? Why? / Why not?

2 Look at the photos. Which person do you think might have a disability, and how do you think the dog is helping? What else do you think dogs can do to help people?

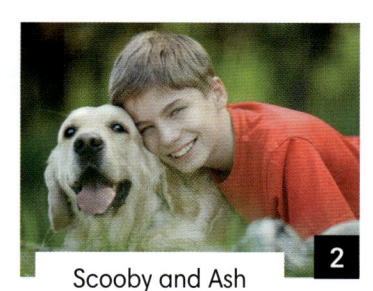

Snoopy and Grace 1

Scooby and Ash 2

3 Look at questions 1–4 below. What do you think Grace's sister will talk about?
1 What does Grace think of her morning routine?
 a It was boring. b It was sad. c It was slow.
2 How old was Grace when she got Snoopy?
 a a baby b a child c a teenager
3 What does Snoopy do to help with Grace's everyday routine?
 a tickles her b washes her feet
 c puts her socks on
4 Based on Grace's sister's account, which adjective best describes Snoopy?
 a busy b funny c clever

4 🔊 2.57 Listen and answer the questions in Exercise 3.

5 Look at the answers for questions 1–4 below. Match the answers to the types of information below.

opinions? feelings? detailed meaning of a word or phrase?
specific information? general topic?

1 What does a puppy trainer do?
 a looks after old dogs
 b teaches young dogs special skills
 c finds new homes for unwanted dogs
2 When the dogs left, Ash felt
 a sad. b bored. c happy for them.
3 Scooby's training was done
 a by Ash on his own.
 b by Ash's stepmum.
 c by Ash and his stepmum together.
4 What is the main thing we learn from Ash's explanation of assistance dogs?
 a They often go to different owners.
 b They take a long time to learn things.
 c They can help with a wide range of needs.

6 🔊 2.58 Listen and answer the questions in Exercise 5.

7 🔊 2.59 **WORD FRIENDS** Match the meaning of *get* (1–6) to the correct words below. Listen and check.

arrive/reach   become   bring/fetch
buy   find   receive

Word Friends

Get can have several meanings:
1 Get a pet = *buy*
2 Get a job = _____
3 Get home = _____
4 Get a letter/phone call / an email = _____
5 Get someone's socks/book / a drink (for someone) = _____
6 Get better/worse   get dressed   get married   get old(er)   get ready   get upset/angry/scared/stressed/bored/excited = _____

8 Choose the correct option.
1 My brother wants to get *a job* / *ready* in the police force.
2 I've just got *dressed* / *a text* from my gran!
3 Shall I get *a glass of water* / *married* for you?
4 The train was late, so we didn't get *home* / *a pet* until midnight.

9 [VOX POPS ▶ 7.3] In pairs, tell your partner about one of the situations below. Describe how you felt and the reasons why you felt that way.
- a time you got a pet
- a time you got bored, scared, angry or stressed
- a time you got an important letter / email / phone call

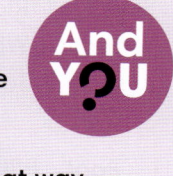

7.6 SPEAKING Identifying people

I can explain who I am talking about.

VIDEO WHO'S THE GUY AT THE BACK?

Tommo: Boo! What are you two up to?
Alisha: I'm just showing Skye the photos from the wedding.
Tommo: Oh, yeah. This one's really funny. You were stressed because you had a bridesmaid's dress that looked like a cream cake!
Alisha: Hey! Give it back.
Skye: Come on, guys. Let's see the other photos.
Tommo: Yeah, it'll be a laugh!
Alisha: Huh! Right, that's my Auntie Lara and my new Uncle Andy in the middle, of course. Then there's my little cousin.
Tommo: Which one?
Alisha: The cute one who's wearing the smart white shirt. He got really bored. He was pulling faces all the time.
Skye: Aww! Who's this guy at the back?
Alisha: Where? Oh, that's, um, Adam. He's the bridegroom's stepbrother.
Skye: Right … He looks nice. Very good looking too.
Tommo: Who? Let's see. Pass it here. Oops!
Alisha: Tommo! Now look what you've done!

OUT of class
Boo!   It'll be a laugh.   What are you (two) up to?   Pass it here.

1 2.60 Listen and check you understand the words in the Vocabulary box.

Vocabulary	People at a wedding
bride bridegroom bridesmaid guests pageboy	

2 7.4 2.61 Listen or watch. What four people are mentioned in the dialogue?

3 Answer the questions.
1 What does Tommo think about the photos?
2 How does Alisha feel when Tommo says 'It'll be a laugh!'?
3 What is the bridegroom's name?
4 How did Alisha's little cousin behave during the wedding?
5 Who is Adam and what does he look like?

4 Work in pairs. Choose a photo from page 132 or 138 and describe a person in it. Follow the instructions.

Speaking	Identifying people

Talking about people in a photo
She's/He's standing/sitting/talking to … / playing with …
She's/He's wearing …
She's/He's in front of/behind/next to/on the left/on the right/near/in the middle/ at the front/at the back.

Asking
Who's this/that boy/girl on the left who is wearing …
Which one/girl/boy/man/woman/guy?

Explaining
The one who is …
The cute/tall one.
Which one do you mean?

- Choose a person to describe.
- Other people ask you questions.
- Answer the questions with one piece of information at a time.

A: Who are you thinking of?
B: A person who is wearing / looks …
A: Where is this person?
B: She's/He's in front of / behind …

5 Work in pairs. Show your partner a photo where there are people he/she doesn't know. Ask and answer questions.

And YOU

Unit 7

7.7 WRITING A short story about friendship

I can write a short story.

1 Look at the pictures and describe what is happening.

2 Read the text and name each person in Exercise 1. What do we find out about each friend?

A friend in need …

Last week I was feeling stressed about my science homework. I asked my friend Nick to help. 'I'd explain it if I was free, but I'm quite busy.' Nick and I get on well, and he's good at science, so I was disappointed.

Next, I went to my neighbour. 'Sorry, Tom. If I understood the homework, I'd help you,' said Christina, 'but it's difficult.'

Just then, a new classmate, Aris, heard us. He is popular, but we don't speak often because he's the kind of person who knows all the answers. He's a big-head. In fact, I fell out with him once because he was so bossy. 'I can help,' he offered.

That day, Aris explained the science homework to me carefully. Afterwards, we sat and chatted. We got to know each other and found we have a lot in common and the same sense of humour. I think we'll be good friends from now on.

3 Read the text again. Match events a–e with descriptions 1–5.

1. ☐ Setting the scene
2. ☐ The first event
3. ☐ The second event
4. ☐ The main event (the climax)
5. ☐ The solution or outcome

a Tom's neighbour can't help him.
b Aris and Tom become friends.
c Tom's friend can't help him.
d Tom has a problem.
e Tom has a surprise offer of help.

4 Study the Writing box. Complete gaps 1–7 with phrases from the text.

Writing A short story

Starting your story and setting the scene
My birthday was a fantastic day.
Have you ever had a really difficult day?
1 _____

Introducing your characters
Nick and I got on well …
2 _____

Using time words and phrases to show order of events
Last week …
Next …
Afterwards …
3 _____ 4 _____ 5 _____

Using direct speech
'I'd explain it if I was free, but I'm quite busy.'
6 _____

Ending your story
All's well that ends well.
I never want to do that again!
7 _____

Writing Time

5 Write a story for a competition in an English language magazine. Follow the instructions:

1. Use the title: *A friend in need.*
2. Write about 100 words.

TIPS
Set the scene and organise the order of events.
Include some speech and use speech marks.
Use relevant past tenses.

Unit 7

WORDLIST Family and friends | Phrasal verb | Talking about friends

adopted /əˈdɒptɪd/
adoption /əˈdɒpʃn/
assistance dog /əˈsɪstəns dɒg/
aunt /ɑːnt/
baby /ˈbeɪbi/
be friends /ˌbi ˈfrendz/
behind /bɪˈhaɪnd/
best friends /ˌbest ˈfrendz/
big-head /ˈbɪg hed/
bossy /ˈbɒsi/
bow tie /ˌbəʊ ˈtaɪ/
bride /braɪd/
bridegroom /ˈbraɪdgruːm/
bridesmaid /ˈbraɪdzmeɪd/
buddy/buddies /ˈbʌdi/ˈbʌdiz/
by blood /ˌbaɪ ˈblʌd/
celebrate /ˈseləbreɪt/
celebration /ˌseləˈbreɪʃn/
chat (v) /tʃæt/
classmates /ˈklɑːsmeɪts/
communicate /ˈklɑːsmeɪts/
confident /ˈkɒnfɪdənt/
cousin /ˈkʌzn/
crowd /kraʊd/
deal with (a problem) /ˌdiːl wɪð ə ˈprɒbləm/
disability /ˌdɪsəˈbɪləti/
disappointed /ˌdɪsəˈpɔɪntɪd/
enemy /ˈenəmi/
fall out (with) /ˌfɔːl ˈaʊt wɪð/
friendship /ˈfrendʃɪp/
friendship bands /ˈfrendʃɪp bændz/
generation /ˌdʒenəˈreɪʃn/
get married /ˌget ˈmærid/
get on with /ˌget ˈɒn wɪð/
go ahead /ˌgəʊ əˈhed/
go out /ˌgəʊ ˈaʊt/

great-grandfather /ˌgreɪtˈgrændˌfɑːðə/
great-grandmother /ˌgreɪtˈgrændˌmʌðə/
great-grandparents /ˌgreɪtˈgrændˌpeərənts/
greeting card /ˈgriːtɪŋ kɑːd/
group /gruːp/
guest /gest/
half-brother /ˈhɑːf ˌbrʌðə/
hang out (with) /ˌhæŋ ˈaʊt wɪð/
have a friend /ˌhæv ə ˈfrend/
in front of /ɪn ˈfrʌnt əv/
international /ˌɪntəˈnæʃnəl/
laugh at (sb/sth) /ˈlɑːf ət (ˌsʌmbədi, ˌsʌmθɪŋ)/
make friends /ˌmeɪk ˈfrendz/
marriage /ˈmærɪdʒ/
married /ˈmærid/
mates /meɪts/
nationality /ˌnæʃəˈnæləti/
near /nɪə/
neighbour /ˈneɪbə/
next to /ˈnekst tə/
on the left /ˌɒn ðə ˈleft/
on the right /ˌɒn ðə ˈraɪt/
origin /ˈɒrɪdʒɪn/
pageboy /ˈpeɪdʒbɔɪ/
parents' evening /ˈpeərənts ˌiːvnɪŋ/
part of the family /ˌpɑːt əv ðə ˈfæmli/
peace /piːs/
pull faces /ˌpʊl ˈfeɪsɪz/
put up with /ˌpʊt ˈʌp wɪð/
related /rɪˈleɪtɪd/
relation /rɪˈleɪʃn/
relative /ˈrelətɪv/
respect (n) /rɪˈspekt/
schoolmates /ˈskuːlmeɪts/

social media /ˌsəʊʃl ˈmiːdiə/
solution /səˈluːʃn/
stepbrother /ˈstepbrʌðə/
stranger /ˈstreɪndʒə/
stressed /strest/
surprise /səˈpraɪz/
uncle /ˈʌŋkl/
wedding /ˈwedɪŋ/
workmates /ˈwɜːkmeɪts/

WORD FRIENDS

come from similar/different backgrounds
enjoy each other's company
get (your/his/her) socks/book / a drink (for someone)
get a job
get a letter / phone call / email
get a pet
get better/worse
get dressed
get home
get married
get on someone's nerves
get old(er)
get to know
get ready
get upset/angry/scared/stressed/bored/excited
have an argument
have something in common
have the same sense of humour
see each other after school/at weekends, etc.
share an interest in
spend time with / spend time on your own

VOCABULARY IN ACTION

1 Use the wordlist to find:
1 four types of friends
2 four phrasal verbs
3 six adjectives
4 five nouns that are NOT people

2 Choose the correct answers.
1 Which person is the same generation as you?
  a your grandfather
  b your mother
  c your half-brother
  d your aunt
2 Which phrase can be used about people who feel very good together?
  a fall out (with)
  b get on well (with)
  c have arguments
  d get on someone's nerves

3 Which person is related to you by blood?
  a half-sister
  b stepdad
  c adopted sister
  d schoolmate

3 In pairs, use the wordlist to describe your relationship with a person in your family.

4 🔊 2.62 **PRONUNCIATION** Listen to the underlined letters and decide how they are pronounced. Listen again and repeat. What is the rule for pronouncing the final -d sound?

/d/ /t/ or /ɪd/?
bor<u>ed</u>   crow<u>d</u>   dress<u>ed</u>   marri<u>ed</u>
relat<u>ed</u>   stress<u>ed</u>

5 Use the wordlist to find more words ending in -d. How are they pronouced?

Revision

VOCABULARY

1 Complete the words in the sentences.
1. Your father's mother's mother is your
   g _ _ _ _ _ **-g** _ _ _ _ _ _ _ _ _ .
2. At a wedding, two people will do this:
   g _ _ **m** _ _ _ _ _ _
3. If you spend time relaxing with friends, you do this. **h** _ _ _ _ _ _ _
4. If you practise speaking English, you
   g _ _ **b** _ _ _ _ _ _ quickly.

2 Match phrases 1–5 with phrases a–e to make sentences.
1. ☐ My best friend is standing in front
2. ☐ My brother and I laugh
3. ☐ Luckily, we don't often have
4. ☐ I sometimes get
5. ☐ My mum and dad both have

a angry with my baby sister.
b at the same things.
c the same sense of humour.
d of me in the photo.
e big arguments.

GRAMMAR

3 Choose the correct answers to complete the song lyrics.

If you ^{1}_____ your friends about your problem, they would help you. (but you don't tell them)
If you didn't keep quiet, they ^{2}_____ understand. (but you don't say anything)
Just ask them, 'What would you do if you ^{3}_____ me?' (you'll be surprised)
If you just ^{4}_____ up, they would hold your hand.

So, would you listen if your friends ^{5}_____ problems? (of course you would)
What would you do if you ^{6}_____ them cry? (you'd go and help them)
So, next time you feel worried, you should speak out. Share things with your friends. Give it a try.

1	a tell	b telling	c told
2	a would	b will	c won't
3	a were	b was	c are
4	a open	b opened	c opens
5	a had	b have	c has
6	a seen	b saw	c see

4 Complete the text with one word in each gap. Then add commas for any of the non-defining relative clauses.

You and your ancestors

For every person on the planet, there are two people ^{1}_____ are their biological parents, four grandparents and eight great-grandparents. Above is a diagram ^{2}_____ shows one person's ancestors for four generations. The top row ^{3}_____ has 16 people shows your great-great-grandparents. It's interesting to think of all the different places ^{4}_____ they lived and the people ^{5}_____ they married. If you go back 200 years in time to the 19th century, you'll probably find as many as 128 ancestors! So a stranger ^{6}_____ you pass in the street could be your long-lost cousin!

great-great grandparents
great grandparents
grandparents
parents
Luisa

SPEAKING

5 Complete the dialogue with questions a–c.

A: Where's Will?
B: ^{1}_____
A: Oh, I've found him. He's holding a book.
B: ^{2}_____
A: He's at the front.
B: ^{3}_____
A: Yes, that's right.

a Is he the one who is wearing glasses?
b I don't know. Which one is Will?
c There are two people holding books. Which one do you mean?

DICTATION

6 🔊 **2.63** Listen, then listen again and write down what you hear.

SELF-ASSESSMENT Think about this unit. What did you learn? What do you need help with?

CULTURE: Is moving house good for you?

Mobile homes in the USA

Some people say that moving house is the most stressful thing in the world. That's why Americans only move home once a decade on average. However, some people are on the move the whole time!

In the USA there are 8.5 million mobile homes. In South Carolina almost twenty percent of all homes are mobile and many people live in trailer parks. These parks, which have a bit of an image problem in the country, are often home to poor or rootless people. But that is not always the case.

In states like Florida there are trailer parks full of retired couples. They often have a great community spirit. Mobile housing expert John O'Reilly explains why: 'People in these parks put up with a little discomfort to feel part of a group and have a sense of identity. The atmosphere is great, people hang out with each other and get on really well. They're like one big happy family.'

Some people stay in the same trailer park for years, but others travel around. For Michael Branston, who has just bought a new trailer with his family in Alabama, choosing a mobile home was all about freedom. 'Even if I could, I wouldn't change my mobile home for a fixed one. Trailer parks are usually quiet, clean and safe and there are no parking problems! We would rather buy our own mobile home than rent an apartment in the city. At least you have a place you can call your own and you're free to move when and where you like. Moving house is great because you see many places and it broadens your horizons. Go ahead and try it!'

GLOSSARY
discomfort (n) a feeling of being uncomfortable
expert (n) someone with special knowledge
retired (adj) a retired person doesn't work because they are old
rootless (adj) often moving from place to place
trailer park (n) caravan park; a place where caravans (trailers) are parked and used as people's homes

EXPLORE

1. How would you feel if you had to move house?

2. Read the article. Mark the sentences T (true) or F (false). Correct the false sentences.
   1. ☐ Trailer parks have a negative image in the USA.
   2. ☐ Trailer parks are always home to poor people or people without families.
   3. ☐ Some people like living in mobile homes in Florida because they want to live alone.
   4. ☐ Some people prefer to live in mobile homes because they don't like to stay in one place.
   5. ☐ According to the article, trailer parks are often dangerous places to live.

3. Read the article again. Answer the questions. Give reasons for your answers.
   1. Does the article present mobile homes in a positive or negative way?
   2. Does the article present moving house in the same way?

EXPLORE MORE

4. ▶ 7.5 Watch with no sound. Order the actions as they appear in the video.
   a. ☐ a family eating together
   b. ☐ a child standing in a big coat
   c. ☐ a man throwing a rope over a reindeer
   d. ☐ 1 white dogs sitting in the snow
   e. ☐ people moving house with reindeer
   f. ☐ a man cutting ice with a knife
   g. ☐ a man putting frozen fish in a sack
   h. ☐ people collecting wood
   i. ☐ a man cutting raw fish

5. In pairs, ask and answer the questions.
   1. Where do you think these people live?
   2. Is it an easy or a difficult life? Why?
   3. Why do you think they move house?
   4. How long do you think they take to move house?

6. ▶ 7.5 Watch with sound. Check your answers to Exercise 5.

7. Were you surprised by the answers? Discuss in pairs.

8. ▶ 7.5 Watch again. Choose the correct option.
   1. The village in the video is home to *two / a few* extended families.
   2. Temperatures in the *autumn / winter* are as low as -40°C.
   3. The Dolgan people use reindeer fur *only for clothes / for clothes and their homes*.
   4. Their favourite food is *raw fish / reindeer meat*.
   5. Over a year, the Dolgan people travel *hundreds / thousands* of miles.
   6. The Dolgan people first came to the Arctic because of the *fishing / reindeer*.

9. Would you like to live like the Dolgan people in the Arctic? Why? / Why not? Do you know of any other kinds of nomadic people in the world?

YOU EXPLORE

10. **CULTURE PROJECT** In groups, prepare a presentation about nomadic people.
    1. Use the internet or other sources to research nomadic people in the world.
    2. Write a short script and think about images or videos to use in your presentation.
    3. Give your presentation to the class.
    4. Report back: what did you learn from the other presentations?

8

No time for crime

VOCABULARY
Criminals | The law
Action verbs | Solving crimes

GRAMMAR
Present Simple Passive and Past Simple Passive | *have/get something done* | Negative prefixes for adjectives

Grammar: Murder in the dark

Speaking: Dress rehearsal

BBC Culture: A famous robbery

Workbook p. 100

BBC VOX POPS ▶

8.1 VOCABULARY Crime

I can talk about crime and criminals.

1 🔊 **3.01** Find the criminals in the picture. Use the words in the Vocabulary A box to complete the sentences. Listen and check.

Vocabulary A	Criminals
burglar pickpocket robber shoplifter ~~thief~~ vandal	

1 The *thief* is wearing a black hat.
2 The _____ is holding a necklace.
3 The _____ are wearing earphones.
4 The _____ is very hot.
5 The _____ can't get out of the window.
6 The _____ is chatting on her mobile.

2 **WORD FRIENDS** Complete the sentences with the verbs below.

breaks into   ~~commits~~   damages   robs   steals

1 A criminal is someone who *commits* a crime.
2 A shoplifter is someone who _____ things from a shop.
3 A bank robber is someone who _____ a bank.
4 A burglar is someone who _____ flats or houses.
5 A vandal is someone who _____ buildings or other things in public places.

3 🔊 **3.02** **WORD BUILDING** Use a dictionary to complete the table with the names of the crimes. Listen and check.

Person	Crime
(bank) robber	1 *(bank) robbery*
burglar	2 _____
pickpocket	3 _____
shoplifter	4 _____
thief	5 _____
vandal	6 _____

4 🔊 **3.03** Look at Exercise 3 again and listen to a person talking about crime. Mark the crimes or criminals you hear.

5 In pairs, discuss which crimes you have heard or have read about where you live.

6 🔊 **3.04** Study the Vocabulary B box, using a dictionary. Choose the correct option.

Vocabulary B	The law
court fine judge law lawyer prison/jail	
punishment reward	

1 £500 *punishment / (reward)* for information on local vandals.

2 Thirty years in *prison / court* for diamond thieves.

3 *Judge / lawyer* decides young thief should work for the community.

4 Old man falls asleep in car park and gets a *fine / reward* of £50.

5 Ex-criminal goes back to school to study and become a *lawyer / court*!

7 🔊 **3.05** Match the pictures with the words from the Vocabulary C box.

Vocabulary C	Action verbs
chase climb push escape pull jump fall trip	

8 **I KNOW!** Add more action verbs to the Vocabulary C box.

9 In pairs, make sentences with the words in the Vocabulary C box.

It's easy to trip when you can't see where you are walking.

10 🔊 **3.06** Listen to the story. Mark the words from the Vocabulary C box that you hear. Which word is NOT in the story?

11 🔊 **3.06** Listen again and make notes. In pairs, retell the story and discuss what you think happened at the end.

12 Complete the text with these words.

> jumped   were chasing   ~~fell~~   tripped
> to escape   pulled   pushed

Crazy crimes!

The thief without a belt
A vandal ¹*fell* and hurt his leg while police officers ²_____ him last night. The vandal told the police he ³_____ because his new trousers were too big and fell down.

The hungry thief
A woman was walking with a fast-food meal when a thief ⁴_____ out of a bush. He ⁵_____ her to the ground and ran off with her burger.

A good phone connection
A shoplifter had a problem when he tried ⁶_____ with an expensive mobile phone. He ⁷_____ the mobile off the shelf, but didn't notice it had a security cable that was one metre long. He got to the door, then suddenly realised he couldn't go any further.

13 In pairs, choose three action verbs and write a funny crime story.

And YOU

Unit 8   95

8.2 GRAMMAR   Present Simple Passive and Past Simple Passive

I can use verbs in the Passive.

Show what you know … The Sherlock Holmes Quiz

1. The Sherlock Holmes detective stories were written 100 years ago by
   a Arthur Conan Doyle.
   b Agatha Christie.
2. Holmes had a famous assistant. What was he called?
   a Doctor Who.
   b Doctor Watson.
3. The stories were first published
   a in a book.
   b in a magazine.
4. Sherlock's flat is located at number 221B of a famous London street, called
   a Sherlock Street.
   b Baker Street.
5. Which famous Sherlock Holmes quote is never really used by Sherlock Holmes?
   a 'Elementary, my dear Watson.'
   b 'My mind is like a racing engine.'

---

1 **CLASS VOTE** What do you know about Sherlock Holmes? In pairs, make a list.

2 🔊 3.07 In pairs, ask and answer the quiz questions. Listen and check.

3 Study the Grammar box. Find more examples of Present Simple Passive and Past Simple Passive in the quiz.

Grammar	Passive
Present Simple Passive Those words are not used.	
Past Simple Passive The detective stories were written by a British author.	

GRAMMAR TIME > PAGE 125

4 Write the Past Simple and past participle form of the verbs below. Use the table on page 127 to help you.

catch   make   see   use   watch
ask   hide   chase

catch – caught – caught

5 Complete the sentences with the past participle form of the verbs in brackets.
1 CCTV cameras are *used* (use) to find clues about many crimes.
2 The thief was _____ (catch) because she talked about her crime on social media.
3 Yesterday evening two car thieves were_____ (chase) by police in fast cars.
4 Sometimes CCTV films are _____ (watch) by special detectives.
5 Last night the witnesses were _____ (ask) questions by police officers.
6 This camera is _____ (hid) so that the shoplifters don't know about it.

6 Complete the text with the passive form of the verbs in brackets. Add *by* where necessary.

The Nancy Drew stories are among the most famous detective stories ever. The first stories about Nancy Drew ¹*were published in the 1930s* (publish/in the 1930s). Different series have appeared since that time. The books ² _____ (create/for teenagers). The Nancy Drew detective stories ³ _____ (write/several different authors). The name Carolyn Keene ⁴ _____ (use/all the authors) but Nancy's name ⁵ _____ (change) in some countries. It may be surprising, but this old series ⁶ _____ (read/thousands of young people) even today, and each year lots and lots of copies ⁷ _____ (sell).

7 Tell the class about a detective story/film you know.

And YOU

96 Unit 8

8.3 READING and VOCABULARY — Who is Sherlock nowadays?

I can find specific detail in an article and talk about solving crimes.

1 **CLASS VOTE** Have you watched any Sherlock Holmes films?

2 Look at the text. What is it?

a story?   a TV review?   an article?

3 🔊 3.08 Read the text. Match the words below with the people in the text.

an actor   a medical school teacher
a detective   a writer   a friend

Who is Sherlock nowadays?

The BBC series, Sherlock, starring Benedict Cumberbatch, has been a big hit. There have been over 250 films about the famous detective, so what's different about the new series?

Many Sherlock Holmes films, like the original stories, are set in the shadows of Victorian London. In those days, the best technology was a magnifying glass to look for fingerprints. However, the BBC series is set in the 21st century, and this adds a fresh perspective and helps to create some clever twists in the plot of each story.

In this modern version, Sherlock has a mobile and a website. He can get information about suspects and witnesses online. He can even check CCTV cameras to look for extra clues, so his job has become very different. His friend Dr John Watson, who is played by Martin Freeman, still helps him. In fact, Watson writes a blog about each of Sherlock's cases, and you can find these online!

Isn't it strange that Sherlock is over 100 years old but he is still popular? Cumberbatch explains that playing Sherlock is 'a form of mental and physical gymnastics'. His character was based on Conan Doyle's teacher at medical school. The teacher, Dr Bell, was very clever and noticed little things. He often looked at his patients and told them about their activities and their illnesses before they even spoke to him! Similarly, Sherlock Holmes solves crimes with the power of his intelligence. What may explain the popularity of the stories today is that it is a chance to find out if you can think as quickly as Sherlock!

4 Read the text again. Choose the correct answer.

1 What has changed for Sherlock in the 21st century?
 a He can do lots of different jobs.
 b He doesn't use a magnifying glass anymore.
 c He has new ways of solving crimes.
 d He's no longer friends with Dr Watson.

2 How did Dr Bell inspire Conan Doyle?
 a He didn't speak to his patients.
 b He wrote lots of notes about his patients.
 c He talked to his patients kindly.
 d He solved problems by finding clues.

3 Why is Sherlock still popular?
 a Because he's been around a long time.
 b Because his character is fascinating.
 c Because he's famous.
 d Because he looks great on screen.

4 What is the writer's main aim in the text?
 a To explain why Holmes is still popular.
 b To describe the old films about Holmes.
 c To tell readers how Conan Doyle wrote these stories.
 d To describe the personality of a detective.

5 🔊 3.09 Complete the sentences with words from the Vocabulary box. Listen and check.

Vocabulary	Solving crimes

case   CCTV camera   clue   detective
fingerprints   magnifying glass   ~~suspect~~   witness

1 The police caught the *suspect* because he put photos on the internet.
2 The burglar didn't wear gloves, so she left _____ on the window.
3 The detectives are working on a very difficult _____.
4 My mum saw a pickpocket, so police asked her to be a _____.

6 **And YOU** Which of these skills are you good at? Would you like to be a detective? In pairs, discuss the ideas below.

spotting clues   thinking quickly
noticing little things   using technology

Unit 8 97

8.4 GRAMMAR *have/get something done*

I can use the construction *have/get something done*.

VIDEO — MURDER IN THE DARK

Alisha: *Murder in the Dark* … that's a great poster for the play, Tommo. Did you design it?
Tommo: Yes, but I want to have some photos taken for it.
Alisha: I've got a good camera. I'll take the photos and you can have the posters printed later.
Tommo: OK, that's sorted!
Alisha: What's happening with the costumes?
Tommo: They're here, look! This is for me … and this is for you …
Alisha: You're joking! I am not wearing this wig. What about Dan?
Tommo: He's going to have a jacket made by his aunt. I gave him my dad's old coat … but he didn't like it. He's so fussy! He wants to have his hair styled today so that he looks like a real detective. He's taking it very seriously. The play should be called *Detective Dan*, not *Murder in the Dark*!
Alisha: Mmhh … What about the furniture?
Tommo: Dad's made these for us. I had them painted this morning.
Alisha: Wow, they're great!
Tommo: Watch out! The paint's still wet!

OUT of class: OK, that's sorted!   Watch out!

1 Discuss in groups. What plays or dramas are shown in your school? Who organises them?

2 ▶ 8.1 🔊 3.10 Study the Grammar box. Watch or listen. Find more examples of *have/get something done* in the dialogue.

Grammar — *have/get something done*

She wants to **have some photos taken** today.
She **has her hair cut** at Angelo's.
We **had the costumes made** for us.
You can **have the poster printed** in town.
I'm going to **have my face painted** for the play.
In spoken English, *get something done* is more common.

GRAMMAR TIME > PAGE 125

3 Match phrases 1–6 with phrases a–f to make sentences.
1 ☐ I'm not happy with my hair. I …
2 ☐ When I do English exercises. I always …
3 ☐ Your coat's dirty. You must …
4 ☐ I love that photo. I should …
5 ☐ I can't see what's written on the board. I'm going to …
6 ☐ If I buy the present here, I can …

a have it printed for my room.
b have my eyes tested.
c have it cleaned.
d have it wrapped.
e had it cut at the weekend.
f have them checked by the teacher.

4 Complete the sentences with the correct form of *have* and the verbs in brackets.
1 The burglar made a mess in the house, but we're going to *have* it *cleaned* (clean).
2 We need to catch the robber. Let's _____ some posters _____ (print) with his photo on.
3 The detective always _____ a coffee _____ (bring) to him when he arrives at work.
4 That girl chased the criminal and then she _____ her photo _____ (take) for the newspaper.
5 I never leave my bike without a lock. I don't want to _____ it _____ (steal).
6 He writes great crime stories. He should _____ them _____ (make) into films.

5 In pairs, say if the sentences are true for you. Correct the false sentences. **And YOU?**
1 I have my bedroom cleaned at the weekend.
2 I have my lunch made every day.
3 I never have my hair coloured.
4 I want to have my nose pierced.
5 We sometimes have pizza delivered to our house.

No, I don't have my bedroom cleaned at the weekend. I clean it myself on Saturday!

98 Unit 8

8.5 LISTENING and VOCABULARY A burglary

I can identify the main points of a monologue and talk about discovering a crime.

1 **CLASS VOTE** Can social media help the police to find criminals? Why? / Why not?

2 🔊 3.11 Listen to the first part of the podcast and look at the pictures. What do you think happened?

3 🔊 3.12 Listen to the second part of Katrina's story. Order the events.

- A ☐ The police went to the burglar's house.
- B ☐ Katrina discovered her laptop was missing.
- C ☐ 1 Katrina and her mum discover the burglary.
- D ☐ A friend told Katrina about a conversation in the park.
- E ☐ Katrina showed the smartwatch box to the police.
- F ☐ The police took fingerprints and photos.
- G ☐ Katrina and her friend started looking on social media.

4 🔊 3.12 Listen again. Check your answers to Exercises 2 and 3.

5 **WORD FRIENDS** Study the phrases below, using a dictionary. Choose the correct option.

> arrest a criminal   interview a witness   look for clues
> search the area   solve a crime   take fingerprints

1 Detectives can *solve a crime* / *take fingerprints* more quickly when there's a good witness.
2 Police want to *interview a witness* / *arrest a criminal* who saw somebody go into the house.
3 We believe the police are going to *search the area* / *arrest a criminal* this evening, but they won't say who it is.
4 The crime took place near the forest, and police officers are *solving a crime* / *searching the area* now.
5 The police couldn't *take fingerprints* / *interview a witness* because the burglar was wearing gloves.
6 The detective is *arresting a criminal* / *looking for clues* at the crime scene, but she hasn't found anything yet.

6 🔊 3.13 Listen to the final part of the podcast. Complete the notes with a word or phrase.

> Date of burglary: ¹ 2nd October
> Time of burglary: between
> ² _____ and _____
> Items stolen: ³ _____
> Call: ⁴ _____
> Reward: ⁵ £ _____

7 [VOX POPS ▶ 8.2] **And YOU**
In pairs, tell your partner what you would do in the situations below.

1 You have your mobile phone stolen in town.
   I'd call the phone company, then I would tell all my friends …
2 You see a person who is shoplifting.
3 Some people are vandalising a wall near your school.

Unit 8 99

8.6 SPEAKING Persuading and reassuring

I can persuade and reassure someone.

VIDEO DRESS REHEARSAL

Miss Jones:	Right, this is our first dress rehearsal for *Murder in the Dark*. We'll start with scene two, after the murder.
Alisha:	I'm so nervous. I can't remember my lines!
Miss Jones:	It's all right, Alisha. I know you can do it. Just take a deep breath.
Alisha:	OK, I'll try.
Miss Jones:	Great. Off you go. Skye, could you give me a hand, please?
Tommo:	Come on, Alisha! You'll be fine.
Lady Harrington (Alisha):	Oh, poor Sir Hugo! What happened? Was he killed by the fall?
Butler (Tommo):	Or … was he murdered?
Lady Harrington (Alisha):	Pardon, Jeeves?
Butler (Tommo):	Nothing, Lady Harrington. Don't worry. The police will be here soon …
Miss Jones:	Hello? Can I help you?
Stranger:	Excuse me, I'm here about the crime.
Miss Jones:	Oh dear! A crime? What happened?
Tommo:	Miss Jones, it's Dan!
Miss Jones:	Dan? Oh my goodness! I didn't recognise you!
Dan:	Do you like my costume? I had it made specially for the play!

OUT of class
Oh my goodness!
Can you give me a hand?
Off you go.

1 In pairs, look at the photo. What do you think is happening?

2 ▶ 8.3 🔊 3.14 Watch or listen and check your answer to Exercise 1. Who is at the door?

Speaking	Persuading and reassuring
Persuading	**Responding**
Come on.	OK, I'll try.
Please!	I don't know.
Just try it. /	I suppose I can do it.
Why don't you try?	
Reassuring	
Don't worry!	It's all right. / OK.
You'll/It'll be fine.	
I know. / I'm sure. / Of course you can do it.	
Just … practise a bit more / try again.	

3 🔊 3.15 Study the Speaking box. Complete the dialogues with one word in each gap. Listen and check.

1 A: Could you come to a rock concert with me?
   B: I don't *know* … I'm not keen on rock concerts.
   A: Please! *The Wild Monsters* are playing.
   B: I _____ I can come, but I haven't got much money.
   A: Don't _____! I'll pay for your train fare.
2 A: I'm scared of water. I can't go in.
   B: Of _____ you can. I'll be with you.
   A: It's too cold.
   B: It's not cold, I promise. You'll be _____.
3 A: Let's go to the fish restaurant.
   B: I never eat fish.
   A: _____ on. _____ try it. It's really good.
4 A: I can't play this song.
   B: I'm _____ you can do it.
   A: But it's really difficult.
   B: Just _____ a bit more.

4 In pairs, role play one of the situations.
- Reassure a friend who's worried about his/her maths test.
- Persuade a friend to go to a party. (he hates parties)
- Reassure your friend that he can succeed in a kayaking competition.

Student A State your problem.
Student B Persuade your partner to do/try something.
Student A Give a reason why you're worried.
Student B Reassure your partner.

5 In pairs, talk about something you find difficult to do. Persuade each other that you can do it.

I can't write the English essay …

And Y?U

8.7 ENGLISH IN USE — Negative prefixes for adjectives

I can form and use negative adjectives.

1 Look at the cartoons. What do you find out about the character of the detectives and the 'criminal'?

> Footprints … more footprints. I hate my magnifying glass. It's so old-fashioned. It's really unfair! The boss gives us all the uninteresting jobs.

> We'll never find out who did all this illegal graffiti. Hey! Wait a minute, Dimwit! There's a can of spray paint. Is it a clue?

> This is like being invisible.

> Don't be stupid, Brains. It's just a piece of rubbish. Put it in the bin. It's obviously unimportant.

> Phew! That was getting a bit uncomfortable.

> Well, it's impossible to find any clues here. There's nothing unusual at all. Let's go home and write a report. Next time, I hope we get an interesting job.

2 Study the information about prefixes. Find more examples of negative prefixes in the cartoons. Complete the table.

Language — Negative prefixes for adjectives

We can use prefixes before an adjective to change its meaning. Prefixes with adjectives usually give the meaning 'not'.

negative prefix	+ adjective		= adjective with negative meaning	
un-	happy		unhappy	
dis-	honest	pleased	dishonest	displeased
im-	patient		impatient	
in-	correct		incorrect	
il-	logical		illogical	
ir-	responsible	regular	irresponsible	irregular

3 Use the table in Exercise 2 to complete the rules 1–4. Add the correct prefix to the words below and use as examples.

friendly   legible   polite   relevant

1 The most common negative prefix is *un-*, e.g. _____ .
2 If the adjective begins with the sound /p/, we usually add _____ , e.g. _____ .
3 If the adjective begins with the sound /r/, we usually add _____ , e.g. _____ .
4 If the adjective begins with the sound /l/, we usually add _____ , e.g. _____ .

4 [VOX POPS ▶ 8.4] In pairs, finish the sentences to make them true for you.

1 If I was invisible, I would …
2 The most impossible thing I've ever done was …
3 One unusual place I'd like to see is …
4 If I saw someone doing something illegal, I would …
5 One really uninteresting film I've watched is …

WORDLIST Criminals | The law | Action verbs | Solving crimes

assistant /əˈsɪstənt/
(bank) robbery /ˈbæŋk ˌrɒbəri/
bin /bɪn/
brain /breɪn/
burglar /ˈbɜːglə/
burglary /ˈbɜːgləri/
case /keɪs/
catch /kætʃ/
CCTV camera /ˌsiː siː tiː ˈviː ˌkæmərə/
chase /tʃeɪs/
climb /klaɪm/
clue /kluː/
correct /kəˈrekt/
court /kɔːt/
crime /kraɪm/
crime scene /ˈkraɪm siːn/
criminal /ˈkrɪmɪnl/
detective /dɪˈtektɪv/
diamond /ˈdaɪəmənd/
dishonest /dɪsˈɒnɪst/
displeased /dɪsˈpliːzd/
(dress) rehearsal /(ˈdres) rɪˌhɜːsl/
e-criminal /ˌiː ˈkrɪmɪnl/
escape /ɪˈskeɪp/
expected /ɪkˈspektɪd/
fair /feə/
fall /fɔːl/
fine /faɪn/
fingerprints /ˈfɪŋgəˌprɪnts/
footprints /ˈfʊtprɪnts/

fussy /ˈfʌsi/
glove /glʌv/
hide /haɪd/
honest /ˈɒnɪst/
illegal /ɪˈliːgl/
illegible /ɪˈledʒəbl/
illness /ˈɪlnəs/
illogical /ɪˈlɒdʒɪkl/
impatient /ɪmˈpeɪʃənt/
impolite /ˌɪmpəˈlaɪt/
impossible /ɪmˈpɒsəbl/
incorrect /ˌɪnkəˈrekt/
invisible /ɪnˈvɪzəbl/
irregular /ɪˈregjulə/
irrelevant /ɪˈreləvənt/
irresponsible /ˌɪrɪˈspɒnsəbl/
item /ˈaɪtəm/
jail /dʒeɪl/
judge /dʒʌdʒ/
jump /dʒʌmp/
law /lɔː/
lawyer /ˈlɔːjə/
legal /ˈliːgl/
legible /ˈledʒəbl/
lock (n) /lɒk/
logical /ˈlɒdʒɪkl/
magnifying glass /ˈmægnɪfaɪɪŋ glɑːs/
mess /mes/
missing /ˈmɪsɪŋ/
murder /ˈmɜːdə/
mysterious /mɪˈstɪəriəs/

necklace /ˈnekləs/
old-fashioned /ˌəʊld ˈfæʃnd/
patient /ˈpeɪʃənt/
pickpocket /ˈpɪkˌpɒkɪt/
pickpocketing /ˈpɪkˌpɒkɪtɪŋ/
pleased /pliːzd/
plot /plɒt/
police officer /pəˈliːs ˌɒfəsə/
polite /pəˈlaɪt/
poster /ˈpəʊstə/
prison /ˈprɪzn/
publish /ˈpʌblɪʃ/
pull /pʊl/
punishment /ˈpʌnɪʃmənt/
push /pʊʃ/
recognise /ˈrekəgnaɪz/
regular /ˈregjulə/
relevant /ˈreləvənt/
report (n) /rɪˈpɔːt/
responsible /rɪˈspɒnsəbl/
reward /rɪˈwɔːd/
robber /ˈrɒbə/
rubbish /ˈrʌbɪʃ/
security cable /sɪˈkjʊərəti ˌkeɪbl/
shadows /ˈʃædəʊz/
shoplifter /ˈʃɒpˌlɪftə/
shoplifting /ˈʃɒpˌlɪftɪŋ/
spot /spɒt/
spy /spaɪ/
suspect /ˈsʌspekt/

theft /θeft/
thief (thieves) /θiːf (θiːvz)/
trip /trɪp/
twist /twɪst/
uncomfortable /ʌnˈkʌmftəbl/
unexpected /ˌʌnɪkˈspektɪd/
unfair /ˌʌnˈfeə/
unhappy /ʌnˈhæpi/
unimportant /ˌʌnɪmˈpɔːtənt/
unintelligent /ˌʌnɪnˈtelɪdʒnt/
uninteresting /ʌnˈɪntrəstɪŋ/
unusual /ʌnˈjuːʒuəl/
vandal /ˈvændl/
vandalising /ˈvændəlaɪzɪŋ/
visible /ˈvɪzəbl/
vandalism /ˈvændəlɪzəm/
witness /ˈwɪtnəs/

WORD FRIENDS

arrest a criminal
break into flats or houses
commit a crime
interview a witness
look for clues
rob a bank
search the area
solve a crime
steal things from a shop
take fingerprints
tell the truth

VOCABULARY IN ACTION

1 Use the wordlist to find:
1 four people who steal things
2 two people who work in a court
3 three verbs that describe actions in which you use your hands

2 In pairs, use the wordlist to describe a situation that is:
1 uncomfortable
A criminal is hiding from a police officer in a bin, but it's hot and very dirty.
2 illegal
3 unfair
4 dishonest
5 impolite

3 Compare your ideas for Exercise 2 with the class.

4 Use the wordlist to complete the sentences. Use the words in the correct form.
1 The man escaped last night and police are **searching** the area now.
2 He _____ a bank when he was young and spent a few years in prison.
3 It's impossible to _____ these new flats because the locks are very strong.
4 We'd like to _____ a witness who was near here at the time of the crime.
5 The detectives are _____ for clues at the crime scene now.

5 🔊 3.16 **PRONUNCIATION** Listen and repeat the pairs of words. Is the stress the same or different when there is a prefix?

1 correct — incorrect
2 honest — dishonest
3 logical — illogical
4 legal — illegal
5 polite — impolite
6 relevant — irrelevant
7 visible — invisible

Wordlist

Revision

VOCABULARY

1 Write the correct word for each definition.
1. This person steals things from people's pockets or bags. **p** i c k p o c k e t
2. This person tries to discover who has committed a crime. **d** _ _ _ _ _ _ _ _ _
3. This is a crime where a person breaks into a building to steal things. **b** _ _ _ _ _ _ _ _
4. This person sees a crime and can say what happened. **w** _ _ _ _ _ _ _
5. A piece of information that helps to solve a crime. **c** _ _ _
6. A building where criminals go for punishment. **p** _ _ _ _ _ _

2 Complete the text with the words below.

> CCTV cameras   fingerprints   ~~murders~~   reward
> shoplift   uncomfortable

Did you know …
1. Most *murders* happen on a Monday.
2. The most popular items that people _____ are electric toothbrushes and smartphones.
3. The best _____ are often found on soap or cheese.
4. There are about 25 million _____ around the world. On average, a person is seen 300 times a day.
5. Police in the USA offered a $5 million _____ for paintings that were stolen from an art gallery. The paintings are still missing.
6. It isn't always _____ in prison. One prison in Norway offers cottages and relaxing activities such as fishing and horse-riding.

3 Read the text again. What surprises you most and why?

GRAMMAR

4 Complete the sentences with the Present Simple passive form of the verbs in brackets.
1. A lot of TV programmes *are made* (make) about crime.
2. The jewellery _____ (hide) in a secret place.
3. Great crime books _____ (write) by ex-detectives.
4. A lot of criminals _____ (catch) abroad.
5. Fingerprint powder _____ (use) to detect fingerprints.
6. A lot of stolen items _____ (sell) on the internet.

5 Make questions in the Past Simple Passive. Read the text and answer them.
1. When/the man/arrest?
   When was the man arrested?
2. Where/the man/find?
3. What/hide/under the man's jacket?
4. Why/the cakes/steal?

Thief caught with cream cakes

Last night, police in Manchester arrested a man who they found in the kitchen of a police station. The man escaped through a window. He was hiding something under his jacket. It was a selection of cream cakes in a box. The man said he was painting the kitchen in the police station when he saw the cakes in the fridge. 'I wanted to take them home for my wife's birthday,' he said.

---

6 Complete the sentences with the correct form of *have something done* and the words in the brackets.
1. We've designed a 'No Time for Crime' poster. We're going to *have it printed* (it/print) later.
2. There was a burglary at the shop, so I _____ (the locks/change).
3. The vandals wrote on the gym wall, so we want to _____ (it/paint).
4. I _____ (my hair/dye) red when I was in town at the weekend.
5. The thieves stole our car and left it in town. We're going to _____ (it/check) before we use it again.

SPEAKING

7 In pairs, role play the situations on page 144. Take it in turns to listen to your friend's problem. Then try to persuade and reassure them.

DICTATION

8 3.17 Listen, then listen again and write down what you hear.

SELF-ASSESSMENT Think about this unit. What did you learn? What do you need help with?

BBC CULTURE

Is chewing gum a crime?

Crime facts from around the world

Countries pass different laws because they often have different attitudes to certain crimes. Punishments vary greatly too. Here are a few facts about laws from some of the safest countries in the world:

Did you know that in Singapore it is illegal to chew gum because it damages the city's pavements and gets stuck in subway doors? You can get a fine or even go to prison for a petty crime like that!

Hong Kong has some of the strangest and strictest laws in the world. For example, it is illegal to play music in the streets. If you are a busker, it's certainly not the place for you!

In Finland fines for certain crimes are based on your income. If you are rich, you pay more! A few years ago the director of mobile phone company, Nokia, was caught speeding and got a fine of over €100,000! Do you think that's fair?

In Iceland, thefts and robberies almost never happen. House burglaries are unknown. People leave the front door to their houses open or their bicycles unlocked on the street. The police are largely invisible.

Of course, some street crime exists in Britain, but there are more CCTV cameras per person here than anywhere else in the world. If you have your bag stolen, there is a good chance that the police will catch the criminal. For that reason, British people feel quite protected. Edinburgh in Scotland is considered to be the country's safest city and it's also a beautiful place to visit!

GLOSSARY
attitude (n) what you think and feel about something
busker (n) someone who plays music in the streets to earn money
income (n) the money you earn
petty crime (n) a crime that is not very serious
vary (v) if things vary they are all different from each other

EXPLORE

1 In pairs, ask and answer the questions.
1. What countries do you think are the safest and the most dangerous in the world?
2. Is there much crime where you live?
3. What kinds of crimes happen, if any? Are they serious or not?
4. Do you think the laws where you live are fair? Why? / Why not?

2 Read the article. Mark the sentences T (true) or F (false). Correct the false sentences.
1. ☐ You cannot chew gum in Singapore because it's bad for you.
2. ☐ The writer thinks that chewing gum is a serious crime.
3. ☐ In Hong Kong there are some unusual laws.
4. ☐ In Finland the punishment varies depending on the money you earn.
5. ☐ The police have a lot to do in Iceland.

EXPLORE MORE

3 Read the article again. Answer the questions.
1. Does the article say that safe countries have similar or different kinds of laws?
2. Do you think CCTV cameras are a good way to make a place safer? Why? / Why not?
3. Which of the countries' laws mentioned in the text do you agree/disagree with? Why?

4 ▶ **8.5** Watch Part 1 of the video. Answer the questions.
1. When did the robbery happen?
2. Where did it take place?
3. Why is it described as a robbery from a film?

5 ▶ **8.5** Watch again. Answer the questions.
1. How did the robbers get from the building to the vault?
2. What was the robbers' biggest challenge?
3. How thick was the concrete wall?
4. How long did it take the specialists to drill the same holes as the robbers?

6 Match words 1–4 with photos A–D.

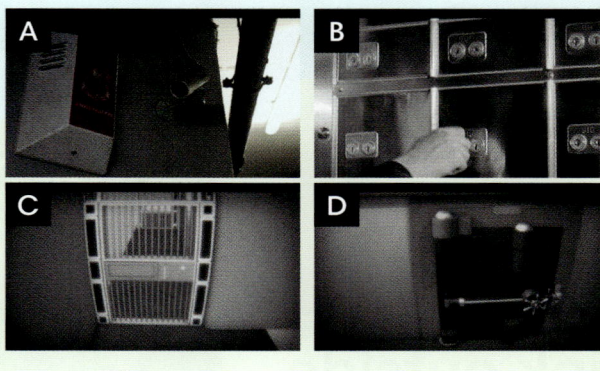

A B C D

1. ☐ security boxes
2. ☐ vault
3. ☐ CCTV camera
4. ☐ security door

7 In pairs, retell the story of how the robbers got to the diamonds. Use the words from Exercise 6 and the photos to help you.

First, they switched off all the CCTV cameras except one. Then they climbed down the lift …

8 ▶ **8.6** Watch Part 2 of the video. Choose the correct option.
1. According to the video, it's *easy / difficult* to open the boxes.
2. The police only discovered the crime *a day / two days* after the robbery.
3. We *know / don't know* exactly how much loot the robbers escaped with.
4. The police *caught / didn't catch* the robbers in the end.
5. The police were *faster / more intelligent* than the robbers with technology.

9 In pairs or groups, ask and answer the questions.
1. Do you think robberies like this still happen in your country? Why? / Why not?
2. What kinds of crimes are committed digitally?

YOU EXPLORE

10 **CULTURE PROJECT** In groups, present a famous film about a robbery.
1. Find out about a film you like.
2. Write notes about what happens in the film.
3. Tell the story to the class.

9 Think outside the box

VOCABULARY
School subjects | Learning and assessment | Describing students

GRAMMAR
Word order in questions | Mixed tenses

Grammar: Could you give me a hand?

Speaking: How was your journey?

BBC Culture:
Two very different schools

Workbook p. 112

BBC VOX POPS ▶
EXAM TIME 3 > p. 136
CLIL 5 > p. 143

9.1 VOCABULARY Education

I can talk about school life.

1 CLASS VOTE What is your favourite school subject? Why?

2 🔊 3.18 Match six words in the Vocabulary A box to the pictures. Listen and check.

Vocabulary A	School subjects

Art   Biology   Chemistry   Citizenship   Cooking   English   French
Geography   Health   History   ICT   Literature   Maths
Music   PE   Philosophy   Physics   Spanish

3 CLASS VOTE Are the subjects below taught in your school? If not, which of them would you add to the school curriculum? Which should be compulsory? Which should be optional or extracurricular?

driving   fashion design   film-making   gardening
karate   photography   yoga

4 I KNOW! In pairs, how many words can you add to each category?

Types of schools: *primary school*, _____
People at school: *head teacher*, *form tutor*, _____
Places at school: *library*, *canteen*, _____

5 🔊 3.19 Study the Vocabulary B box. Then choose the correct options. Listen and check.

Vocabulary B	Learning and assessment

Learning
learn   memorise   revise   study

Types of assessment
performance   practical exam   project   speaking exam   written exam

1 (memorise) / revise a poem
2 revise / learn for a speaking exam
3 learn / study for the whole night
4 revise / learn about the ancient Romans

6 In pairs, match the pictures A–D to the types of assessment in the Vocabulary B box.

7 🔊 3.20 Listen and match the speakers to the photos.

A

B

C

D

8 In pairs, discuss which types of assessment you might have for different school subjects. Which types do you like? Which do you dislike? Why?

9 🔊 3.21 Complete the text with words and phrases from the Vocabulary C box. Which words are NOT in the text? Listen and check.

Vocabulary C	Describing students

confident   creative   hard-working   intelligent   lazy
talented/gifted

good at: critical thinking   general knowledge
problem solving   teamwork

Life skills are important, too!

It's easy to think that school life is all about how ¹*intelligent* you are, in other words, your *ability* to understand things. However, good life skills help you more than intelligence, at school and beyond.

One key skill is how ²_____ you are. That is, *you believe that you can do things successfully*. It's important to build this skill because it helps with many areas of life. Once you believe in yourself, you can start being ³_____, *using your imagination*, which is helpful in all subjects, not just arts.

Another life skill, which is a new school subject in some areas, is ⁴_____. This teaches you *how to think clearly and ask questions*. Part of this subject also involves ⁵_____. Students develop *the ability to identify a problem and work out a solution*. Also, students learn *how to work well with others* which is all part of another key skill, ⁶_____.

Of course, traditional skills are important, too, such as ⁷_____, *knowing information about the world around you*. And don't forget about being ⁸_____, which means that *you always put in a lot of effort*, as that's the secret to many people's success.

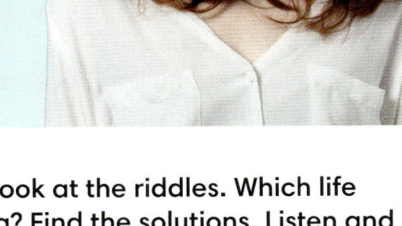

10 🔊 3.22 Work in pairs. Look at the riddles. Which life skill is each of them testing? Find the solutions. Listen and check.

A You have two minutes to think of as many uses as possible for paper clips.

B Two boys are registering at a new school. When they fill out their forms, the head teacher sees that they have the same parents. He also notices that they share the same birthday. 'Are you twins?' asks the head teacher. 'No,' reply the boys. Is it possible?

11 How would you describe yourself as a student? Which skills could you improve and how?

And YOU?

9.2 GRAMMAR Word order in questions

I can make questions with the correct word order.

VIDEO COULD YOU GIVE ME A HAND?

Alisha: Hey, Tommo. What are you doing?
Tommo: I'm getting ready for my water safety test tomorrow. I'm just checking the life jacket.
Skye: Cool. Will you get a certificate?
Tommo: Yeah, definitely … if I pass! Have you ever been kayaking?
Skye: No, I haven't tried it. I did windsurfing once, though.
Tommo: Did you enjoy it? Who taught you?
Skye: No, not much. My dad taught me, but it was really hard.
Tommo: Could you guys give me a hand moving this?
Alisha: Sure. Is it heavy?
Tommo: No, it's quite light, but you have to be careful with it.
Alisha: Where do you want it? Here, near the water?
Tommo: Yeah, that's great. OK, thanks. I think I'm ready.
Alisha: Good luck!
Skye: Are you going to become an instructor?
Tommo: I hope so. Maybe one day!

OUT of class
Good luck!
Where do you want it?
I hope so.

1 Have you got any certificates? What were they for and when did you get them?

2 🎬 9.1 🔊 3.23 Look at the photo. What are Tommo, Alisha and Skye doing? Watch or listen and check.

3 Study the Grammar box. Find more examples of questions in the dialogue.

Grammar	Word order in questions

Yes/No questions
Inversion
You are hungry. → **Are** you hungry?
You have finished. → **Have** you finished?
I enjoyed it. → **Did** you enjoy it?
She cycles. → **Does** she cycle?

Wh- questions
Question word + inversion
Why are you hungry?
Why did you enjoy it?

Subject questions
Who taught you? My dad taught me.

Object questions
Who did they see? They saw Tommo.

GRAMMAR TIME > PAGE 126

4 Match the responses with the questions in Grammar box.

1 A: _____   3 A: _____
   B: Yes, I have.   B: No, I didn't.
2 A: _____   4 A: _____
   B: Yes, I am.   B: Yes, she does.

5 Write questions for these sentences.

1 Yes, I had pasta for dinner last night.
   Did you have pasta for dinner last night?
2 No, I left home at six-thirty this morning.
3 Yes, we're going to Italy for our holidays.
4 Yes, I saw two films at the cinema last week.
5 No, I'm not going to do anything tonight.

6 Write subject and object questions about the underlined words.

1 A fire started in the science lab yesterday.
   What happened in the science lab?
   Where did the fire start?
2 Class 12D had a maths test this morning.
3 Everyone in my class has read this book!
4 Tom saw me when I was at the burger bar.

7 In pairs, ask and answer the questions in Exercise 5. Some of your answers may be false. Say if your partner's sentences are true or false.

And YOU?

9.3 READING and VOCABULARY — Does intelligence change?

I can find specific detail in an article and talk about intelligence.

Bright sparks!

1 _____

Is modern education rubbish? Are today's teenagers poor learners who can't think for themselves? Not according to a report from researchers in Scotland. The good news is that young people are more intelligent than their great-grandparents were!

2 _____

Intelligence Quotient (IQ) tests are a way of measuring general intelligence. An average score in a given population is 100 points. Scientist Steven Pinker has taken a look at IQ test results over many years and made notes about what he found. Every few years, people did better in the tests, so the test writers made changes and the tests became harder.

3 _____

If some average modern teenagers went back in time, their IQ score would be higher than the people around them. If your IQ is 100 now, and you travelled back to 1950, you would probably have an IQ of 118. If you went back to 1910, you would have an IQ of 130. That's better than 98 percent of other people in 1910! To look at it another way, an average person from 1910 who visited us today would have an IQ measurement of only 70.

4 _____

Now, why are people getting cleverer? In order to find the reasons, we have to ask 'How have people changed?' We have made improvements in diets and health, and because they influence the brain, this is the main reason. Answers to vocabulary, maths or general knowledge questions haven't changed so much, but we have become better at problem solving. We have made progress with puzzle questions, such as 'GLOVE is to HAND as SHOE is to what?' This is also because we live in a fast-paced digital world where we have to think and react quickly, and we can't be afraid of making mistakes.

---

1 **CLASS VOTE** Do you think intelligence can be measured? Why? / Why not?

2 🔊 3.24 Read the text quickly. Match headings a–f with paragraphs 1–4. There are two extra headings.
- a Why are tests so hard?
- b IQs have improved
- c A new report
- d What are the reasons?
- e Tests have changed
- f Intelligence has no use

3 🔊 3.24 Read the text again. Mark the sentences T (true) or F (false).
1. ☐ Researchers believe that humans are cleverer now than in the past.
2. ☐ Steven Pinker based his report on IQ tests which he took himself.
3. ☐ Test writers had to make the tests more challenging.
4. ☐ Some teenagers travelled a long way for an experiment.
5. ☐ A change in lifestyle is responsible for the better test scores.
6. ☐ Big improvements were made in answers to all types of questions.

4 In pairs, write two *Wh*- questions about the article and ask the class.

5 **WORD FRIENDS** Complete the Word Friends with *make* or *take*. Sometimes more than one answer is possible.
1. *make* changes
2. _____ a test/exam
3. _____ sense
4. _____ notes
5. _____ progress
6. _____ a look
7. _____ an improvement
8. _____ a mistake

6 In pairs, discuss other reasons for the test results. What's your opinion? Use the ideas below to help you.

We take more tests.
More people go to college and university.
We learn a lot from TV and magazines.
Schools are better.
Parents talk to their children more.
We read more books.

Unit 9

9.4 GRAMMAR Mixed tenses

I can use a variety of tenses.

Babar Ali – the youngest head teacher in the world

Babar Ali is probably the youngest head teacher in the world, and right now he is working very hard. He sometimes travels and gives talks about his school in order to raise money. The school has already grown and has hundreds of students, so he is opening other branches.

How did this start? He was walking back from school one day when he saw some children in his neighbourhood who didn't have money for school books, uniforms or transport. Babar decided to help them. When he got home, he started teaching children in his backyard. The school grew, and soon many people were talking about it.

The holidays finish soon. This year, Babar Ali is going to train some more of his pupils to become teachers. In fact, some of his original pupils are starting to work as teachers this term. In this way, they will change the lives of more children.

Imagine you enter a school in India, and you meet the head teacher who is a man in his twenties!

1 CLASS VOTE Do you think you would be a good teacher? Why? / Why not?

2 3.25 Read the article quickly. What was Babar Ali's idea? Was it a good one?

3 Study the Grammar box. Match each paragraph with the time: past, present or future. Find more examples of each tense in the text.

Grammar | Mixed tenses

Talking about the present
Present Simple: She often walks to school.
Present Continuous: I am studying now.

Talking about the past
Past Simple: I visited her yesterday.
Past Continuous: She was working.

Talking about the present and the past
Present Perfect: Our school has grown.

Talking about the future
will: This school will change lives.
going to: I am going to train as a teacher.
Present Continuous: She is starting work tomorrow.
Present Simple: The autumn term starts in September.

GRAMMAR TIME > PAGE 126

4 Choose the correct options.

Hi Nadim,
Thanks for your email. I ¹have / ('m having) / 've had a great time in India, it's really amazing here. We ²stay / 're staying / 've stayed with some of my cousins.
We ³get up / 're getting up / 've got up early most mornings. We usually ⁴have / are having / have had breakfast outside. Then we visit some tourist sites. I ⁵see / 'm seeing / 've seen elephants and monkeys but I ⁶don't go / am not going / haven't been to the famous Babar Ali school yet. I'm looking forward to it!
See you soon,
Leyla x

5 Complete the sentences with the Past Simple or Past Continuous form of the verbs in brackets.
1 What _were you doing_ (you/do) in town yesterday?
2 Where _____ (you/go) on holiday last year?
3 We _____ (not come) to visit last weekend.
4 I _____ (watch) TV when I heard the phone.
5 They _____ (not work) when the teacher came in.

6 Use *will* or *going to* to answer the questions.
1 Are you going to study this evening?
2 Will you study at college in a few years?
3 What plans do you have for the weekend?
4 What places will you travel to in the future?

7 [VOX POPS ▶ 9.2] In pairs, tell your partner about your first school and first teacher.

And YOU

9.5 LISTENING and VOCABULARY — Awkward moments

I can identify specific information in a dialogue and talk about awkward moments.

1 **CLASS VOTE** Have any of these 'awkward moments' ever happened to you? In pairs, discuss what you would say or do in each situation. Which is the most embarrassing?
- you call your teacher 'mum' by accident
- you're playing with your pen when it flies across the classroom
- you realise your T-shirt is dirty

2 🔊 3.26 Listen to four dialogues. Choose the correct answers.

1 What does the teacher want the girl to do before the test?

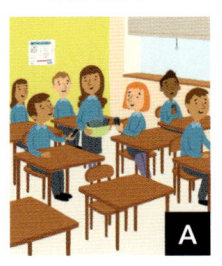

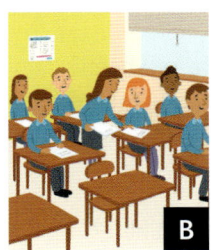

2 Where are all the other students now?

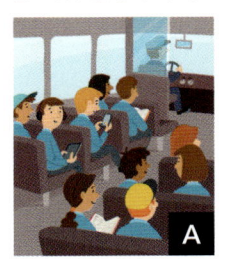

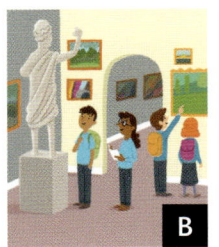

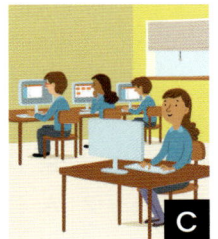

3 What happened to the boy's form?

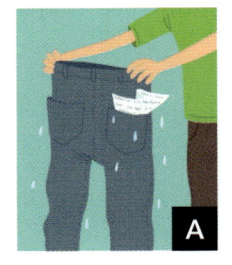

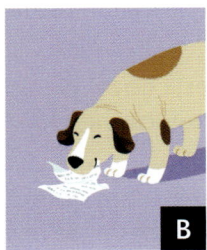

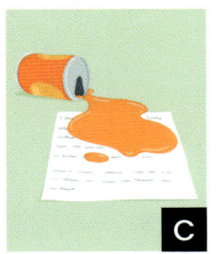

4 What were the students doing?

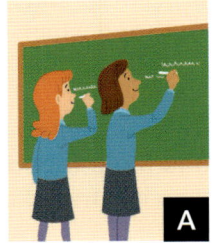

3 🔊 3.26 Listen again. Which situation is most embarrassing? How would you behave?

4 🔊 3.27 Study the Vocabulary box. Choose the correct options. Listen and check.

Vocabulary	Phrasal verbs
calm down fill in (a form) get on hand in/out	
look over look up mess about/around	

1 The teacher asked us all to *hand in* / *look up* our homework on time.
2 Pupils who finish early should *get on* / *look up* with some extra reading.
3 Please don't *mess about* / *hand out* in the art lesson.
4 Make sure you *get on* / *look over* all your answers before you finish.
5 You can *look up* / *look over* any words you don't know in a dictionary.
6 We have to *fill in* / *calm down* this form with our name and number.

5 🔊 3.28 Choose the correct answers. Listen and check.

1 Who's ready to hand in their essay?
  a Yes, I will.
  b I've just finished it.
  c No, it wasn't difficult.

2 Are we going to look over the test papers now?
  a Yes, I will.
  b No, it isn't.
  c Yes, we are.

3 Did the teachers see you when you were messing about?
  a No, they didn't.
  b No, I wasn't.
  c Where were they?

4 Could you all calm down, please?
  a Yes, Miss.
  b No, I couldn't.
  c Thank you, Miss.

6 🔊 3.28 Listen again. What was the 'awkward moment' in each dialogue?

7 [VOX POPS ▶ 9.3] Write a short paragraph about an 'awkward moment' that has happened to you.

And YOU?

9.6 SPEAKING   Exchanging personal information

I can have a casual conversation.

VIDEO — HOW WAS YOUR JOURNEY?

Ed: Dan! Great to see you! Sorry I couldn't meet you at the airport.
Dan: That's all right. It was easy by taxi. It's good to be here.
Ed: How was your journey?
Dan: Tiring! I'm feeling shattered.
Ed: Tell me about it! Let's put your bag in my locker, and then we'll get you a drink.
Dan: The college looks amazing. Do you like it here?
Ed: Yeah. I've made some good friends already. What about you? How have you been?
Dan: Everything's fine. The house is quiet without you, though.
Ed: Oh! So, do you miss me?
Dan: Not really. Well … only sometimes!
Ed: Ha! Oh, there's Miguel. Let me introduce you. Hey, Miguel! Come and meet my brother, Dan.
Miguel: Nice to meet you, Dan. Have you been to New York state before?
Dan: No, we lived on the west coast when we were little. I can't wait to look around.
Miguel: So what are you guys doing this evening?
Ed: We're having a drink here, and then I'm going to show Dan around. Would you like to join us?
Miguel: Sure thing. I'd love to.

OUT of class
Great to see you!   Tell me about it!
I'm (feeling) shattered.
Let me introduce you.

1 **CLASS VOTE** Have you ever changed school? What was it like?

2 9.4 3.29 Watch or listen and answer the questions.
1 How is Dan feeling?
2 Does Ed like his American college?
3 Is this Dan's first time in New York state?
4 What are their plans?

3 3.30 Use the Speaking box to match the questions with the responses. Listen and check.

Speaking	Exchanging personal information

Past
How have you been?
How was your journey?
Have you been to the USA before?

Present
Do you like it here?

Future
What are you guys doing this evening?
Would you like to join us?

1 A: _____
   B: That would be great. Thanks.
2 A: _____
   B: Fine. What about you?
3 A: _____
   B: Well, it's interesting, but I miss home.
4 A: _____
   B: Yes, I have. We had a holiday in Florida when I was little.
5 A: _____
   B: Well, there's a great pizza restaurant near here. We're going to try it.

4 3.31 Listen to Miguel, Dan and Ed. Write down the three questions they ask. Which is past, which is present and which is future?

5 Work in groups of three. Role play one of the situations. Students A and B are friends, and they meet Student C, who is a friend of Student A.
1 at a party
2 at the cinema
3 in a sports club

9.7 WRITING — A letter giving information

I can write a letter giving information.

1 CLASS VOTE What information would you give a school exchange partner who was coming to your school?

2 Read the letter from an exchange partner. What does she want to know?

Hi Kyla,

As you know, I'm arriving next Monday evening. I'm attaching a recent photo so you can see what I look like! I know it will be term time, so please can you tell me a few things about your school? Like, is it big and do you wear uniforms? Also, are you going to meet me at the airport, or shall I get a taxi?

See you soon,

Nadia

3 Read Kyla's reply. Does she include all the information that Nadia asked for?

Dear Nadia,

Thanks for your letter. I'm looking forward to meeting you as well.

You asked about my school. Well, there are about a thousand pupils, and the teachers are friendly. We wear uniforms, but I can lend you a spare one if you like. I have basketball club after school on Fridays, so you're welcome to come along.

Of course we're going to meet you on Monday! I'll be at the airport with my parents. We'll have a big card with your name on, but here's a photo, too, just in case! Don't worry about anything, we're going to have fun!

Best wishes,

Kyla

4 Look at the phrases in colour. What do they mean? Why does Kyla use them?

5 Underline and name the tenses in Kyla's letter. Match each tense with its function.

a past event   regular habits
something happening now   plans   a promise

6 Study the Writing box. Complete gaps a–d with sentences from Kyla's letter.

Writing — A letter giving information

1 Starting your letter
Dear (name), …
It was good to hear from you.
a _____
It was nice to hear your news.

2 Making it clear why you're writing
You wanted to know about my school. Well, …
You asked for information about the school here.
b _____

3 Giving useful information
There are about a thousand pupils.
I can lend you a uniform / PE kit / bag.
c _____

4 Making arrangements
We'll definitely meet you.
We'll be there at 7.15 p.m.
d _____

5 Before you finish
I'm really looking forward to seeing you (again).
We're going to have a great time.
It will be good to meet you at last.

6 Ending your letter
All the best, / See you soon,

Writing Time

7 Read Jack's letter and then write a reply.

Hi Bryan,

As you know, I'm arriving next week by train. What are the plans for meeting me? Shall I phone you from the station, or take a taxi? Should I bring anything special with me (e.g. warm clothes, sports equipment, hiking boots, etc.)? I'm not sure about the weather, and your plans for the weekend. Please, let me know.
Jack

In your letter, you should
1 thank Jack for his letter and say why you're writing
2 reply to all the questions
3 express your feelings about the visit

WORDLIST — School subjects | Learning and assessment | Describing students | Phrasal verbs

ability /əˈbɪləti/
Art /ɑːt/
average /ˈævərɪdʒ/
awkward /ˈɔːkwəd/
Biology /baɪˈɒlədʒi/
board /bɔːd/
brain /breɪn/
brainstorm /ˈbreɪnstɔːm/
branch /brɑːntʃ/
calm down /ˌkɑːm ˈdaʊn/
certificate /səˈtɪfɪkət/
cheat /tʃiːt/
Chemistry /ˈkemɪstri/
Citizenship /ˈsɪtɪzənʃɪp/
college /ˈkɒlɪdʒ/
compulsory /kəmˈpʌlsəri/
confident /ˈkɒnfɪdənt/
Cooking /ˈkʊkɪŋ/
copy /ˈkɒpi/
creative /kriˈeɪtɪv/
critical thinking /ˌkrɪtɪkl ˈθɪŋkɪŋ/
curriculum /kəˈrɪkjʊləm/
driving /ˈdraɪvɪŋ/
education /ˌedjʊˈkeɪʃn/
educational research /ˌedjʊˌkeɪʃnəl rɪˈsɜːtʃ/
effort /ˈefət/
essay /ˈeseɪ/
examiner /ɪɡˈzæmɪnə/
experiment /ɪkˈsperɪmənt/
extracurricular /ɪkˈsperɪmənt/
fashion design /ˈfæʃn dɪˌzaɪn/
fill in (a form) /ˌfɪl ɪn ə ˈfɔːm/
film-making /ˈfɪlm ˌmeɪkɪŋ/
gardening /ˈɡɑːdnɪŋ/
general knowledge /ˌdʒenrl ˈnɒlɪdʒ/
Geography /dʒiˈɒɡrəfi/
get on /ˌɡet ˈɒn/
gifted /ˈɡɪftɪd/
hand in/out /ˌhænd ˈɪn/ˈaʊt/
hard-working /ˌhɑːd ˈwɜːkɪŋ/
head teacher /ˌhed ˈtiːtʃə/
Health /helθ/
Humanities /hjuːˈmænətiz/
ICT /ˌaɪ siː ˈtiː/
imagination /ɪˌmædʒɪˈneɪʃn/
improvement /ɪmˈpruːvmənt/
influence /ˈɪnfluəns/
information /ˌɪnfəˈmeɪʃn/
instructor /ɪnˈstrʌktə/
intelligence /ɪnˈtelɪdʒəns/
intelligent /ɪnˈtelɪdʒənt/
IQ /ˌaɪ ˈkjuː/
lazy /ˈleɪzi/
learn /lɜːn/
learner /ˈlɜːnə/
life skill /ˈlaɪf skɪl/
Literature /ˈlɪtərətʃə/
locker /ˈlɒkə/
look over /ˌlʊk ˈəʊvə/
look up /ˌlʊk ˈʌp/
marks /mɑːks/
Maths /mæθs/
measure /ˈmeʒə/
memorise /ˈmeməraɪz/
mess about/around /ˌmes əˈbaʊt/əˈraʊnd/
miss a lesson /ˌmɪs ə ˈlesn/
Music /ˈmjuːzɪk/
optional /ˈɒpʃənl/
pass /pɑːs/
PE /ˌpiː ˈiː/
performance /pəˈfɔːməns/
Physics /ˈfɪzɪks/
population /ˌpɒpjuˈleɪʃn/
practical exam /ˌpræktɪkl ɪɡˈzæm/
presentation /ˌprezənˈteɪʃn/
problem solving /ˈprɒbləm ˌsɒlvɪŋ/
progress /ˈprəʊɡres/
project /ˈprɒdʒekt/
pupil /ˈpjuːpl/
raise money /ˌreɪz ˈmʌni/
revise /rɪˈvaɪz/
school exchange /ˈskuːl ɪksˌtʃeɪndʒ/
Science /ˈsaɪəns/
score /skɔː/
shattered /ˈʃætəd/
solution /səˈluːʃn/
speaking exam /ˈspiːkɪŋ ɪɡˌzæm/
study /ˈstʌdi/
subject /ˈsʌbdʒɪkt/
talented /ˈtæləntɪd/
teamwork /ˈtiːmwɜːk/
technical /ˈteknɪkl/
term /tɜːm/
train /treɪn/
uniform /ˈjuːnɪfɔːm/
written exam /ˌrɪtn ɪɡˈzæm/

WORD FRIENDS
make changes
take a test/an exam
make sense
take/make notes
make progress
take a look
make an improvement
make a mistake

VOCABULARY IN ACTION

1 Use the wordlist to find:
1. four types of test or assessment
2. five adjectives to describe students
3. three life skills
4. two synonyms of the word 'learn'

2 In pairs, use the wordlist to discuss which subjects:
1. are useful for you
2. are not very useful for you
3. are hard to understand
4. are fun
5. you would like to try in the future

3 Use four words from the wordlist to describe an 'ideal' student. Compare with a partner. Are your ideas the same?

4 Complete the sentences with the words below.

mistake   notes   progress   sense   test

1. My sister's taking her driving _____ today.
2. It doesn't make _____ to me.
3. Listen and take _____.
4. My marks are improving, so I'm making _____.
5. I didn't get 100 percent in the exam because I made a _____ in one question.

5 🔊 3.32 **PRONUNCIATION** Listen to the intonation in each question and repeat.

Do you like it here?
What are you doing this evening?
Would you like to join us?
Did you enjoy the film?
Have you been here before?
Are you going to visit your family?

6 Does the intonation rise or fall in questions? In pairs, ask the questions from Exercise 5 with the correct intonation.

Revision

VOCABULARY

1 Write the correct word for each definition.

1 great poems, novels and other books
   l _ _ _ _ _ _ _ _ _ _

2 a piece of paper you get when you pass an exam
   c _ _ _ _ _ _ _ _ _ _

3 If you have an exam tomorrow, you should do this. r _ _ _ _ _ _

4 a person who teaches you a special skill, like driving
   i _ _ _ _ _ _ _ _ _

5 a presentation using dance, music, acting or movement
   p _ _ _ _ _ _ _ _ _ _

2 Complete the questions.

1 Do you prefer to relax and not work hard? Are you l a z y?

2 Are you shy and quiet or are you
   c _ _ _ _ _ _ _ _ ?

3 Can you work well with other people? Are you good at t _ _ _ _ _ _ _ _ ?

4 Do you know a lot about the world? How's your
   g _ _ _ _ _ _ _ _ _ _ _ _ ?

5 Can you use your imagination? Are you
   c _ _ _ _ _ _ _ _ ?

6 Do you have some natural skills, for example in sport or music? Are you
   t _ _ _ _ _ _ _ _ _ ?

3 In pairs, ask and answer questions from Exercise 2.

GRAMMAR

4 Complete the text with the correct form of the verbs in brackets.

The latest news in education...

A: Lunchbox thieves?
Recently, strange things ¹have happened (happen) in the UK. At some schools, teachers ² _____ (take) food items out of pupils' lunch boxes! Are teachers hungry? No, they ³ _____ (put) unhealthy snacks in the bin! Pupils and their parents ⁴ _____ (feel) shocked.

B: Police to get pupils out of bed!
Another UK school says it is going to ⁵ _____ (send) ex-police officers to get pupils out of bed! Apparently the officers are going to ⁶ _____ (take) lazy students to school by car. This way, pupils won't ⁷ _____ (miss) any lessons, so they will ⁸ _____ (do) better in their exams, which ⁹ _____ (start) in three months.

C: Parents must behave!
Last week we ¹⁰ _____ (read) an interesting report about a head teacher who was angry with parents who ¹¹ _____ (not come) to any parent-teacher evenings. What was his idea? He ¹² _____ (want) lazy parents to pay a fine. However, other people ¹³ _____ (not like) his plan, so he was very unpopular!

5 Make questions from the prompts. In pairs, answer them.

1 what / teachers / do / with unhealthy snacks?
2 pupils and parents / feel / happy about this?
3 why / one school / send police officers to get students / out of bed?
4 this / help / students?
5 who / become / famous / last week?
6 he / popular?

SPEAKING

6 In pairs, role play the situation. Imagine you are an exchange student in the UK. Choose a character from page 144 and introduce yourselves. Add two more questions and extra information of your own.

Angelina? That's a nice name. Where are you from?
France. I live in Paris.
Have you ever been to the UK before?

DICTATION

7 🔊 3.33 Listen, then listen again and write down what you hear.

BBC CULTURE

Can school be fun?

Another way to learn: A day in the life of a student at an alternative school

Adam

'I go to a Steiner school. It's very different to the traditional schools that my friends go to. First of all, our learning is far more creative and interactive. We don't sit in class and memorise facts; we get up and do practical stuff, which I think is really alternative.

For example, today we had a Biology lesson. As we were learning all about the body, the teacher asked us to make clay models and draw pictures of different body parts. It was much more fun than just reading information in a book. Also, we did this in a group, so we learnt from each other. Then we took it in turns to give presentations about a subject of our choice. I gave a talk about modern-day allergies. I researched this topic because I think it's really fascinating.

Anyway, it's great that we have the freedom to do that. And the other positive thing is that there are no tests – we just revise the material in our own time!

We also usually only have one academic subject per week. It's just two or three hours in the morning, then the rest of the day we do gardening, arts and crafts. Today we did singing and dancing – my favourites! One thing that they discourage at my school is the computer. We aren't allowed to sit in front of a screen for a long time. I don't like this, but I understand the reasons – we can do that at home.

Here the teachers are very different too – they are your friends. They don't just instruct you; they help you achieve your potential. I love that. I actually look forward to going to school!'

GLOSSARY
achieve (v) to succeed in doing something
allergy (n) a medical condition that makes you ill when you eat, touch or breathe something
clay (n) a type of material that is used to make pots
discourage (v) to try to make someone want to do something less often
in turns (phrase) one after another

EXPLORE

1 In pairs, ask and answer the questions.
1. Describe something you have learnt recently that was fun or interesting. Why was it a good learning experience?
2. What makes a lesson interesting or boring for you? Give examples.

2 Read the article. Mark the sentences T (true) or F (false).
1. ☐ Adam knows that his school is alternative.
2. ☐ He would like to read more in class.
3. ☐ He chose a subject he liked for his presentation.
4. ☐ The students study academic subjects at the same time.
5. ☐ Adam would like to spend longer on the computer.
6. ☐ He thinks that the teachers are similar to those in traditional schools.

3 Read the article again. In pairs, ask and answer the questions.
1. What information in the text surprises you about this alternative school?
2. How does the 'day in the life' compare to daily life at your school? Which do you prefer? Why?

EXPLORE MORE

4 ▶ 9.5 Watch Part 1 of the video. Which school would you prefer to go to? Why?

5 ▶ 9.5 Watch again. Choose the correct option.
1. At King's School order and *creativity* / *discipline* is important.
2. Today's class is a *Maths* / *Leadership* class.
3. The girl interviewed wants to be a *teacher* / *banker*.
4. The Steiner school is more *formal* / *informal* than King's.
5. At the Steiner school academic studies start at *six* / *seven* years old.

6 ▶ 9.6 Watch Part 2 of the video. Complete the text with the words below. There are two extra words.

> memory   movements   fourteen   words
> alternative   English   forty   colours

In the UK there are ¹_____ schools which specialise in teaching dyslexic children. Dyslexia affects reading and spelling, and your short-term ²_____. So, the students learn new ³_____ with shapes and ⁴_____. Kara attends an ⁵_____ lesson. In the class the students spell out words with physical ⁶_____.

7 What's your opinion of the different schools from the video? Discuss in pairs.

I think the school that specialises in helping dyslexic children is great.

YOU EXPLORE

8 **CULTURE PROJECT** In groups, prepare a presentation based on the question: 'What would your ideal school be like?'
1. Use these notes to help you:
   - practical tasks / academic tasks: what's the right balance?
   - use of computers: a lot or a little?
   - how much freedom of choice?
   - discipline: important or not?
2. Write a short script to describe your ideas. Think about images or videos to use in your presentation.
3. Give your presentation to the class. Whose ideal school is the best? Why?

GRAMMAR TIME

1.2 Present Simple, Present Continuous and state verbs

Present Simple
We use the Present Simple for facts, permanent situations and routines.
They sing in a band.
She doesn't use her tablet every day.

Time expressions
every day/week/month/year
once/twice/three times a month
on Mondays/weekdays/holiday
always/usually/often/sometimes/rarely/never

Present Continuous
We use the Present Continuous for actions that are happening at or around the time of speaking.
They're playing a computer game right now.
I'm recording songs this week.

Time expressions
now, at the moment, this morning/afternoon, this year, these days

State verbs
State verbs express opinions, preferences, mental states and perception.
love, like, hate, prefer, want, need, understand, think, feel, hear, see
They don't normally have a continuous form, even if they refer to the time of speaking.
I want to see your new mobile phone.

1 Complete the text with the correct form of the verbs below.

> (not) like   dance   go   make   prefer   show   ~~think~~   wear

I ¹*think* one of the favourite pastimes for my generation is watching music videos on YouTube. My favourite is the one by Ylvis called 'What does the fox say'. Do you want to watch it? Look, there's a fancy dress party and all the people ²_____ animal costumes. They ³_____ in the forest and ⁴_____ crazy animal sounds! It's amazing, although a bit old now! My sister ⁵_____ music videos – she ⁶_____ videos about shopping where people ⁷_____ shopping for clothes or cosmetics and then ⁸_____ the viewers what's in their shopping bags … Not my kind of thing, really.

2 Write a similar text about what kinds of videos you like and describe your favourite one.

1.4 Verb + ing and verb + to-infinitive

Verbs followed by the -ing form:
avoid, can't stand, enjoy, finish, (not) mind, miss, practise, stop
I avoid using flash in my camera.
The -ing form is also used after prepositions.
I'm looking forward to seeing my grandpa.
Verbs followed by the to-infinitive:
agree, allow, ask, choose, decide, forget, hope, learn, offer, plan, try, want, would like/love
I hope to become a good photographer in the future.
Some verbs can be followed by either the to-infinitive, or the -ing form:
like, love, hate, prefer, start
I love taking photos of cats. / I love to take photos of cats.

1 Complete the sentences with the correct form of the verbs in brackets.

1. Martha's parents often allow her _____ (stay up) late at night.
2. I would love _____ (buy) a new camera.
3. My boyfriend is crazy about _____ (watch) old silent movies.
4. Why don't you practise _____ (play) this song again?
5. Please, try _____ (stay) calm.
6. Would you mind _____ (help) me with this poster?

2 Choose the correct option.

A: What are you planning ¹*to do / doing* at the weekend, Josh?
B: I don't know. I want ²*to write / writing* the French essay. Finish ³*to write / writing* it, in fact.
A: Doesn't sound very exciting!
B: Well, no, it doesn't. I can't stand ⁴*to learn / learning* French. What about you, Jessica?
A: Well, I'm trying ⁵*to earn / earning* some money for a new camera. My old one is broken. I can help my uncle in his garden. He is offering ⁶*to pay / paying* me five pounds an hour. In fact, he wants me ⁷*to bring / bringing* a friend too … There's enough work for two people with planting apple trees.
B: That's great! I need some cash. And I'm really good at ⁸*to plant / planting*!
A: Really? That's new!

Grammar Time

GRAMMAR TIME

2.2 Past Simple: regular and irregular verbs

We use the **Past Simple** to talk about actions and situations that finished in the past. We often mention when these actions/situations happened.
We saw a storm yesterday.
We didn't see the storm.
Did you see the storm?

Some verbs in English have regular Past Simple forms.
happen–happened, move–moved, study–studied, travel–travelled

Some verbs are irregular. (See page 127 for a list of irregular verbs.)

Time expressions
yesterday
two hours/days/weeks/years ago
last week/year/night
in 2001

1 Complete the sentences with the correct form of the verbs in brackets.

1 I _visited_ (visit) my aunt in August.
2 I last _____ (see) a rainbow two weeks ago.
3 It _____ (rain) a lot last summer.
4 I _____ (take) a lot of photos on holiday.
5 I _____ (study) for the Maths test last night.
6 I _____ (have) fried eggs for breakfast yesterday.

2 In pairs, make questions from the the prompts and time expressions below. Then ask and answer the questions.

> yesterday   the day before yesterday
> last Monday / Friday / Saturday   a month ago
> last year   two years ago   in 2007   in June 2010

1 What / you / have / for lunch / ?
2 What films / you / see / ?
3 Where / you / go / on holiday / ?
4 What sports / you / do / ?
5 What video games / you / play / ?
6 What mobile phone / you / have / ?

A: *What did you have for lunch the day before yesterday?*
B: *Uhm … OK, I remember. I had some spaghetti.*

3 Write ten true sentences about yourself, using the Past Simple and ten different time expressions.

2.4 Past Continuous and Past Simple

Past Continuous
We use the Past Continuous to describe an activity that was in progress in the past or to describe a scene in the past.
At seven o'clock I was talking to friends online.
It was snowing.
She was doing her homework. She wasn't playing games.
They were swimming. They weren't running.
Was she sleeping? Yes, she was. No, she wasn't.

Past Continuous and Past Simple
We use the Past Continuous and Past Simple to talk about an activity that was in progress when something else happened.
I was walking in the forest when I suddenly saw a bear.
Anne called me while I was doing the Maths homework.

1 Complete the sentences with the Past Simple or the Past Continuous form of the verbs in brackets.

1 When you _____ (call), I _____ (take) a shower.
2 The weather was perfect last Christmas: it _____ (snow) and the sun _____ (shine).
3 A: What _____ (you / do) at ten o'clock last Wednesday?
   B: I'm not sure … I _____ (not sleep). I think I _____ (watch) a film on television.
4 A: _____ (you / play) games on your mobile when the teacher _____ (come) into the classroom?
   B: No, I _____ ! I _____ (look) for some information about Asia on the internet.

2 Complete the text with the correct forms of the words below.

> appear   break   fall   come   hear   ~~hike~~
> run   shout   try

Last winter I ¹_was hiking_ in the mountains with my friend Jake when we ² _____ a strange sound. We were quite scared. There was lots of snow on the top of the mountain and it ³ _____ down on us really quickly. It was an avalanche! 'Run,' Jake ⁴ _____ . We ⁵ _____ when we both ⁶ _____ down the slope and my friend ⁷ _____ his leg! I ⁸ _____ to call my dad from my mobile phone when a helicopter ⁹ _____ in the sky and we were saved!

GRAMMAR TIME

3.2 Present Perfect with *ever*, *never*, *just*, *already* and *yet*

The Present Perfect form is *have/has* and the past participle. For regular verbs, the past participle is the same as the Past Simple form. Many past participles are irregular (see page 127).

We use the Present Perfect to talk about:

- life experience up to now with *ever* (in questions) and *never* (in negatives).
  Have you **ever** eaten pizza with bananas?
  I've **never** been to this restaurant.
- actions that finished a short time ago with *just*.
  I'm not hungry. I've **just** had a sandwich.
- actions that are (or are expected to be) completed by now with *already* (in affirmative sentences) and *yet* (in negatives and questions).
  I've **already** cooked lunch.
  I haven't cooked lunch **yet**.
  Have you cooked lunch **yet**?

1 Complete the sentences with the correct form of the words in brackets.

1. We can eat pizza now! The delivery _____ (just / arrive).
2. Joshua _____ (already / wash) the dishes so we can relax.
3. A: _____ (the kids / have lunch / yet)?
   B: No, they _____.
4. A: _____ (you / do the shopping / yet)?
   B: Yes, I _____ (just / return) from the shops.
5. These almond biscuits are absolutely amazing! I _____ (never / eat) better ones!
6. We are still working on a cookery project for school and we _____ (not finish / yet).

2 In pairs, ask and answer questions about the things listed below. Use *ever*.

	YOU	YOUR PARTNER
try snails		
watch a horror film		
make a cake		
cook a family dinner		

Have you ever tried snails? Yes, I have.

3 You are preparing a party with your friend. Write them a note to say what you have already done and what you haven't done yet.

Hi, Mark! I've already bought some crisps and nuts, but I haven't bought any soft drinks yet …

3.4 Present Perfect with *for* and *since*; Present Perfect and Past Simple

Present Perfect with *for* and *since*
We use the Present Perfect with *for* and *since* to describe an unfinished action that started in the past and still continues.
Use *for* with:
a week / a month / a year / ages, etc.
They have owned this restaurant **for** two years.
Use *since* with:
2012 / March / last Tuesday / the day we met, etc.
I've had this dishwasher **since** February.

Present Perfect and Past Simple
Use the Past Simple in sentences with a reference to a specific time in the past.
I went to this pizzeria **last Sunday**.

Use the Present Perfect to talk about life experiences up to now.
I've been to this pizzeria. It's really nice.

We use the Present Perfect with times and dates when we want to say how long something has lasted (*for* how long or *since* when).
I've known my best friend for ten years.

1 Complete the sentences with *since* or *for*.

1. I've lived in this house _____ I was born.
2. I've known him _____ ten years.
3. I've had this furniture _____ two months.
4. I've haven't seen him _____ yesterday.

2 Write sentences from the prompts.

1. Maria / get / her mobile phone / for Christmas / two years ago.
2. She / win / her skiis in a skiing competition / last year.
3. She / make / her jumper herself / last winter.
4. She / find / her favourite book in a park / three weeks ago.

Maria got her mobile phone for Christmas two years ago.

3 Write how long Maria has had her favourite things, using *since* or *for*.

Maria has had her mobile phone since Christmas two years ago.

GRAMMAR TIME

4.2 Comparatives and superlatives

Comparative
To compare two people or things, we use the comparative form + *than*.
The theatre is more interesting than the cinema.
(not) as + adjective + as
We can also use *(not) as + adjective + as*.
The cinema is not as interesting as the theatre.
The film adaptation is as good as the book.
Superlative
The superlative form is used to compare one person or thing with the rest of a group. We usually use *the* with superlative adjectives.
Omen is the scariest horror film I've seen.
too / (not) enough
We use *too* and *(not) enough* with adjectives to say what we expect from a situation.
The screen is too dark. = The screen is not bright enough.

1 Write the comparative and superlative forms of the adjectives below. Then write six sentences using these forms.

> amusing   big   dramatic   dry   heavy
> large   sad   strange

2 Complete the text with the words below.

> the best   bigger   the biggest   cheaper
> closer   as comfortable as   comfortable enough
> more expensive   too expensive

Well, I often go to the cinema, and here are my three favourites. Multi-Film and MacroMovie are two typical multiplex cinemas. MacroMovie is ¹_____ to the city centre, and it has ²_____ screens (probably ³_____ in the city), and it's also ⁴_____ than the other cinemas so I don't go there so often. The tickets are ⁵_____ if you ask me … The seats in Multi-Film cinema are ⁶_____ in Macromovie, but the tickets are ⁷_____. I often choose Chaplin cinema. Maybe the chairs aren't ⁸_____, but I think the quality of sound is ⁹_____ of all the cinemas.

3 In pairs, discuss three cinemas you know. Use Exercise 2 to help you.

A: OK, I think … is the cheapest.
B: Yes, and it's also the closest to the city centre.

4 Write a paragraph comparing two actresses or two TV programmes.

4.4 Quantifiers: *some, any, much, many, (a) few, (a) little, a lot of, lots of*

Countable and uncountable nouns
We use quantifiers with nouns to talk about quantity. Countable nouns refer to things we can count, e.g. a bracelet, three bracelets. Uncountable nouns refer to things we cannot count, e.g. substances and liquids (rice, milk), things that are being described together (furniture, jewellery) and abstract ideas (love, peace).
a lot / lots of*, *much* and *many
Use *a lot / lots of* with all nouns in affirmative sentences.
I've got a lot / lots of furniture/T-shirts.
Use *much* with uncountable nouns and *many* with countable nouns in negatives and questions.
How much furniture have you got? How many T-shirts have you got?
I haven't got much furniture. I haven't got many T-shirts.
some* and *any
Some and *any* are used with both countable and uncountable nouns. We use *some* in affirmative sentences and *any* in negatives and questions.
I've got some furniture/T-shirts.
Have you got any furniture/T-shirts?
I haven't got any furniture/T-shirts.
***a few, few* + countable nouns**
***a little, little* + uncountable nouns**
I've got a few T-shirts. (= some T-shirts)
I've got few T-shirts. (= not many T-shirts)
I've got a little furniture. (= some furniture)
I've got little furniture. (= not much furniture)

1 Read the texts. Choose the correct answers.

I only wear sports clothes, so in my wardrobe there aren't ¹_____ smart dresses. I've got ²_____ T-shirts and ³_____ hoodies. I haven't got ⁴_____ jewellery, only ⁵_____ bracelets.   *Marika*

I like smart clothes, so in my wardobe there're ⁶_____ suits and ⁷_____ white shirts. I haven't got ⁸_____ trainers. I hate sports shoes!   *Rob*

1 a any   b some   c much
2 a lots of   b a lot   c much
3 a a little b a few   c much
4 a much   b many   c any
5 a a little b little   c a few
6 a a few   b few   c any
7 a some   b any   c much
8 a much   b few   c any

2 Write a paragraph about the clothes and accessories you have got. Use the correct quantifiers.

Grammar Time 121

GRAMMAR TIME

5.2 Talking about the future

Use **will/won't** to talk about predictions or decisions made at the moment of speaking.
I don't think he'**ll win** the competition.
Wait, I'**ll help** you.

Use **be going to** to talk about intentions and plans, or to make predictions based on things we know now.
I'**m going** to take up kayaking.
Look at the sky: it'**s going** to rain.

We use the **Present Continuous** to talk about fixed arrangements.
We'**re having** a competition next month.

We use the **Present Simple** to talk about timetables and schedules.
My basketball training **starts** in October.

1 Circle the correct option.
1 *I'm going to buy* / *I'll buy* a new tennis racket, so I'm looking for some offers on eBay.
2 No, I'm sorry. I can't visit you on Tuesday evening. *I'm having / I'll have* guests.
3 In our school, all extra-curricular classes *are going to start / start* in October.
4 Look at Susan! She looks really pale. She *isn't going to finish / doesn't finish* the race.
5 Bob, I've arranged an interview with *Newsweek*. They *are coming / are going to come* tomorrow at 6.30.
6 A I'm starving.
   B *I'm going to make / I'll make* you a sandwich.

2 Complete the questions with the words below.

    having   going (x2)   meeting   will (x2)

1 What do think the weather **will** be like tomorrow?
2 Are you _____ to get a summer job during the holidays?
3 Are you _____ any extra-curricular classes tomorrow?
4 Are you _____ your friends tonight?
5 Do you think people _____ read books in the future?
6 Are you _____ to organise a birthday party?

5.4 First Conditional + *if/unless*

Use the **First Conditional** (If + Present Simple, *will*) to talk about things that will (or won't) happen in the future under certain conditions.
If you **like** gymnastics, you'**ll love** slacklining.
You'**ll love** slacklining if you **like** gymnastics.
Will you **try** slacklining if you **have** a chance?

if not/unless
If the condition is negative, use *if not* or *unless*.
You won't be good at slacklining **if** you **don't practise**.
You won't be good at slacklining **unless** you **practise**.

time clauses with *when*
Notice the difference between a First Conditional sentence and a time clause with *when*.
I'll tell Jack about the competition **if** he comes. (Jack may or may not come.)
I'll tell Jack about the competition **when** he comes. (Jack will come and then I will tell him.)

1 Complete the sentences with the correct form of the verbs in brackets.
1 We _____ (go) skiing if it _____ (snow).
2 I _____ (show) her some skateboarding tricks when she _____ (come) round.
3 Your team _____ (lose) the volleyball match if they _____ (not change) a few players.
4 If the train _____ (not be) late, the footballers _____ (arrive) at Brighton at 5 p.m.
5 The training _____ (not start) if the coach _____ (be) ill.
6 I _____ (take up) jogging when the weather _____ (get) better.

2 Choose the correct answers. In pairs, ask and answer the questions.
1 Will you do your English homework _____ home?
   a if you return
   b when you return
   c when you'll return
2 Will you buy a new tennis racket _____ some money for Christmas?
   a if you get
   b when you'll get
   c if you'll get
3 Will you go cycling at the weekend _____ nice?
   a when the weather will be
   b if the weather is
   c when the weather is

122 Grammar Time

GRAMMAR TIME

6.2 Modal verbs for obligation, prohibition and advice

Obligation and prohibition
To express obligation, use *must* and *have to*. *Must* is used when the speaker feels something is necessary. *Have to* is used for external rules and obligations.
I **must** go now. I don't want to be late.
We **have to** wear uniforms.

To express lack of obligation, we use *don't have to*.
She **doesn't have to** work in July.

Mustn't expresses prohibition.
You **mustn't** smoke during the flight.

Advice
Use *should/shouldn't* and *ought to* to give advice. *Ought to* is more formal than *should*.
You **should/shouldn't** take the train.
You **ought to** pack your luggage now.

Must, *should* and *ought to* are modal verbs. They have the same form in all persons singular and plural. Questions are formed with inversion.
She **must/should/ought to** leave now.
Must/Should she leave now?
Ought she **to** leave now?

Questions and negatives with *have to* are formed with auxiliaries.
She **has to** go now.
She **doesn't have to** work hard.
Does she **have to** pack now?

1 Complete the second sentence so that it means the same as the first sentence. Use the verbs in brackets.

1 Wearing suits and white shirts is obligatory in Joanna's office.
   Joanna _____ in the office. (has)
2 Is it a good idea for us to check out before breakfast?
   _____ before breakfast? (should)
3 Don't take your passport. It's not necessary.
   You _____ passport. (have)
4 You should buy new sunglasses.
   You _____ . (ought)
5 Smoking is forbidden at the airport.
   You _____ at the airport. (mustn't)
6 Is it necessary for Sue to take a sleeping bag?
   _____ a sleeping bag? (does)

6.4 Modal verbs for speculation

We use a modal verb + infinitive to speculate about the present.

We use *must* + infinitive when we strongly believe that something is true.
She **must feel** exhausted after the trip. (= I'm sure she feels exhausted.)

We use *might*, *may* or *could* + infinitive when we think something is possibly true.
It **might/may/could be** cold at night in the mountains. (= It's probably cold.)

We use *can't* + infinitive if we believe something is not true.
This rucksack **can't weigh** more than 20 kilos. It's so small! (= I'm sure it doesn't weigh more than 20 kilos.)

1 Complete the dialogues with the words below.

1

might   can't   must

A: Look at him! He ¹_____ be exhausted!
B: Oh, yes! He ²_____ be an experienced cyclist! Look at his rucksack! It's weird!
A: Yeah. He ³_____ be an artist or something.

2

can't   must   could

A: The water ⁴_____ be freezing! Look, nobody's swimming.
B: No, it ⁵_____ be freezing, not with this sunny weather. The water is always quite warm here.
A: I'm not going in, anyway. It ⁶_____ be muddy or full of seaweed … Brr …

2 Complete the text with one word in each gap.

Hi Mark,
I'm writing about the cruise. I've analysed all the pros and cons and I finally think it ¹m_____ not be the best idea because a cruise in the Mediterranean ²m_____ cost a fortune! Looking at the sea ³c_____ be a bit boring. Also you usually get to the harbour in the evening. It ⁴c_____ be frustrating because it's too late to go sightseeing.
Let's go sailing instead. I think it's more exciting and it ⁵m_____ be cheaper too!
Let me know what you think.
Martha

GRAMMAR TIME

7.2 Second Conditional

We use the **Second Conditional** (*If* + Past Simple, *would* + infinitive) to talk about imaginary situations in the present and future.
If I had a brother, I'd share my room with him.
(= I haven't got a brother, so I don't share my room.)
If I had some money, I would buy my sister a new mobile phone.
I would buy my sister a new mobile phone if I had some money.

Notice the difference between First and Second Conditionals:
I'd be very happy if my grandma visited me. (= it's not very probable)
I'll be very happy if my grandma visits me. (= it's probable)
In the first and third person singular, the form of the verb *to be* after *if* is *was* or *were*.
If I were/was taller, I'd become a model.

1 Order the words to make Second Conditional sentences.

1. behave / if / how / you / were / me / would / you / ?
   How _would you behave if you were me?_
2. if / laugh / feel / at him / Chris / wouldn't / so unhappy / his stepmother / didn't
   Chris _____
3. if / your aunt / would / your family / do / didn't / help / you / what / ?
   What _____
4. get on well / would / do / if / with your mum / what / you / didn't / you / ?
   What _____
5. I / were/ with your grandma / you / I / quarrel / wouldn't / all the time / if
   If _____

2 Complete the Second Conditional sentences with the correct form of the verbs in brackets.

A good friend:
1. _would help_ (help) me if I _were_ (be) in trouble.
2. _____ (give) me some money if I _____ (not have) any.
3. _____ (buy) me some medicine if I _____ (be) ill.
4. _____ (not be) angry with me if I _____ (do) something wrong.
5. _____ (not complain) if I _____ (not be) in a good mood.

7.4 Defining and non-defining relative clauses

We use relative clauses to give information about people, things and places. We use *who* to refer to people, *which* to refer to things and *where* to refer to places.
We use defining relative clauses to give essential information about people, things and places.
I've just seen a man who lives on my street. (this piece of information is essential to identify the man)
Non-defining relative clauses are used to give additional information.
I've just seen Frank Jones, who lives in my street. (information not essential to identify who I'm talking about)
In defining relative clauses *who* and *which* can be replaced with *that*:
This is the woman that asked about you.
In non-defining relative clauses we use commas.
This is Maria Kennel, who is going to work with us.

1 Complete the questions with *who*, *which* or *where*.

1. That's the hospital _where_ I was born.
2. What's the name of the teacher _____ taught you in Year 1?
3. What's the title of the film _____ you went to see at the cinema?
4. What's the name of the person _____ taught you to sail?
5. What is the address of the kindergarten _____ the picnic is going to take place?

2 Combine the sentences using relative clauses with *who*, *which* or *where*. Add commas where necessary. In which sentences could you use *that*?

1. During my brother's wedding, I met an elderly lady. She used to know my great-grandmother.
2. She told me a lot of things. I had no idea about them.
3. My great-grandmother lived in a village near Edinburgh. Edinburgh is the capital of Scotland.
4. The lady told me about a house. My great-grandmother lived there.
5. She had Shetland ponies. She often rode them.

GRAMMAR TIME

8.2 Present and Past Simple Passive

We use the passive when we think *what* happens is more important than *who* does it, or when we don't know who does it.

To say who performed an action, use *by*.
The book **was published** *by* Puffin.
Who **was** the book **published** *by*?

We form the passive with the correct form of the verb *to be* and the past participle.

Present Simple Passive
I **am** often **punished** at school for my naughty behaviour.
The performance **is based** on Agatha Christie's novel.
The tickets for the performance **aren't sold** online.
Are shoplifters always **caught by the police**?

Past Simple Passive
The witness **was interviewed** yesterday.
The criminals **were arrested** on Monday.
He **wasn't found** guilty.
Who **were** the robbers **punished** by?

1 Complete the second sentence so that it means the same as the first sentence.

1. Someone damaged the school gate last night.
   The school gate _____.
2. Nobody uses CCTV cameras just for fun.
   CCTV cameras _____.
3. Nobody saw the suspect in Hyde Park on Sunday.
   The suspect _____.
4. Did the police chase the robbers?
   Were _____?
5. Do people find fingerprints on food as well?
   Are _____?
6. Someone stole my aunt's bag.
   My aunt's bag _____.

2 Complete the text with the words below.

| is based   wasn't completed   were published
| was published   is sold   ~~were written~~   wasn't written

The Millenium is a series of best-selling Swedish crime novels. They ¹*were written* by Stieg Larsson, who created two fantastic characters, the rebellious hacker Lisbeth Salander and the curious journalist Mikael Blomkvist. Because of Larsson's sudden death in 2004, the series ² _____. Only three books of the series ³ _____ out of ten planned. The first book, *The Girl with the Dragon Tattoo* ⁴ _____ in 2005, after Larsson's death. The series ⁵ _____ in over fifty countries. In 2015, a new book in the series appeared. It ⁶ _____ by Larsson but by David Lagercrantz, a Swedish author and crime journalist. The book ⁷ _____ on Larsson's characters and ideas in his novels.

8.4 *have/get something done*

We use *have/get something done* to talk about things that we don't do ourselves and that somebody else (usually a professional) does them for us.
I **made** my costume. (= I made it myself.)
I **had** my costume **made**. (= Somebody else made it for me.)
Get is more informal and is used more often in spoken English.

1 Complete the questions with the correct form of the words in brackets.

1. How often do you *have your hair cut*? (have / your hair / cut)
2. Have you ever _____? (have / your bike / repair)
3. Do you sometimes _____ (have / your photos / print) or do you only keep them in your computer?
4. Would you ever _____ (have / your hair / dye) blue or green?
5. Are you going to _____ (have / a tattoo / do) in the future?
6. Do you think people should _____ (have / their houses / clean) or should they clean them themselves?

2 Complete the text with the words below.

| my hair cut   some photos taken
| my dress made   my nails painted
| them repaired   it styled

Hi Jessie,
How are you? How are the preparations going for the end-of-year party? I've already had ¹_____. I'm really lucky as my aunt works in a small clothing company and I got a discount. The dress is red and it's got little red roses at the front. I'm going to wear my red high-heels. They are the same colour as the dress, and I had ²_____ last week. Anyway, I don't want to have ³_____ although it's a bit long now … My mum says it brings bad luck before the exams! I'm only going to have ⁴_____ before the party. And I'm not going to have ⁵_____. I'll paint them myself. By the way, remember we're having ⁶_____ on Monday for the album. Do you know what we should wear then?
Best,
Martha

GRAMMAR TIME

9.2 Word order in questions

To form **object questions**, move the verb or an auxiliary before the subject of the sentence.

- With the Present Simple or Past Simple of the verb *to be*, swap the verb and the subject.
  He was talented. → Was he talented?

- With verb forms composed of an auxiliary verb and the main verb, e.g. *have got*, Present and Past Continuous, Present Perfect, *be going to*, Future Simple, modal verbs, we move the auxiliary verb before the subject of the sentence.
  They have failed the test. → Have they failed the test?
  What have they failed?
  She will succeed next time. → Will she succeed next time? When will she succeed?
  She studies abroad. → Does she study abroad?
  Where does she study?
  They passed the test → Did they pass the test?
  What did they pass?

To form **subject questions**, use *who* or *what*, with the same word order as in the affirmative sentence. Don't use inversion or auxiliary verbs to form subject questions.
Cristina often helps Sue in science. → Who often helps Sue in science?
PE makes me tired. → What makes you tired?

1 Order the words to make questions.

1. do / most useful / what subjects / you / find / ?
   What subjects do you find most useful?
2. you / how many / take / tests / did / ?
3. doing / at 5 p.m. / yesterday / what / you / were / ?
4. you / a gap year / going / to take / are / ?
5. cheated / in a test / you / have / ever / ?

2 Write one subject question and one object question, using the words in brackets.

1. My dad has bought me a new English dictionary. (Who …? What …?)
   Who has bought you a new English dictionary?
   What has your dad bought you?
2. Jessica is going to take a French exam tomorrow. (Who …? When …?)
3. Mark wants to study in Belgium. (Who …? Where …?)
4. The accident happened in the science lab. (What …? Where …?)
5. A giant spider bit the French teacher. (What …? Who …?)
6. The teachers were absent because of the strike. (Who …? Why …?)

9.4 Mixed tenses

Talking about the present
Use the Present Simple for facts and routines. Use the Present Continuous for actions happening at or around the moment of speaking.

Talking about the past
Use the **Past Simple** for finished actions in the past. Use the **Past Continuous** for actions that were in progress at some time in the past, or when another action took place.

Talking about the present and the past
The **Present Perfect** is used to talk about events that finished in the past (without saying when), or to talk about past events when their effects are visible in the present or continue up to the present.

Talking about the future
Will is used to talk about predictions and decisions taken at the moment of speaking. ***Be going to*** is used for general plans and predictions based on evidence in the present. The **Present Continuous** is used to talk about arrangements and the **Present Simple** for timetables and schedules.

1 Complete the sentences with the correct form of the verbs in brackets.

1. I *am sunbathing* (sunbathe) in Ibiza at the moment. (Present Continuous)
2. At 7 a.m. today I _____ (still / sleep). (Past Continuous)
3. I _____ (go) to the dentist this afternoon. (Present Continuous)
4. My karate training _____ (start) in November. (Present Simple)
5. I _____ (never / copy) an essay from the internet. (Present Perfect)

2 Choose the correct option.

I ¹(remember) / 'm remembering my first day at this school very well. It ²rained / was raining when I ³entered / was entering the building. I ⁴didn't know / haven't known anybody. In the classroom I instantly ⁵noticed / was noticing a nice girl and I quickly ⁶sat / was sitting next to her. Now Sylvia and I ⁷are / have been friends for three years! In three months I ⁸am going to finish / have finished this school. I ⁹'ve already chosen / already choose a secondary school. I hope my results ¹⁰will be / were good enough to get in to the school!

Grammar Time

IRREGULAR VERBS LIST

INFINITIVE	PAST SIMPLE	PAST PARTICIPLE
be [biː]	was/were [wɒz/wɜː]	been [biːn]
become [bɪˈkʌm]	became [bɪˈkeɪm]	become [bɪˈkʌm]
begin [bɪˈgɪn]	began [bɪˈgæn]	begun [bɪˈgʌn]
break [breɪk]	broke [brəʊk]	broken [ˈbrəʊkən]
bring [brɪŋ]	brought [brɔːt]	brought [brɔːt]
build [bɪld]	built [bɪlt]	built [bɪlt]
burn [bɜːn]	burned [bɜːnd]/ burnt [bɜːnt]	burned [bɜːnd]/ burnt [bɜːnt]
buy [baɪ]	bought [bɔːt]	bought [bɔːt]
can [kæn]	could [kʊd]	been able to [biːn ˈeɪbl tə]
catch [kætʃ]	caught [kɔːt]	caught [kɔːt]
choose [tʃuːz]	chose [tʃəʊz]	chosen [tʃəʊzn]
come [kʌm]	came [keɪm]	come [kʌm]
cost [kɒst]	cost [kɒst]	cost [kɒst]
cut [kʌt]	cut [kʌt]	cut [kʌt]
do [duː]	did [dɪd]	done [dʌn]
draw [drɔː]	drew [druː]	drawn [drɔːn]
dream [driːm]	dreamed [driːmd]/ dreamt [dremt]	dreamed [driːmd]/ dreamt [dremt]
drink [drɪŋk]	drank [dræŋk]	drunk [drʌŋk]
drive [draɪv]	drove [drəʊv]	driven [drɪvn]
eat [iːt]	ate [et]	eaten [iːtn]
fall [fɔːl]	fell [fel]	fallen [fɔːln]
feed [fiːd]	fed [fed]	fed [fed]
feel [fiːl]	felt [felt]	felt [felt]
fight [faɪt]	fought [fɔːt]	fought [fɔːt]
find [faɪnd]	found [faʊnd]	found [faʊnd]
fly [flaɪ]	flew [fluː]	flown [fləʊn]
forget [fəˈget]	forgot [fəˈgɒt]	forgotten [fəˈgɒtn]
forgive [fəˈgɪv]	forgave [fəˈgeɪv]	forgiven [fəˈgɪvn]
get [get]	got [gɒt]	got [gɒt]
give [gɪv]	gave [geɪv]	given [gɪvn]
go [gəʊ]	went [went]	gone [gɒn]
grow [grəʊ]	grew [gruː]	grown [grəʊn]
hang [hæŋ]	hung [hʌŋ]	hung [hʌŋ]
have [hæv]	had [hæd]	had [hæd]
hear [hɪə]	heard [hɜːd]	heard [hɜːd]
hide [haɪd]	hid [hɪd]	hidden [hɪdn]
hit [hɪt]	hit [hɪt]	hit [hɪt]
hold [həʊld]	held [held]	held [held]
hurt [hɜːt]	hurt [hɜːt]	hurt [hɜːt]
keep [kiːp]	kept [kept]	kept [kept]
know [nəʊ]	knew [njuː]	known [nəʊn]
learn [lɜːn]	learned [lɜːnd]/ learnt [lɜːnt]	learned [lɜːnd]/ learnt [lɜːnt]
leave [liːv]	left [left]	left [left]
lend [lend]	lent [lent]	lent [lent]
let [let]	let [let]	let [let]
lie [laɪ]	lay [leɪ]	lain [leɪn]
lose [luːz]	lost [lɒst]	lost [lɒst]
make [meɪk]	made [meɪd]	made [meɪd]
meet [miːt]	met [met]	met [met]
pay [peɪ]	paid [peɪd]	paid [peɪd]
put [pʊt]	put [pʊt]	put [pʊt]
read [riːd]	read [red]	read [red]
ride [raɪd]	rode [rəʊd]	ridden [rɪdn]
ring [rɪŋ]	rang [ræŋ]	rung [rʌŋ]
run [rʌn]	ran [ræn]	run [rʌn]
say [seɪ]	said [sed]	said [sed]
see [siː]	saw [sɔː]	seen [siːn]
sell [sel]	sold [səʊld]	sold [səʊld]
send [send]	sent [sent]	sent [sent]
set [set]	set [set]	set [set]
shine [ʃaɪn]	shone [ʃɒn]	shone [ʃɒn]
show [ʃəʊ]	showed [ʃəʊd]	shown [ʃəʊn]
sing [sɪŋ]	sang [sæŋ]	sung [sʌŋ]
sit [sɪt]	sat [sæt]	sat [sæt]
sleep [sliːp]	slept [slept]	slept [slept]
speak [spiːk]	spoke [spəʊk]	spoken [ˈspəʊkən]
spell [spend]	spelt [spelt]/ spelled [speld]	spelt [spelt]/ spelled [speld]
spend [spend]	spent [spent]	spent [spent]
stand [stænd]	stood [stʊd]	stood [stʊd]
steal [stiːl]	stole [stəʊl]	stolen [ˈstəʊlən]
sweep [swiːp]	swept [swept]	swept [swept]
swim [swɪm]	swam [swæm]	swum [swʌm]
take [teɪk]	took [tʊk]	taken [ˈteɪkən]
teach [tiːtʃ]	taught [tɔːt]	taught [tɔːt]
tell [tel]	told [təʊld]	told [təʊld]
think [θɪnk]	thought [θɔːt]	thought [θɔːt]
understand [ˌʌndəˈstænd]	understood [ˌʌndəˈstʊd]	understood [ˌʌndəˈstʊd]
wake [weɪk]	woke [wəʊk]	woken [ˈwəʊkən]
wear [weə]	wore [wɔː]	worn [wɔːn]
win [wɪn]	won [wʌn]	won [wʌn]
write [raɪt]	wrote [rəʊt]	written [rɪtn]

CULTURE 1 — Explore India

1 Read about India. How many people live in India?

2 Read about India again. Answer the questions.
1. Which is the largest city in India?
2. Which two languages are the most important in India?
3. Why is 1947 an important date in India's history?
4. Which two religions do most Indians practise?
5. What can you find in most Indian food?

3 In pairs, answer the questions.
1. Do people speak different languages in your country?
2. Which religions are important in your country?
3. What food is popular in your country?

4 Write a short paragraph about your country. Use your answers to Exercise 3 and the India examples to help you.

India

India is the second largest country in Asia and the largest in South Asia. More than 1.2 billion people live in India and it has the second largest population in the world. Its capital and largest city is New Delhi. Other big cities are Mumbai, Kolkata and Bangalore.

Languages
India has many different cultures and people speak over 1,600 languages and dialects there. The official language of India is Standard Hindi, but English is also very important in business and education. The reason for this is that India was part of the British Empire. It became independent in 1947. Other important languages are Bengali, Telugu, Marathi, Tamil, Urdu, Gujarati and Punjabi.

Religion
In India, religion is very important. India is the home of two major world religions: Hinduism and Buddhism. Nearly 80% of the population of India practise Hinduism, but today only 0.8% of the population practise Buddhism. Another important religion is Islam – about 14% of Indians are Muslims. In fact, India has the second largest population of Muslims in the world after Indonesia.

Food
Indian food varies from place to place and different cultures have different cuisines. Indians eat a lot of rice and most Indians use spices in their food. The most important spices are pepper, chilli pepper, black mustard seed, cumin, turmeric, ginger and coriander.

CULTURE 2 — Explore New Zealand

1 Read about New Zealand. Where is it?

2 Read about New Zealand again. Answer the questions.
1. Where did the Maoris come from?
2. Who was the first European to sail to New Zealand?
3. Who made the first map of New Zealand?
4. Why did European and North American ships come to New Zealand?
5. In which century did New Zealand become part of the British Empire?

3 In pairs, answer the questions.
1. Where is your country?
2. Were there famous explorers in your country in the past?
3. What are some important dates in your country's history? Why are they important?

And YOU

4 Write a short paragraph about the history of your country. Use your answers to Exercise 3 and the New Zealand examples to help you.

New Zealand

New Zealand is a country in the south-western Pacific Ocean. It has two large islands, the North Island and the South Island, and its capital is Wellington.

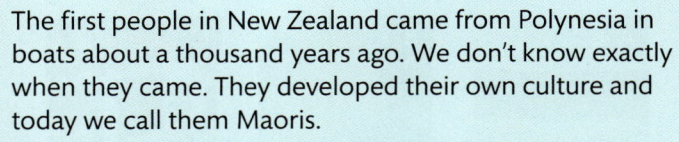

The first people in New Zealand came from Polynesia in boats about a thousand years ago. We don't know exactly when they came. They developed their own culture and today we call them Maoris.

For a long time the Maoris were the only people in the country. Then, in 1642, the Dutch explorer, Abel Tasman, arrived with two ships. Unfortunately, there was a fight between the Europeans and the Maoris and many people died. Tasman left and Europeans did not come again for many years.

In 1769, the British explorer, James Cook, sailed to New Zealand and made the first maps of its coastline. After that, many European and North American ships arrived. They wanted to hunt for whales in the Pacific and trade with the Maoris.

In the nineteenth century, many British people came to live in New Zealand and they bought land from the Maoris. In 1840, the British government signed an agreement with the Maoris, the Treaty of Waitangi, and New Zealand became part of the British Empire. In 1893, New Zealand became the first country in the world to give women the right to vote.

Today New Zealand is a quiet country famous for kiwi birds, spectacular landscapes and the filming location of *The Lord of the Rings*.

EXAM TIME 1 — Listening

1 🔊 **3.34** There are seven questions in this part. For each question, choose the correct answer A, B or C.

Tip: Remember you will hear each recording twice, so you have time to check your answers.

Example: Which film do they want to see? (C)

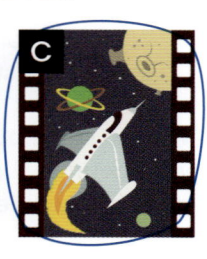

1 What does the girl want to buy for her mum's birthday?
A / B / C

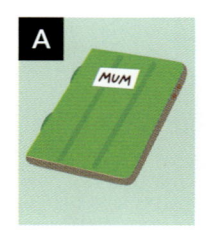

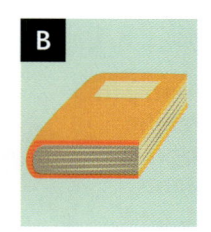

2 What is the view from the girl's window?
A / B / C

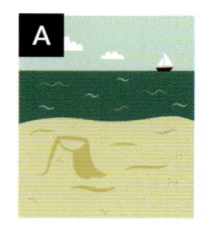

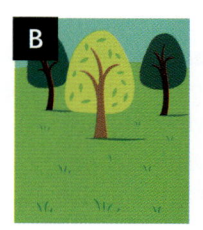

3 What did the boy do at the weekend?
A / B / C

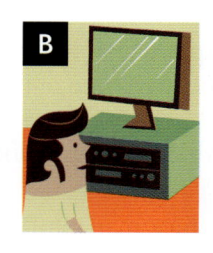

4 What was the weather like yesterday?
A / B / C

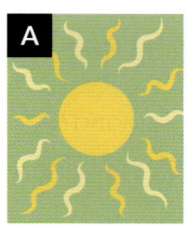

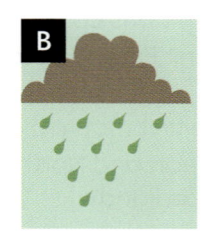

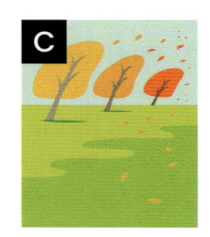

5 What did the boy make for dinner?
A / B / C

6 Where is the boy's phone?
A / B / C

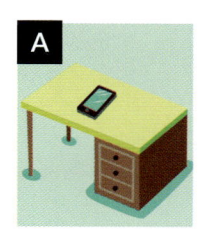

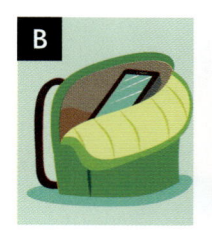

7 What is the boy's sister's job?
A / B / C

EXAM TIME 1 — Listening

2 🔊 **3.35** You will hear a teacher talking about a school trip to a science exhibition. Complete the gaps with the missing information.

VISIT TO SCIENCE EXHIBITION

Day of trip: ¹ _____

Name of exhibition: ² _____

Exhibition is also going to: ³ _____

You can have a conversation with a robot called: ⁴ _____

The trip will begin at: ⁵ _____

Students should take: ⁶ _____

3 🔊 **3.36** You will hear a conversation between a girl, Kelly, and a boy, Dan, about a TV documentary called *All Change!* Decide if each sentence is correct or incorrect. If correct, choose the letter A for YES. If incorrect, choose the letter B for NO.

		YES	NO
1	Dan enjoyed the documentary last night.	A	B
2	Kelly agrees with Dan about the number of environmental documentaries on television.	A	B
3	Kelly and Dan both go skiing regularly.	A	B
4	One of Dan's friends was once near an avalanche.	A	B
5	Kelly and Dan agree about the importance of documentaries like these.	A	B
6	Dan is persuaded to watch the next documentary in the series.	A	B

EXAM TIME 1 — Speaking

1 Students A and B, choose TWO questions to ask your partner.

1. Tell us about your English teacher.
2. What's your favourite season? Why?
3. What do you do in your free time?
4. What's your favourite meal?

2 Work in pairs. Look at the picture and do the task together.

Tip: Talk about all the pictures first before you decide which is best.

A friend from another country is coming to stay with you. Talk together about the activities you could do with him on his first Saturday afternoon, and then decide which is best.

EXAM TIME 1 — Speaking

3 Work in pairs. Take turns to tell your partner about a photograph. Your photographs will be of people eating meals.

Tip: Describe everything you can see in the photograph: the people, their clothes, the place and the things you can see there.

Student A

It's your turn first. Look at the photograph and tell Student B what you can see in it.

Student B

Tell Student A what you can see in the photograph.

4 Work in pairs. Talk to each other about the sort of meals you like to have and where you like to eat them.

Tip: This should be a conversation, so remember to ask your partner questions to give them a chance to say something.

EXAM TIME 2 — Listening

1 🔊 **3.37** There are seven questions in this part. For each question, choose the correct answer A, B or C.

Tip: Remember to listen to the whole conversation before you choose your answer, because the correct answer is sometimes at the end.

Example: Which film do they want to see?

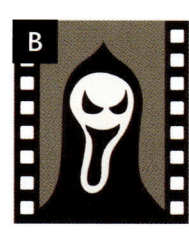

4 What time will the boy go to the theatre?

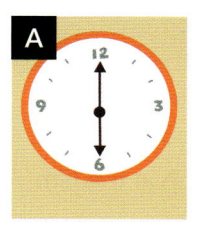

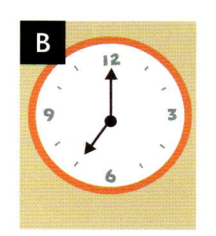

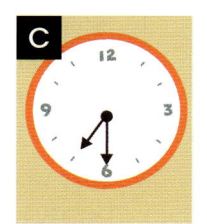

1 What holiday do the boy and girl want to go on?

5 What is the girl definitely going to take camping?

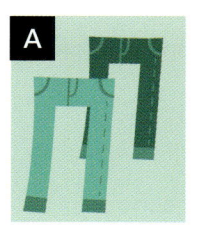

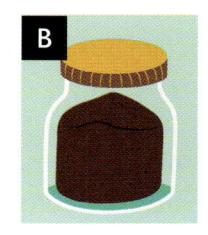

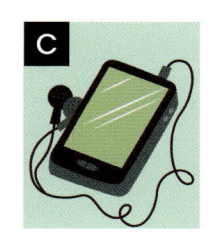

2 What did the girl watch last night?

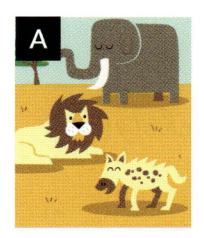

6 What was the boy doing yesterday afternoon?

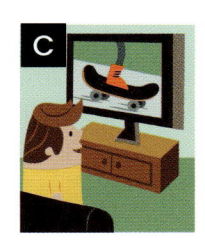

3 What did the boy do first at the Leisure Centre?

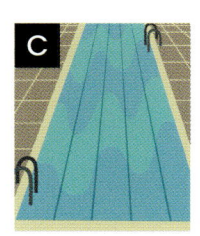

7 What does the girl want to get in town?

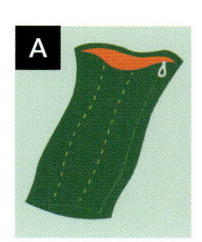

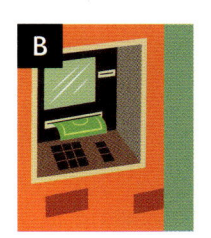

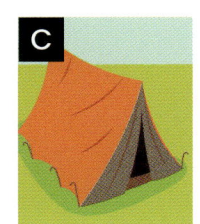

EXAM TIME 2 — Listening

2 🔊 **3.38** You will hear part of an interview with a girl called Suzy who has just got a role in a major film. For each question, choose the correct answer a, b or c.

Tip: Before you hear the recording, use the time you have to read the questions, so that you know what sort of information you are going to listen for.

1 How is Suzy feeling at the moment?
   a She is worried that it may be too hard.
   b She is excited about starting work.
   c She is surprised that she got the part.

2 Suzy won't be swimming much in the film because
   a she can't swim.
   b she hasn't got a good style.
   c her character doesn't swim much.

3 What sort of film has she been in before?
   a a comedy
   b a historical film
   c an educational film

4 Why didn't Suzy go to drama school?
   a She got the part in the film.
   b She wasn't accepted by a drama school.
   c She was advised to do it later.

5 How does Suzy think she'll change because of the film?
   a She'll become more confident.
   b She'll be a better actress.
   c She'll learn more about jobs in film-making.

6 When this filming ends, Suzy
   a will start another film.
   b would like to do some travelling.
   c is going to drama school.

3 🔊 **3.39** You will hear some information about an open-air music concert. Complete the gaps with the missing information.

Tip: You may hear several pieces of information that sound like the right answer, for example different dates, but only one of them is correct. Listen carefully before you make a choice.

MUSIC IN THE PARK

Dates of festival: 1 _____ August

Parking: 2 _____ entrance

Singers: 3 _____

Dance competition categories: hip hop, salsa and 4 _____

Dancers will appear on TV show:
5 _____

Book here for cheapest tickets:
6 _____

EXAM TIME 2 — Speaking

Tip: Remember to try to extend your answers to some of the questions, with reasons and examples.

1 Students A and B answer the questions below.
1. What's your name?
2. What's your surname? How do you spell that?
3. Where do you come from?
4. Do you study English at school? Do you like it?

2 Students A and B, choose TWO questions to ask your partner.
1. How often do you go out with friends?
2. Tell me something about your favourite band or singer.
3. Do you enjoy watching or doing sport?
4. What did you do on your last holiday?

3 Work in pairs. Look at the picture and do the task together.

Tip: Make sure you each get an opportunity to talk. Try not to talk all the time or let your partner do all the talking.

Two teenagers from your country want to go on holiday together for a week in the summer. Talk together about the different types of holiday they could go on, and then decide which holiday is best.

EXAM TIME 3 — Listening

1 🔊 **3.40** There are seven questions in this part. For each question, choose the correct answer A, B or C.

Tip: Before you listen, look at the pictures and think about which words you might hear.

Example: Which film do they want to see?

1 When will the boy and girl's granddad go to a restaurant?

2 What did the girl take with her on her walk?

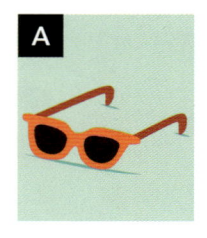

3 Where will the new students be this afternoon?

4 Where did the accident happen?

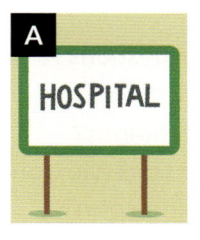

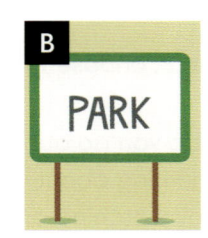

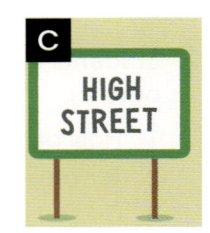

5 What is the new after-school club?

6 What time is the girls' swimming race?

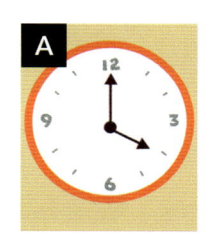

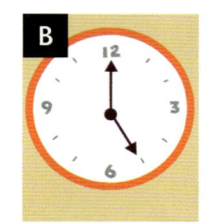

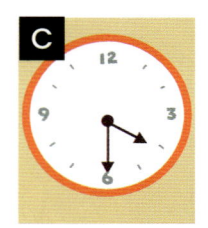

7 Which subject did both the boy and the girl fail?

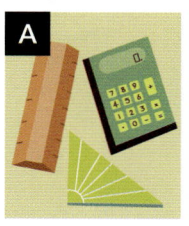

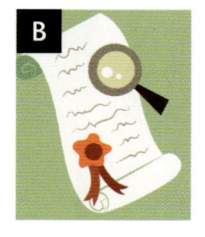

EXAM TIME 3 — Listening

2 🔊 **3.41** You will hear a girl called Debby talk about her trip to France. For each question, choose the correct answer a, b or c.

Tip: Sometimes it helps to read just the questions and not the options before you listen for the first time. Try to answer the question and then check if your answer is one of the options.

1. Where did Debby stay while she was in France?
   a a short distance from Paris
   b in the centre of the town
   c near a theme park
2. How did Debby feel about her French language skills?
   a She wishes she could speak as quickly as the French.
   b She was surprised at how much she could understand.
   c She thinks she doesn't speak well because of limited vocabulary.
3. What does Debby say about French food?
   a She enjoys it because it's unusual.
   b She could only eat some things her host mother cooked.
   c She would like to have tried more fish dishes.
4. Why didn't they go to an art exhibition?
   a It was outside and the weather was bad.
   b She'd seen the exhibition in London.
   c It wasn't open.
5. Debby is next going to see her French friend again
   a in two weeks' time.
   b this autumn.
   c next year.
6. In the future, Debby wants to
   a become a teacher.
   b become a writer.
   c use French in her job.

3 🔊 **3.42** You will hear some information about a crime museum. Complete the gaps with the missing information.

Tip: It's important to spell easy basic words correctly when you fill in missing information, so check your spelling at the end.

CRIME MUSEUM

The museum has been open for 1 _____.

The person who finished the work on the museum's collection was 2 _____.

Visitors can get written information about the exhibits from a 3 _____.

Ned and John Carson killed people from London's 4 _____.

A policeman caught them in 5 _____.

The gang of thieves that carried out a robbery left some 6 _____, which are in one of the museum rooms.

EXAM TIME 3 — Speaking

1 Work in pairs. Take turns to tell your partner about a photograph. Your photographs will be of students learning.

Tip: Don't worry if you can't remember a specific word. Try to explain it in another way.

Student A

It's your turn first. Look at the photograph and tell Student B what you can see in it.

Student B

Tell Student A what you can see in the photograph.

2 Work in pairs. Talk to each other about the things you learned at your first school and the things you study now.

Tip: Use linking words to contrast things in the past and things now, such as *but*, *whereas* and *however*.

ART — 3D printer sculpture

CLIL 1

Art from technology

When people think about sculpture, they usually think about statues made of materials like stone, metal, wood or even ice! Sculptors use special tools to make these with their hands. Sometimes they make casts of their sculptures. They fill the casts with hot metal to make bronze sculptures.

Today there is a new and interesting type of sculpture. Technology is progressing very fast and is changing many parts of our lives – even art! 3D printers are becoming very important for manufacturing, making things like machine parts and furniture, and also in fashion, making shoes, accessories, and even clothes. Now artists are also using them to create sculptures.

First the artist makes a digital model on the computer. Then the 3D printer prints it out. They print layers of material to build up the object. This is called an 'additive process' because it adds different layers of different shapes. They can make very fine pieces like tiny flowers and insects, and big, colourful, modern pieces – from life-size statues of people to huge dinosaurs! They print big statues in sections. To make bronze sculptures, they make casts from the printed objects.

It's even possible to have 3D printed selfies! We can have small statues of ourselves on our wedding cake or we can have small models of our whole family on our desk. Nearly everything is possible with 3D printing today.

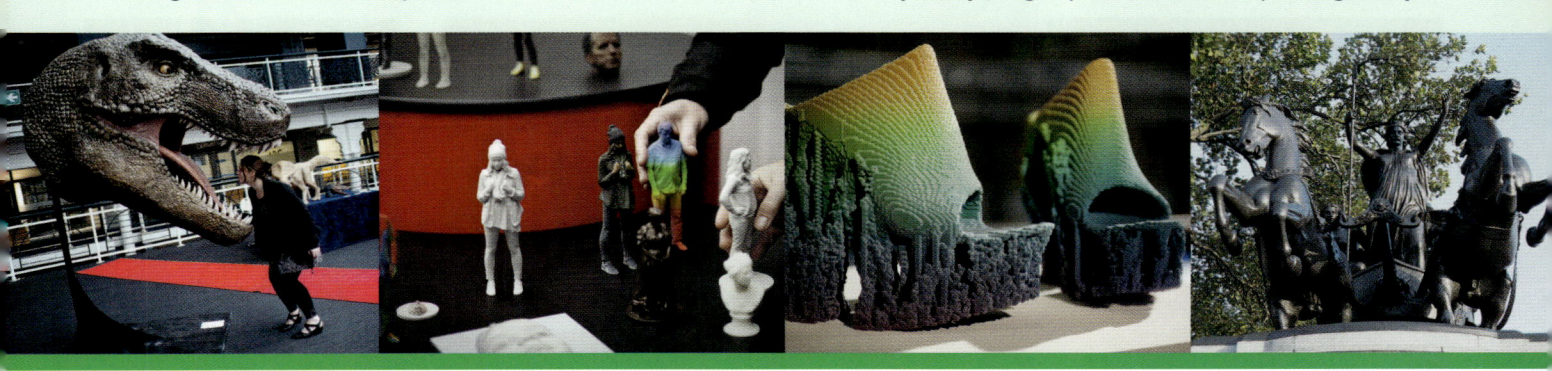

1 Do you have a favourite sculpture? What do you know about it? Tell the class.

2 Read the article. Answer the questions.
 1 What materials do sculptors often use?
 2 How do they make bronze sculptures?
 3 What sort of things do 3D printers usually create?
 4 What is the first step in 3D printer sculpture?
 5 What is the next step called? Why?
 6 What can some people put on their wedding cakes?

3 What new information did you learn from the text? What was the most interesting part? Discuss in pairs.

4 Read the text about 3D printing and art. Do you think this is a good idea? Why? / Why not? Discuss in pairs.

> One artist, Cosmo Wenman, wants to digitally scan famous sculptures from museums all over the world and put the files online. His idea is that everyone can print out their own copies on a 3D printer. He wants these sculptures to belong to everyone.

5 Look at the photos. Which of these sculptures would you like to create with a 3D printer? Discuss in pairs.

6 **PROJECT** Use the internet to find out about an artist who uses 3D printing. Make notes about the things below.
- his/her nationality and experience
- the types of sculpture he/she makes
- any other interesting information

7 **PROJECT** Write a paragraph about the artist. Add pictures.

SCIENCE — Cooking

CLIL 2

Cooking and science

Heston Blumenthal is an English chef. He is important because he has made people think about the science of cooking. Heston uses complicated scientific techniques all the time in his cooking and some equipment that he uses in his kitchen is from a science laboratory!

Science is part of all cooking. Every time we cook something, there is a chemical change. A chemical change means that we create a new substance. The process is irreversible – the ingredient cannot change back. To do this, we need energy – in cooking that means a high temperature. When we use heat in cookery, we change both the taste and the texture of the ingredients.

Here are some examples of chemical changes that happen when we cook. A cake looks and tastes very different before and after cooking. With the heat of the oven, it rises. This is because the baking powder ($NaHCO_3$) in the mixture changes at a high temperature. It produces carbon dioxide (CO_2) and the cake grows. But there was no CO_2 in the cake before! Another example is when we toast bread. The carbohydrates in the bread break to form carbon (C). This makes the bread brown and hard, a change in texture and colour. Proteins in meat and eggs change too. The protein molecules take the energy from the heat and change shape. The meat gets harder and red meat becomes brown. Clear egg whites become solid and white.

Chefs like Heston Blumenthal use their knowledge about chemical changes in food to create new tastes and textures. Heston's famous bacon-and-egg ice cream is made using liquid nitrogen!

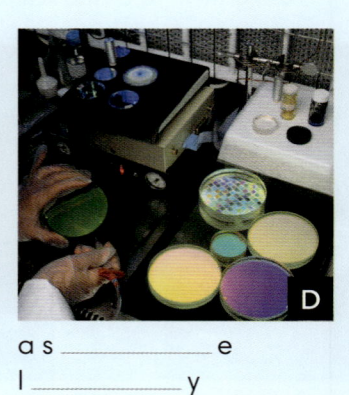

A l_____d n_____n
B p_____n m_____s
C h_____h t_____e
D a s_____e l_____y

1 Why do you think some people say cooking is an art and others say it's a science? Discuss in pairs.

2 Read the article quickly and find words to complete the captions for photos A–D.

3 Read the article again. Answer the questions.
  1 Who is Heston Blumenthal and why is he important?
  2 What does 'a chemical change' mean?
  3 What happens to make a cake rise?
  4 What happens when bread becomes toast?
  5 What happens when we cook meat and eggs?
  6 Which of Blumenthal's dishes is made using liquid nitrogen?

4 What new information did you learn from the text? What was the most interesting part? Discuss in pairs.

5 Think of a raw ingredient which changes when cooked. Then, in pairs, take turns to describe the ingredient before and after cooking. Can your partner guess what you are describing?

  A: Before cooking they're small, round, white and hard. After cooking at a high temperature they're light, brown and break easily.
  B: Potatoes which become crisps!

6 **PROJECT** Use the internet to research another chemical change that happens to food during cooking. Make notes about the things below.
  - what happens and why
  - examples of meals where this happens
  - any other interesting information

7 **PROJECT** Prepare a short presentation. Write a paragraph about the chemical change. Add pictures and diagrams.

DRAMA — Zigger Zagger

Zigger Zagger

There are many plays and films about football but Peter Terson's *Zigger Zagger* (1967) is one of the best. It was also probably the first play to show football hooliganism – fighting between supporters from different clubs. In the 1960s, football hooliganism was causing a lot of problems and in *Zigger Zagger*, Terson tried to show why this was happening. He also wanted to show how difficult life was for young people at that time.

Zigger Zagger is about a boy called Harry who is from a poor family. When he leaves school, he doesn't know what to do with his life. Harry is passionate about football and supports his local team, City End. Zigger Zagger is the name of the dangerous, angry leader of the City End fans. He offers Harry excitement at the match and after it. His world is full of singing, shouting and fighting. Les is a relative of Harry's who wants Harry to get a good job, a wife and a house. At first, Harry follows Zigger Zagger but then realises that his life is crazy and wrong.

If you see this play, you'll never forget it. The setting is a football ground and on the stage the supporters are in rows like in a stadium. They face the audience all through the play. The main characters act on the stage in front of them, and the supporters sing and shout and wave scarves between the scenes. Peter Terson wrote the play for the National Youth Theatre and the first performance in London had a cast of almost ninety young people – most of them were acting the parts of football fans. It's loud and scary but a very exciting and important play.

1 Describe the photo. How do football club supporters show their support for their team in your country?

2 Have you ever seen a play or film with a story about sport? If so, did you enjoy it? Why? / Why not?

3 Read the article about *Zigger Zagger*, a play about sport. Complete the fact file.

> **ZIGGER ZAGGER**
> Writer: [1] _____
> Written in (year): [2] _____
> Topic: [3] _____
> Main characters: [4] _____
> Setting: [5] _____
> Theatre that first performed it: [6] _____
> Number of people in the first cast: [7] _____

4 Would you like to see this play? Why? / Why not?

5 Look at two film posters about sport. In pairs, discuss your ideas about what the film may be about and then compare your ideas with the class. Think about the following:
- main character or characters
- the supporting characters
- the challenge the characters face
- the ending

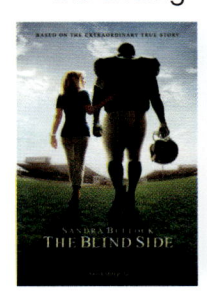

6 **PROJECT** Use the internet to research another play about sport. Make notes about the things below.
- the writer
- the story
- the cast
- why the play is important or interesting
- any other interesting information

7 **PROJECT** Write a paragraph about the play. Add pictures.

GEOGRAPHY | International Date Line

CLIL 4

Imaginary lines around the Earth

Tonga and Samoa are two islands in the South Pacific. They are 557 miles apart. If you flew from Tonga to Samoa, the journey would take you two hours, but you would arrive twenty-two hours before you left! It might be 5 November when you leave Tonga and 4 November when you arrive in Samoa. Why? Because you would cross the International Date Line (IDL). This can be confusing for travellers and cause problems with hotel bookings!

The IDL – an imaginary line, not a real one – goes from north to south. There are two other important imaginary lines across the Earth: the Equator, which divides the world into the northern and southern hemispheres, and the Prime Meridian (which goes through London), dividing the world into the western and eastern hemispheres. The IDL is on the opposite side of the world to the Prime Meridian. The world is always turning and as we travel around the world (east or west), our days become shorter or longer. The IDL tells all the countries in the world where the beginning of one day and the end of another come together.

The IDL starts at the North Pole and goes down to the South Pole and crosses through the Pacific Ocean. But it isn't a straight line – it has several zigzags in it! This is so that it is the same date in one country. For example, the line zigzags east to go through the Bering Straits so that Alaska and Russia are on different sides. The country of Kiribati used to be on the eastern side but it decided to change to the western side. It wanted to be the first country in the world to celebrate the new millennium in 2000!

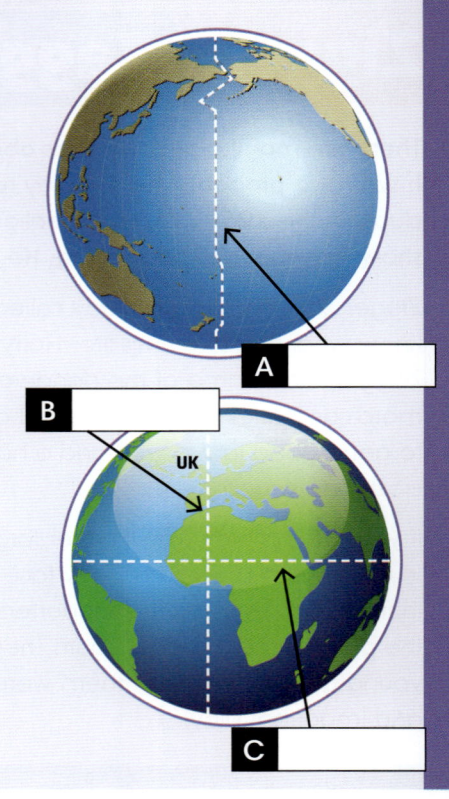

1 Read the article quickly. Label the lines A–C on the maps.

2 Read the article again. Mark the sentences T (true) or F (false).

1. ☐ It takes twenty-two hours to fly from Tonga to Samoa.
2. ☐ The IDL is on the other side of the world from the Prime Meridian.
3. ☐ The International Date Line goes in a straight line from north to south.
4. ☐ It is the same time and day in Russia and Alaska.
5. ☐ Kiribati is on the eastern side of the IDL.

3 What new information did you learn from the text? What was the most interesting part? Discuss in pairs.

4 Read about how the problem of losing a day was first discovered. In pairs, take turns to make, ask and answer the questions.

1. who / Ferdinand Magellan?
2. why / he / famous?
3. what / the crew / discover?
4. what / the year?
5. what / happen / seventeenth century?
6. what / happen / 1884?

History of the IDL

In 1519 the explorer Ferdinand Magellan was the first person to sail round the world. During the journey, the crew kept careful records. When they got home, they discovered that they had lost a complete day. The date they had was a day behind the people in their country. This was the beginning of the idea of an international date line and in the seventeenth century it started to appear on maps. It became official in 1884, after an international meridian conference. However, there is still no law that says the IDL exists.

5 **PROJECT** Use the internet to find out about one of the other imaginary lines around the Earth. Make notes about the things below.

- where it goes
- its purpose and when it was named
- any other interesting information

6 **PROJECT** Prepare a short presentation. Write a paragraph about the imaginary line you have chosen and add a map with labels. Share your presentation with the class.

SCIENCE   Forensics

Forensics

The crime scene
When there is a crime, the police often use forensic scientists to help them find the criminal. At nearly every crime scene there is some evidence that scientists can check. This might be blood, hair, fingerprints or other very small things that they can analyse. The forensic scientist uses special equipment in a police laboratory to carry out experiments. They use a powerful microscope (an electron microscope) to check both the evidence and samples from suspects. Forensic scientists also study dead bodies to find out how and when they died. This is called an autopsy or post-mortem. All this information helps the police.

Fingerprints
Everyone has different fingerprints. These are the lines and circles on the tips of our fingers. When we touch something, we leave a print. Scientists can use special powder to copy these prints. These are compared to records of fingerprints to find out who left them.

Blood splatter
Blood is very important to forensic scientists. The way that it falls gives lots of information. For example, if it's on a wall (blood splatter), it can show where a killer was standing and how fast the blood was travelling. Sometimes it even shows the shape of the killer!

DNA
DNA is like a genetic fingerprint. Everyone's DNA is different (apart from identical twins). So if a criminal leaves DNA at a crime scene, the forensic scientist can use it. DNA can be found in many things such as blood, hair, teeth, bone and saliva (from inside our mouths). We leave our DNA everywhere – on clothes and cups, in hairbrushes and on toothbrushes.

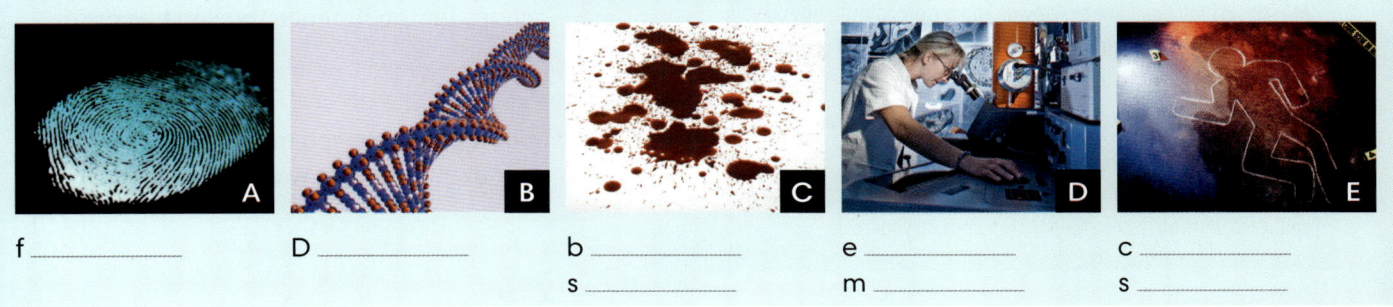

A f_____ B D_____ C b_____ s_____ D e_____ m_____ E c_____ s_____

1. What do you think a forensic scientist does? Discuss in pairs.

2. Read the article quickly and find words to complete the captions for photos A–E.

3. Read the article again. Answer the questions.
   1. What is a forensic scientist?
   2. Where does a forensic scientist work?
   3. What can they find out?
   4. What are fingerprints and how does a forensic scientist check them?
   5. What can blood splatter show?
   6. What is DNA and where is it found?

4. Do you think it is a good idea for the police to keep samples of everyone's DNA to help solve crimes? Why? / Why not?

5. In pairs, choose and read one of the texts, A or B. Tell your partner the information in your text and how it helps forensic scientists.

   A Hair
   Our hair falls out all the time and a criminal often leaves hair at a crime scene. Scientists can analyse hair and find out if the colour is natural and if it is an animal or human hair. They can also get an idea of the age, race and gender of the person. There are fourteen things a hair can tell the scientist! If the hair has a root, it can also give DNA.

   B Shoes
   Shoes can leave prints. These can tell scientists about a criminal's size, the way he/she walks and the type of shoe that he/she wore. Shoes also leave dirt. Scientists can sometimes learn where the person lives or works, if he/she has pets, where he/she walks and even which field or path he/she has walked on.

6. **PROJECT** Find out how the police solved a famous crime using forensics. Make notes about the crime and the evidence.

7. **PROJECT** Prepare a short presentation. Write a paragraph about the crime and the forensic work involved. Add pictures.

STUDENT ACTIVITIES

Unit 1 — Lesson 1.5 Exercise 2

ANSWER KEY

Mostly As: You're obviously busy with other things in life, and that's great. Have fun and enjoy real time with your friends!

Mostly Bs: You know it's there when you need it, but technology isn't the most important thing in your life.

Mostly Cs: You're internet crazy! You love going online and checking messages from friends. Make sure you take time to do other things, too.

Unit 3 — Revision SPEAKING Exercise 7

MENU

Food
- Pizza with cheese and tomato
- Chicken salad
- Fresh bread rolls with tuna or cheese
- Ice cream — any flavour!

Drinks
- Fruit juice   Smoothies
- Coffee   Tea   Water

Unit 7 — Lesson 7.1 Exercise 7

ANSWER KEY

Mostly As: You don't like big crowds and are probably happy on your own. You know how to be a good friend to a few special people.

Mostly Bs: You love having lots of friends. You give your opinion honestly, and you don't mind if other people agree. You are happiest when you're busy and in a crowd.

Mostly Cs: You know how to get a balance. You can have fun when you want, but you're not afraid to do things on your own.

Unit 8 — Revision SPEAKING Exercise 7

A: Your parents want you to stay with your cousins for the summer. You don't want to.

B: Your teacher says you must study more for your exams, but you want to do more sport.

Unit 9 — Revision SPEAKING Exercise 5

Personal details: Selma, 14
From: Mexico
Been to the UK before? No, this is the first time.
Interests: football, art, food
While in the UK, would like to … go to Madame Tussauds and to a football match!

Personal details: Angelina, 15
From: France
Been to the UK before? Yes, three times.
Interests: photography, old films, acting
While in the UK, would like to … see some musicals at the theatre; improve my accent

Personal details: Tomek, 16
From: Poland
Been to the UK before? Yes, once.
Interests: nature and animals, handball
While in the UK, would like to … go to London Zoo, and eat fish and chips!

Personal details: Selim, 15
From: Turkey
Been to the UK before? No, this is the first time.
Interests: football, history, architecture
While in the UK, would like to … visit Stonehenge and go to a football match